Welcome to the world of investing "factor factories," where innumerable attributes have been "identified" to improve the risk/return attributes of diversified portfolios. Berkin and Swedroe provide the research and evidence showing that the "secret sauce" of properly diversified portfolios includes just eight. I highly recommend it.

— JOHN A. HASLEM, PROFESSOR EMERITUS OF FINANCE,
ROBERT H. SMITH SCHOOL OF BUSINESS, UNIVERSITY OF MARYLAND

The typical finance professional or student is exposed to a bewildering array of investment strategies that are claimed to deliver substantial alphas. For the first time, Berkin and Swedroe present a lucid exposition of what strategies are the most pertinent, and how these strategies should be implemented. The work is an invaluable tool for both financial advisors as well as students aiming to achieve a better understanding of how excess returns can be generated in portfolios.

— A. SUBRAHMANYAM, GOLDYNE AND IRWIN HEARSH
DISTINGUISHED PROFESSOR OF FINANCE, UCLA

What makes this book so valuable — and so unlike the vast majority of books on investing — is that its conclusions are firmly based on independent, peer-reviewed evidence. I highly recommend it.

— ROBIN POWELL, FOUNDER OF THE EVIDENCE-BASED INVESTOR BLOG

Berkin and Swedroe apply a novel framework to evaluate the market's most profitable anomalies and offer a roadmap that any investor can follow to better market outcomes. I'll be referencing this for years to come.

— ADAM BUTLER, CEO, RESOLVE ASSET MANAGEMENT

An incisive study that offers clarity to your investing decisions. With expected returns on major asset classes near all-time lows, understanding market factors is essential to accentuating portfolio returns and reaching financial goals. Berkin and Swedroe have delivered a must-read book for today's investor.

— BILL SCHULTHEIS, AUTHOR OF "THE COFFEEHOUSE INVESTOR"

A whirlwind tour de force along the frontiers of modern finance. A comprehensive guide to factor investing: what they are and which ones are the most useful. Your tour concludes with how a prudent investor might use them to improve a portfolio through diversification into the factors that drive returns while mitigating market risk. Thoroughly researched and clearly presented. Highly recommended.

— FRANK ARMSTRONG, PRESIDENT AND FOUNDER, INVESTOR SOLUTIONS INC.

YOUR

COMPLETE GUIDE

TO

FACTOR-BASED

INVESTING

THE WAY SMART MONEY INVESTS TODAY*

Andrew L. Berkin & Larry E. Swedroe

*** FOREWORD BY CLIFF ASNESS OF AQR**

Copyright © 2016 by Andrew L. Berkin & Larry E. Swedroe

978-0-692-78365-8 (paperback)
978-0-692-78365-5 (ebook)

BAM ALLIANCE Press
8182 Maryland Ave.
Suite 500
St. Louis, MO 63105
thebamalliance.com

Design by Alan Dubinsky

Larry E. Swedroe and Andrew L. Berkin are co-authors of "The Incredible Shrinking Alpha: And What You Can Do to Escape Its Clutches" (2015).

Mr. Swedroe has authored nine other investment books:

"The Only Guide to a Winning Investment Strategy You'll Ever Need: Index Funds and Beyond — The Way Smart Money Invests Today" (1998)

"What Wall Street Doesn't Want You to Know: How You Can Build Real Wealth Investing in Index Funds" (2000)

"Rational Investing in Irrational Times: How to Avoid the Costly Mistakes Even Smart People Make Today" (2002)

"The Only Guide to a Winning Investment Strategy You'll Ever Need: The Way Smart Money Invests Today" (2005 revised edition)

"The Successful Investor Today: 14 Simple Truths You Must Know When You Invest" (2006)

"Wise Investing Made Simple: Larry Swedroe's Tales to Enrich Your Future" (2007)

"Wise Investing Made Simpler: Larry Swedroe's Tales to Enrich Your Future" (2010)

"The Quest for Alpha: The Holy Grail of Investing" (2011)

"Think, Act, and Invest Like Warren Buffett: The Winning Strategy to Help You Achieve Your Financial and Life Goals" (2012)

Mr. Swedroe has co-authored five other books:

"The Only Guide to a Winning Bond Strategy You'll Ever Need: The Way Smart Money Preserves Wealth Today," co-author Joe H. Hempen (2006)

"The Only Guide to Alternative Investments You'll Ever Need: The Good, the Flawed, the Bad, and the Ugly," co-author Jared Kizer (2008)

"The Only Guide You'll Ever Need for the Right Financial Plan: Managing Your Wealth, Risk, and Investments," co-authors Kevin Grogan and Tiya Lim (2010)

"Investment Mistakes Even Smart Investors Make and How to Avoid Them," co-author R.C. Balaban (2011)

"Reducing the Risk of Black Swans: Using the Science of Investing to Capture Returns with Less Volatility," co-author Kevin Grogan (2014)

CONTENTS

CONTENTS

ACKNOWLEDGMENTS

For all their support and encouragement, Larry thanks his colleagues at Buckingham and The BAM ALLIANCE, with special thanks to Dan Campbell, Sean Grover, and Kevin Grogan for their help with all the data. In addition, Sean provided the analysis for Appendix I. Larry also thanks Mark McLennan of AQR Capital for all his help in providing source material. Larry would also like to thank the research staff at Dimensional Fund Advisors for their help and support over the years, while specifically acknowledging Jim Davis, Marlena Lee, and Weston Wellington. He especially thanks his wife, Mona, the love of his life, for her tremendous encouragement and understanding during the lost weekends and many nights he sat at the computer well into the early morning hours. She has always provided whatever support was needed — and then some. Walking through life with her has truly been a gracious experience.

Andy thanks his colleagues at Bridgeway Capital Management for their enthusiastic support of this book specifically and his professional and personal life more generally. Andy also thanks his family, especially his wife, Joy, and son, Evan, for their encouragement and understanding.

Larry and Andy both express their great appreciation for the editorial assistance provided by Nick Ledden and the production assistance of Leslie Garrison. We also express our gratitude to Ronen Israel and Antti Ilmanen of AQR; Tobias Moskowitz, professor of finance at Yale; Ed Tower, professor of economics at Duke; and Adam Butler of ReSolve for reviewing the book and providing many helpful suggestions. The usual caveat applies that any remaining mistakes are ours. And, finally, we express our great appreciation to Cliff Asness for providing the foreword for our book, as well as helpful suggestions. Cliff's contributions to the understanding of how markets work is only exceeded by his wit.

FOREWORD

At its most basic level, factor-based investing is simply about defining and then systematically following a set of rules that produce diversified portfolios. Imagine I systematically always chose to own a diversified portfolio of stocks with some well-defined, shared characteristic and to avoid, sell, or even short (Larry and Andrew focus on factors that are always as short as they are long) a diversified portfolio with the opposite characteristic. Once you define a factor, some questions immediately arise: Did it make money in the past? Will it make money, after costs, in the future? Why does it make money? One classic example of a factor is going long a very diversified set of stocks that are "cheap" and short stocks that are "expensive," where cheap and expensive are measured by comparing a stock's price to its fundamentals, such as book value, earnings, or sales. Another example is going long stocks with good momentum, meaning they've been doing relatively well lately, and short stocks with bad momentum. There are many others, and in fact, that in and of itself can be a bit of a problem.

Professor John Cochrane famously said that financial academics and practitioners have created a factor "zoo."[1] He didn't mean it as a compliment. Other researchers have forcibly reminded us recently of the dangers of "data mining."[2] While in some fields, this may indeed be praised, in finance, it's generally seen pejoratively. In finance, it means that smart people with even smarter computers can find factors (adding to the "zoo") that have worked in the past but are not "real." In other words, they are the product of randomness (together with selection bias) and, thus, their past success won't repeat in the future. To see this, say there were no real factors, you'd nonetheless find many characteristics that delivered strong historical returns if you tested enough possible candidates (or enough candidate rules for creating diversified factors). But they would have no efficacy going forward, as we started out assuming no factors are "real," so these were just the result of searching through enough random returns to find factors that accidentally looked good. Such is the power of big data and big computing. The zoo of factors is a result of this fact and, importantly, the powerful incentive, both for academic publication and real-world asset gathering for managers, to find historically powerful factors.

The harm in doing so is real. You might be tempted to think that believing in a factor that isn't truly real is a neutral

---

1 In the book, Larry and Andrew also refer to this comment from Cochrane's 2011 presidential address to the American Finance Association.

2 E.g., Harvey, Liu, and Zhu (2015).

event. No harm, no foul. That is not the case. It's not that you simply fail to make the money the illusory factor randomly made in the past. It's worse. On top of the factor failing, you still pay trading costs and a management fee to implement it. You still take risk (randomness without a positive expectation of gain is not good!). And because you take risk in this fictitious factor, you likely take less risk elsewhere — perhaps foregoing risk that truly is compensated. So, all in all, data mining over factors is a real problem, and one that's dangerous to your wealth.

Here's where Larry and Andrew come in — thankfully. They do, at least, two very important things in this book. First, they offer an extremely useful guide to understanding which of the factors are indeed real. Second, they do it in such a way that a non-super-geek interested reader can really benefit. These are very important, but not easy, tasks — and they do them superbly.

To start, Larry and Andrew show us that the factor zoo isn't quite as crazy as it seems. They don't go through every factor on which anyone has written a paper (nobody should do that!). Instead, they recognize that many of the seemingly separate factors are variations on a theme, and these themes make the zoo far easier to navigate. These themes are things like value, size, momentum, carry, and others (not esoteric quantitative jargon but categories that stem from the basic intuitive language of investing). Indeed, that many factors are variations on a theme not unique unto themselves is, in fact, one of the things they insist upon. They correctly look on a theme that works[3] only under one very specific formation and without other reasonable ways to express it, as highly suspect (e.g., if the only value factor that was historically effective was price-to-earnings and not price-to-anything-else, they'd argue — and I'd agree — that our faith in the value effect would be severely shaken).

Next, they give us a wonderfully intuitive and quite specific list of criteria that researchers and practitioners must satisfy to have us believe in, and more importantly invest in, a factor. These are persistence (does the factor historically deliver reasonably reliable returns?), pervasiveness (does it, on average, deliver these returns in a variety of locales and asset classes if such tests apply?), robustness (as just discussed this is the idea that it shouldn't be dependent on one very specific formulation but fails to work if other related versions are tested), intuitiveness (does it make sense to us or are we just going by historical performance?), and, finally, investability. Notice, aside from investability, all of these come down to some aspect of "do we believe the historical results are real and not just data mining?" Investability is the one that differs, implicitly asking the all-important question: "OK, even if we believe the factor is real, can a practical investor really

---

3   As usual, I use the word "works" as a statistician and financial economist not a regular person. To a statistician, if something works a little more often than it doesn't for long enough, we start to find it unlikely that it was random. To a financial economist, if we find enough of these, even if each one fails fairly often on its own, you can start to build a pretty good portfolio.

make money from it after costs?" That's a very important final question and one Larry and Andrew always make sure to include an answer to.

While those five are the most important, they also often discuss two additional criteria. Both are relevant even if a factor already is deemed persistent, pervasive, robust, intuitive, and investable. First, they ask whether today is different from the past. It's always possible that a factor was real, not just the result of data mining, but that its day has just passed. Markets can wise-up to behavioral factors, and risk premia can be priced to lower levels than the past.[4] Larry and Andrew aren't interested in a factor's past glory, but its future benefits. Second, they make sure to ask, OK, even if this is real, is it already covered by the other factors we believe in?" An example of both is "low-risk investing." They make a strong case that low-risk investing is more expensive today than in the past and is historically, perhaps, covered already by some of the other factors (e.g., value and profitability). Note, I don't totally agree, and I'm more bullish on low-risk investing than they are. While perfect

4   Another important thing Larry and Andrew do throughout the book, particularly in the area of "intuition," is discuss for each factor the possibility that it's a result of rational assumption of risk (you get paid to go long some stocks and short others because it's a risk proposition in an economically important way) or the result of other investor errors (you get paid to go long some stocks and short others as other investors make errors and misprice these stocks). Some observers believe that only the former explanations can justify expectations of sustained future performance. I would not go that far (nor do they).

agreement is too much to ask for, credible factor researchers and investors will often agree on far more than they disagree, and that's certainly the case for me with Larry and Andrew. While I might quibble with their conclusions, this is the right way to think about choosing factors and the right questions to ask. The reader is well served to follow their lead and ask these same questions about factors.

It's not just low risk that doesn't quite make their cut. Default risk (often called credit risk in other contexts) doesn't either. Again, I don't totally agree. Adapting an old joke, you can put three researchers in a room and get four opinions. Still, I love that they are not just summing up the literature uncritically. Rather, they are willing to make some bold statements. Having five important criteria for choosing factors would have few teeth and little credibility if all factors and factor themes passed all the tests. You are reading great stuff, but more importantly, honest stuff here!

Explaining what the factors are, and how to choose whether you believe in them, forms the bulk of this very useful book. But there is more. They devote a whole chapter to the question of whether publication itself ruins future factor returns (does it still work when the cat is out of the bag?).[5] They explain the issues here and share the important results that although you

5 This is really a test of the combination of the cat being out of the bag, so publication actually affects the investing world, and the possibility that published results were just the result of data mining and not "real" to begin with.

make somewhat less after publication, the bulk of the factor returns on which they report do survive, to my great relief.

All this and I haven't even discussed the appendices! You get a couple of free mini-books tacked on here, so please make sure to read them. A great example is their review of the findings that are very similar to factor investing in the world of sports betting. They do this not to encourage sports betting or the starting of profitable book-making operations by their readers (actually, I can't swear to that). Rather, once again, they are trying to understand if these factor themes are indeed pervasive. When something works in a place you haven't yet looked, you actually get more confident about your original findings. Remember, there's always a chance those original findings were random luck, not real, and the result of data mining, not truth. In other words, if value investing wasn't a real phenomenon, but just data mining, just because it works for stocks wouldn't imply it works for sports betting (as it wasn't real — it was random!). On other hand, if you have an "intuitive" theory (one of the five criteria!) for why it works for stocks, and that same intuition applies to sports betting, you would expect it to work there, too. Finding it does is a wonderful confidence-builder, even if you never watch sports, let alone bet on them. That is, after seeing similar intuition hold up for sports betting, you should have somewhat more confidence in that intuition leading to real, not random, returns for stocks.

Vitally, Larry and Andrew always stress that no investing plan, diversifying across good factors included, survives too much impatience. Although they strive to show us factors that work more often than they don't, and work better and more consistently in combination, Larry and Andrew don't go down the cheap, easy, and false path of promising an easy road. Rather, they stress that belief in the factors you choose is vital not just to make sure they are real, and not just data mining, but because without well-formed, strongly held beliefs (perhaps stemming from persistence, pervasiveness, robustness, intuition, and investability!), nobody will stick with their investing process through the inevitable tough times. Good and wise advice. It's not hard to give back more than all the positives of a good investment process by falling down on this last vital hurdle.

Finally, I'd contrast their work with the legion of investing books telling you how to actively pick stocks just like Warren Buffett (actually, Larry and Andrew do this, too, but I'll let them tell you about it). Those books are, in my view, far easier to write than this one. There are always great stories when it comes to individual companies: fascinating tales of greatness and woe that end wonderfully for the sage stock picker who is the hero of this tale. In contrast, Larry and Andrew have taken on the task of describing an inherently quantitative affair. Factors don't have made-for-TV endings. Success is measured by less thrilling statements like, "and then the factor had a +1 standard deviation decade," versus discretionary stock-picking stories that end with "and then the company I invested in invented the iPod!" Of course, while the stories are better in the world of discretionary stock picking, it has one small problem (just a small one, mind you): It generally doesn't work! This is not the place to dive into such a contentious issue (so I'll just assert it), but both economic logic and a large body of research has shown that discretionary stock picking is, in broad generality (with obvious exceptions like Mr. Buffett), not the path to riches. So they could've gone with the better and easier stories, and written an easier (for them and the reader) and maybe more entertaining book. Instead, they went with stuff that they, and I, believe actually helps. I think they made the right choice.

To sum up, this is a great book. It surveys the increasingly important area of factor investing, suggesting concrete ways to navigate the factor "zoo." I am confident that you will enjoy your journey through the factor zoo as much as I did.

— Cliff Asness, Co-Founder of AQR Capital Management

INTRODUCTION

If a poll was taken asking investors to name the greatest investor of all time, it is safe to say that the vast majority would likely respond, "Warren Buffett." Thus, we could say that a major goal of investors the world over is to find Buffett's "secret sauce." If we could identify it, we could invest like him — assuming we also had his ability to ignore the noise of the market and avoid the panicked selling that causes so many investors to incur the higher risk of stocks while ending up with lower, bond-like returns. This book is in part about the academic community's search for that secret sauce — specifically the characteristics of stocks and other securities that both explain performance and provide premiums (above market returns). Such characteristics can also be called factors, which are simply properties or a set of properties common across a broad set of securities. Thus, a factor is a quantitative way of expressing a qualitative theme. For example, in Chapter 3 we will discuss the value factor, which can be measured by a number of different metrics, such as price-to-book, price-to-cash flow, price-to-earnings, and price-to-sales. But this book is also about how practitioners use that academic research to build portfolios, and how you as an investor can benefit from that knowledge.

What you will learn is that while Buffett is considered by many to be a peerless stock picker, we now know that his success has not been due to such skill. Instead, it is attributable to his identification of certain key characteristics, or factors, that would deliver above-market returns. In other words, if you knew what characteristics to look for, you could replicate his record of successful equity selection by investing in funds that own the stocks with those key traits. It is important to understand that in no way does this detract from what Buffett, or his mentors (legendary value investors Benjamin Graham and David L. Dodd) accomplished. After all, they discovered these characteristics decades before the academics. In fact, it is often the case that academics uncover important stock characteristics by studying the performance of investors who have outperformed the market. Their goal, then, is to determine if these investors' successes were the result of exposure to a common factor or factors, or instead a result of stock-picking and/or market-timing skill. With that said, once the secret sauce of great investors has been discovered, there is no longer any need for investors to perform any fundamental research on individual stocks. You can now achieve the results of these legends of finance by investing in low-cost, passively managed (meaning there is no individual stock picking or market timing) exchange-traded funds (ETFs) or mutual funds that provide exposure to these factors.

Our journey will take you through the land of academic research with an extensive review, citing more than 100 academic papers, of the more than 50-year quest to uncover the secret of successful investing. Our objective is not to convince you to adopt any one viewpoint or our specific interpretation of the research on factor investing, but rather to provide you with the information and data you need to make your own informed investment decisions. Along the way, you will come across some technical terms — we have included a glossary to provide an explanation of these terms, while allowing for ease of reading.

Given the great rewards available to those who could identify these factors, it should not be a surprise that there has been a great amount of effort expended in this pursuit. In their 2014 paper, "Long-Term Capital Budgeting," authors Yaron Levi and Ivo Welch examined 600 factors from both the academic and practitioner literature. And authors Campbell R. Harvey (past editor of The Journal of Finance), Yan Liu, and Heqing Zhu in their 2015 paper "...and the Cross-Section of Expected Returns," reported that 59 new factors were discovered between 2010 and 2012 alone. In total, they studied 315 factors from top journal articles and highly regarded working papers. These investment characteristics had become so numerous and exotic that, in his 2011 presidential address to the American Finance Association, John H. Cochrane of the University of Chicago coined the term "zoo of factors."

FACTORS: A NONTRADITIONAL VIEW

Traditionally, most portfolios have been constructed primarily from public equities and bonds. The risks associated with the equity portion of those portfolios are typically dominated by exposure to market beta, or how much assets tend to move with the stock market. (We will cover market beta in detail in Chapter 1.) And because equities are riskier (specifically, more volatile) than bonds, market beta's share of the risk in a traditional portfolio split 60/40 between stocks and bonds is actually much greater than 60 percent. In fact, it is typically more than 80 percent. This result is due to the annual volatility of a market portfolio of stocks being about 20 percent, while the annual volatility of a high-quality intermediate bond portfolio is only about 5 percent. Thus, stocks contribute far more to unwanted volatility and downside risk than their portfolio weight might naively imply.

The severe financial crisis of 2008, with its large stock market drop, led many investors (including institutions) to search for diversifying alternatives. Among the usual suspects were private equity and hedge funds. Unfortunately, the evidence demonstrates that the correlation of both of these alternatives to equities is quite high. For example, Niels Pedersen, Sébastien Page, and Fei He, authors of the 2014 study "Asset Allocation: Risk Models for Alternative Investments," found that for the period from December 1991 through December 2012, the correlations of private equity funds and hedge funds to stocks were 0.71 and

0.79, respectively. Most of the returns of these types of alternative investments are explained by the returns of stocks — the same beta risk they are trying to reduce through diversification. This is the same conclusion that Clifford Asness, Robert Krail, and John Liew reached in their 2001 study, "Do Hedge Funds Hedge? Be Cautious in Analyzing Monthly Returns."

Making matters worse is that alpha, true outperformance defined as returns above the appropriate risk-adjusted benchmark, has proven to be very elusive. The historical evidence on the performance of private equity and hedge funds, as presented in Larry Swedroe and Jared Kizer's book, "The Only Guide to Alternative Investments You'll Ever Need: The Good, the Flawed, the Bad, and the Ugly," is not supportive. Other traditional alternative investments, such as real estate investment trusts (REITs) and infrastructure, also have a relatively high correlation with stocks. Among traditional alternatives, the only two that showed almost no correlation to equities were commodities and timberland.

However, there is a nontraditional way to think about diversification. Rather than viewing a portfolio as a collection of asset classes, one can view it instead as a collection of diversifying factors. Support for such factor-based investing strategies is provided by Antti Ilmanen and Jared Kizer in their 2012 paper "The Death of Diversification Has Been Greatly Exaggerated." Their work, which won the prestigious Bernstein Fabozzi/Jacobs Levy Award for the best paper of the year, made the case that factor diversification is more effective at reducing portfolio volatility and market directionality than asset class diversification.

WHAT FACTORS SHOULD YOU CONSIDER?

In his role as Director of Research for Buckingham Strategic Wealth and The BAM ALLIANCE, Larry Swedroe has been researching academic literature and writing about it for more than 20 years. His more than 3,000 articles and blog posts serve as the source material for much of this book.

Our objective is to bring clarity out of complexity and opaqueness. What you will learn is that, within the "factor zoo," you need only a handful of factors to invest in the same fashion that has made Buffett a legend. You will also learn that you can invest like the previously mentioned paragons of finance in a low-cost, tax-efficient way.

To determine which exhibits in the factor zoo are worthy of investment, we will use the following criteria. For a factor to be considered, it must meet all of the following tests. To start, it must provide explanatory power to portfolio returns and have delivered a premium (higher returns). Additionally, the factor must be:

- Persistent — It holds across long periods of time and different economic regimes.
- Pervasive — It holds across countries, regions, sectors, and even asset classes.
- Robust — It holds for various definitions (for

example, there is a value premium whether it is measured by price-to-book, earnings, cash flow, or sales).

• Investable — It holds up not just on paper, but also after considering actual implementation issues, such as trading costs.

• Intuitive — There are logical risk-based or behavioral-based explanations for its premium and why it should continue to exist.

The 600 exhibits in the factor zoo cover many different categories. Some are related to macroeconomic variables; others are related to asset characteristics. Some factors have risk-related explanations, others are attributed to behavioral considerations, and many have arguments for both.

The good news is that from among all these factors to choose, you can focus on just eight that meet our criteria. What about all those other factors? Some have not passed the test of time, fading away after their discovery, perhaps because of data mining or random outcomes. Or, perhaps the factors worked only for a special period, regime, or narrow band of securities. And many factors have explanatory power that is already well captured by the factors we recommend. In other words, they are variations on a common theme (such as the many definitions of value). We will briefly discuss some of these other factors in the appendices.

Our quest to find that special set of factors able to explain the vast majority of the differences in returns among diversified portfolios is really a journey through time and the history of what are called asset pricing models. This journey begins about 50 years ago with the development of the first asset pricing model, the capital asset pricing model (CAPM).

THE CAPITAL ASSET PRICING MODEL

Building on the work of Harry Markowitz, the trio of John Lintner, William Sharpe, and Jack Treynor are generally given most of the credit for introducing the first formal asset pricing model to explain what drives returns. They developed the CAPM in the early 1960s.

The CAPM provided the first precise definition of risk and how it drives expected returns. It allowed us to understand whether an active manager who outperforms the market has generated alpha, or whether that outperformance could be explained by exposure to some common factor. This is an important issue because active managers charge relatively high fees for the "promise" of alpha. In other words, if an active manager's above-market performance was due to loading (beta) on common factors, investors paid a high price for the promise of alpha but actually received beta. And that exposure can be obtained far more cheaply.

THE CAPM: A ONE-FACTOR MODEL

The CAPM looks at risk and return through a "one-factor" lens: The risk and the return of a portfolio are determined only by its exposure to market beta. This specific market beta is the measure of the sensitivity of the equity risk of a stock, mutual fund, or portfolio relative to the risk of the overall market. It is called systematic, nondiversifiable risk because no matter how many stocks you own, you cannot diversify away the risk of market beta. Market beta will be the first stop on our tour of the factor zoo.

CHAPTER 1
MARKET BETA

There are many misperceptions about the meaning of market beta. To bring clarity to the subject, we will begin with a definition that explains both what market beta is and what it is not. And we will also explain why it is important.

First, market beta is not volatility, though the two are related. Market beta expresses the degree to which an asset tends to move with the broad market. It is defined mathematically as the correlation (a measure of how much two variables change together) between the asset's return and the market's return, multiplied by the ratio of the asset's volatility to the market's volatility (as measured by the standard deviation of returns). By definition, a market portfolio consisting of all stocks (for example, the Vanguard Total Stock Market Index Fund) has a beta of exactly one. A beta of more than one means that the asset has more risk than the overall market. A beta of less than one means it has less risk than the overall market. However, beta is not just the percentage of stocks in the asset allocation of a portfolio. To demonstrate this point, we will consider two portfolios.

Investor A owns a portfolio that is 100 percent invested in "high-flying" technology stocks. The beta of Investor A's portfolio might be 1.5. If the market goes up 10 percent, we would expect this portfolio to go up 15 percent (10 percent × 1.5). And if the market drops 10 percent, we would expect this portfolio to go down 15 percent. Investor B owns a portfolio that is also invested 100 percent in equities. However, Investor B's portfolio is much more conservative, invested in more "defensive" stocks (such as utilities, supermarkets, and drug stores) that are not as susceptible to changes in economic growth. The beta of this portfolio might be only 0.7. Thus, if the market rose (fell) by 10 percent, we would expect this portfolio to rise (fall) by only 7 percent.

You can also build a portfolio that has only a 70 percent allocation to stocks, but if the beta of those stocks is, say, 1.43, then the portfolio will have a beta of one (70 percent × 1.43). Obviously, the market beta of a portfolio is an important determinant of its risk and expected return.

We will now examine market beta against the criteria we established. We will begin by looking at the premium that market beta has provided over the standard benchmark, the return on the one-month U.S. Treasury bill (a "riskless" investment). Note that in finance, premiums are typically measured as the difference in the average annual (not the annualized, or compound) return of two factors. In other words, they are what are called long/short portfolios. Thus, in the case of market beta, we calculate the annual average return to the total U.S. stock market and subtract the annual average return of the one-month U.S. Treasury bill. From 1927 through 2015, the U.S. market beta premium has been 8.3 percent. Not only has there been a large premium, but it has been persistent as well.

PERSISTENT

Table 1.1 shows the persistence of the market beta premium over the period from 1927 through 2015. Observe that the premium has been positive in about two-thirds of calendar years, and for longer horizons, the persistence has been even greater.

TABLE 1.1: ODDS OF OUTPERFORMANCE (%)

	1-YEAR	3-YEAR	5-YEAR	10-YEAR	20-YEAR
MARKET BETA	66	76	82	90	96

In addition to its high level of persistence, the Sharpe ratio (a measure of risk-adjusted returns, defined in the Glossary) of the market beta premium was 0.4, the second highest of all the premiums we will discuss. The highest Sharpe ratio was 0.61 and the lowest was 0.06.

While the market beta premium has shown high persistence — and the longer the horizon, the greater its persistence becomes — it is important to note that no matter how long the horizon, there was still the chance of a negative outcome. For example, at the five-year horizon, it was negative 18 percent of the time. At the 10-year horizon, it was still negative 10 percent of the time. And at the 20-year horizon, it was negative 4 percent of the time. This must be the expected result. If this were not the case, there would be no risk associated with investing in equities as long as you had the ability to wait out a bear market. It is precisely the risk of underperformance that explains why the premium exists. This must be true for all the factors we will examine. If there was no risk, investors would bid up the price of stocks with those characteristics until the premium disappeared.

The important takeaway is that if you want to earn the expected (but not guaranteed) premium from a factor, you must be willing to accept the risk that there will almost certainly be long periods when the premium will turn out to be negative. These are the times in which you took the risk, but were not rewarded. The risk of underperformance is why it is critical that investors do not assume more risk than they have the ability, willingness, or need to take. It is also why discipline is so crucial to successful investing. You must have the ability to be patient, ignoring even long periods of underperformance. This fact is why Warren Buffett stated: "The most important quality for an investor is temperament, not intellect." He also said: "Success in investing doesn't correlate with IQ once you're above the level of 25. Once you have ordinary intelligence, what you need is the temperament to control the urges that get other people into trouble in investing."

Unfortunately, our lengthy experience has taught us that most investors believe three or even five years is a long time, and 10 years is an eternity. However, as we've just demonstrated, 10 years is not even close to being long enough to draw conclusions. The failure to understand this, and the impatience that results, is why so many investors have poor experiences. They end up selling after periods of poor performance (when prices are low and future expected returns are now high) and buying after periods of good performance (when prices are high and future expected returns are now low). Buying high and selling low is not a prescription for success. Yet, it is what most investors do.

PERVASIVE

In their 2011 publication "Equity Premiums Around the World," authors Elroy Dimson, Paul Marsh, and Mike Staunton found that since 1900 market beta has been positive in virtually every country and region around the globe. In the 2016 Credit Suisse Global Investment Returns Yearbook, Dimson, Marsh, and Staunton revisited market beta and presented the evidence on the equity risk premium (ERP) for 21 developed countries, from the perspective of a U.S. investor. From 1900 through 2015, the premium, as measured against one-month U.S. Treasury bills, was positive in every case, ranging from about 3.1 percent in Belgium to 6.3 percent in South Africa (Table 1.2). The U.S.

market was tied for eighth place with a premium of 5.5 percent. The global ERP was 4.2 percent, the world ex-U.S. premium was 3.5 percent, and in Europe it was 3.4 percent. Over the last 50 years of this period (1966–2015), again all premiums were positive, ranging from 1.4 percent in Austria to 6.6 percent in Sweden. The U.S. premium was 4.4 percent (ninth highest), the global premium was 4.1 percent, the world ex-U.S. premium was 4.5 percent, and in Europe it was 5.4 percent. Clearly, the market beta premium has been pervasive. And you can see that the United States was not the country with the highest returns.

TABLE 1.2: EQUITY RISK PREMIUMS AROUND THE WORLD

COUNTRY	ERP 1966–2015 (%)	ERP 1900–2015 (%)
AUSTRALIA	3.5	6.0
AUSTRIA	1.4 *	5.5
BELGIUM	3.4	3.1 *
CANADA	2.3	4.1
DENMARK	4.8	3.4
FINLAND	6.1	5.9
FRANCE	4.9	6.2
GERMANY	3.9	6.1
IRELAND	4.8	3.7
ITALY	1.5	5.8
JAPAN	4.0	6.2
NETHERLANDS	5.2	4.4
NEW ZEALAND	3.2	4.4
NORWAY	4.2	3.1 *

TABLE 1.2: EQUITY RISK PREMIUMS AROUND THE WORLD

COUNTRY	ERP 1966–2015 (%)	ERP 1900–2015 (%)
PORTUGAL	3.9	4.7
SOUTH AFRICA	5.9	6.3 **
SPAIN	3.7	3.3
SWEDEN	6.6 **	3.9
SWITZERLAND	5.2	3.7
UNITED KINGDOM	4.6	4.3
UNITED STATES	4.4	5.5
WORLD	4.1	4.2
WORLD EX-U.S.	4.5	3.5
EUROPE	5.1	3.4

* SMALLEST
** LARGEST

INVESTABLE

Market-like portfolios have low turnover, minimizing trading costs. In addition, the cost of trading in the form of bid-offer spreads has fallen sharply, as has the cost of commissions. And finally, competition between indexed mutual funds and ETFs has driven expense ratios lower. Today, you can invest in a U.S. total market ETF for as little as 0.03 percent, and in a total international market ETF for as little as 0.13 percent.

Two examples demonstrate the investability of the market beta factor. First, over the period from September 1976 (its first full month from inception) through 2015, the Vanguard 500 Index Fund Investor Shares (VFINX) returned 10.8 percent annually, while the S&P 500 index itself (which does not have either expenses or trading costs) returned 11.1 percent. And it is important to note that the expense ratio of VFINX has fallen over time. Second, for the period from May 1992 (its first full month from inception) through 2015, the Vanguard Total Stock Market Index Fund Investor Shares (VTSMX) returned 9.2 percent annually and the total U.S. equity market returned 9.3 percent. The benchmark for the total U.S. equity market is the Center for Research in Security Prices (CRSP) 1–10 index (1–10 represents the 10 deciles of stocks as ranked by market capitalization).

INTUITIVE

There are clear and simple risk-based rationales for investors to expect a positive excess return to market beta. The first is that the risk of owning equities is highly correlated with the risks of the economic cycle. Thus, in recessions, investors who earn a wage or own a business are exposed to the "double whammy" of bear markets and either job layoffs or reduced business income (or even bankruptcy). Given the large body of evidence demonstrating that individual investors are, on average, highly risk averse, it should be no surprise that they have demanded a large equity premium as compensation for accepting the risk of this double whammy, especially because the risks of unemployment or the loss of business income are basically uninsurable. Investors might be forced to sell stocks (because of the loss or diminution of earned income) at the worst possible time.

A second explanation for the equity premium's large size is that a large percentage of equities, if not the vast majority, are owned by high-net-worth individuals. As net worth increases, the marginal utility (the increase in satisfaction from consuming an extra unit of something) of wealth decreases. While more wealth may indeed be better than less, when individuals attain a level of wealth at which there is no longer a need to take risk, only a large risk premium might be enough to induce them to take the risk.

There is also a third explanation, and it is related to the investment life cycle and borrowing constraints. Given their long investment horizon and the size of the equity premium, young investors generally would like to invest in equities. However, they have limited ability to do so because of their typically lower levels of income, their consumption desires (such as buying a house), and constraints on their ability to borrow in order to invest in the stock market. This combination prevents much equity investment from occurring. Older investors, with their shorter investment horizons, generally have both less ability and willingness to take equity risk. They are also in the withdrawal stage of their investment life cycle. Thus, they tend to reduce their equity holdings as a percentage of their total assets. The result is that the risk of holding equities is concentrated in the hands of the middle-aged, saving consumer. This group is likely to be saving not only for retirement, but also for the college education of their children. They are also likely to be more risk averse than younger investors. After all, they must concern themselves with minimizing the risks of the aforementioned double whammy at a time when they are closer to retirement.

Another intuitive explanation for the equity premium is that the volatility of stocks is much greater than it is for riskless one-month U.S. Treasury bills. The annual standard deviation of the U.S. stock market has been about 20 percent compared to about 3 percent for the one-month U.S. Treasury bill.

We can also observe the risks involved with owning stocks by looking at periods when returns were the most negative. For example, the worst one-year return for the total U.S. equity market was −43.5 percent, which occurred in 1931. On the other hand, the one-month U.S. Treasury bill has never experienced a loss in a calendar year. And the worst total loss for U.S. stocks occurred from September 1929 through June 1932, when the equity market lost more than 83 percent. During that period, the one-month U.S. Treasury bill returned 6 percent. That is an underperformance of almost 90 percentage points. *That* is risk.

The following table provides a summary of the data on the market beta premium.

TABLE 1.3: MARKET BETA (1927–2015)

	MARKET BETA
ANNUAL PREMIUM (%)	8.3
SHARPE RATIO	0.40
1-YEAR ODDS OF OUTPERFORMANCE (%)	66
3-YEAR ODDS OF OUTPERFORMANCE (%)	76
5-YEAR ODDS OF OUTPERFORMANCE (%)	82
10-YEAR ODDS OF OUTPERFORMANCE (%)	90
20-YEAR ODDS OF OUTPERFORMANCE (%)	96

Market beta clearly meets all of our criteria for considering an allocation to that factor. But, as is the case with all factors, how much you allocate to it will depend on your unique ability, willingness, and need to take risk. Your allocation should also depend on what other risky investments are in your portfolio, as well as how the risk of those assets mixes (correlates) with the risks of the entire portfolio. The situation is analogous to cooking, where a good chef focuses not just on the quality of the ingredients, but also on how well their flavors interact. In short, the risk of an asset should never be viewed in isolation. The only right way to think about an investment is to consider how its addition impacts the risk and expected return of the entire portfolio.

THE CAPM WAS FLAWED

The single-factor CAPM was the financial world's operating model for about 30 years. However, like all models, it was, by definition, flawed or wrong. If such models were perfectly correct, they would be laws (such as laws we have in physics). Over time, we learned that the CAPM was only able to explain about two-thirds of the differences in returns of diversified portfolios. As a simple example: If Portfolio A returned 10 percent and Portfolio B returned 13 percent, the difference in market betas of the two portfolios roughly would be able to explain only 2 percentage points of the 3 percentage-point difference in returns. The remaining percentage-point difference might be explained by luck, skill (at either picking stocks or timing the market), or perhaps by some as yet unidentified factor(s). Over time, anomalies that violated the CAPM began to surface. And eventually, other factors were "discovered."

THE FAMA–FRENCH
THREE-FACTOR MODEL

In 1981, Rolf Banz's paper "The Relationship between Return and Market Value of Common Stocks" found that market beta does not fully explain the higher average return of small stocks. In 1983, Sanjoy Basu's paper "The Relationship between Earnings' Yield, Market Value and Return for NYSE Common Stocks: Further Evidence" found that the positive relationship between the earnings yield (earnings-to-price ratio, or E/P) and average return is left unexplained by market beta. And in 1985, Barr Rosenberg, Kenneth Reid, and Ronald Lanstein found a positive relationship between average stock returns and book-to-market (B/M) ratio in their paper "Persuasive Evidence of Market Inefficiency." The latter two studies provided evidence that, in addition to a size premium, there also was a value premium.

A 1992 paper by Eugene Fama and Kenneth French, "The Cross-Section of Expected Stock Returns," basically summarized and explained these anomalies in one place. The essential conclusion from the paper was that, as mentioned previously, the CAPM explained only about two-thirds of the differences in returns of diversified portfolios, and that a better model could be built using more than just the single factor. Fama and French proposed that, along with the market beta factor, exposure to the factors of size and value further explains the differences in returns of diversified portfolios.

The Fama–French three-factor model greatly improved upon the explanatory power of the CAPM, accounting for more than 90 percent of the differences in returns between diversified portfolios. To see the impact of the new and improved model, we return to our simple example. If Portfolio A returned 10 percent and Portfolio B returned 13 percent, the difference in market betas between the two portfolios would be able to explain 2 percentage points of the 3 percentage-point difference in returns. With the addition of the size and value factors, the Fama–French model roughly would be able to explain more than

2.7 percentage points of the difference in returns. Again, the remaining 0.3 percentage points might be explained by either skill at picking stocks or timing the market, or perhaps by some other yet unidentified factor(s).

We will now turn to the size factor and examine it against the established criteria.

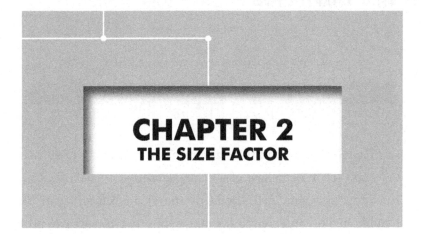

CHAPTER 2
THE SIZE FACTOR

Our discussion of the size factor will again begin with a definition. As we explained, all factors are long/short portfolios. Thus, the size factor is calculated by taking the annual average return of small-cap stocks and subtracting the annual average return of large-cap stocks. The factor is thus referred to as SMB, or small minus big. Small-cap stocks are the stocks within deciles 6–10 of the CRSP index, and large-cap stocks are those within deciles 1–5 of the CRSP index. From 1927 through 2015, the U.S. size premium was 3.3 percent.

PERSISTENT

The size premium has been persistent, though not to the same extent as market beta. Table 2.1 shows the persistence of the size premium over the period from 1927 through 2015. Again, we see a pattern in which the chances of success increase as the time period lengthens, although with somewhat lower values.

TABLE 2.1: ODDS OF OUTPERFORMANCE (%)

	1-YEAR	3-YEAR	5-YEAR	10-YEAR	20-YEAR
SIZE	59	66	70	77	86

The Sharpe ratio of the size premium over this period was 0.24, the second smallest of all the premiums we will discuss. However, alternate definitions of the size premium can be notably higher, and combining size with other factors can also be very effective.

PERVASIVE

To determine if the size premium has been pervasive, we will first compare the return of the MSCI EAFE Index (which captures the returns of large- and mid-cap stocks from developed markets around the world — Europe, Australasia, and the Far East — excluding the United States and Canada) to the return of the Dimensional Fund Advisors (DFA) International Small-Cap Index. For the period from 1970 through 2015, the MSCI EAFE Index returned 9.5 percent, while the DFA Small-Cap Index returned 14.5 percent.

MSCI has produced an EAFE small-cap index since 1999; thus, we only have a relatively short period to consider. With that in mind, from 1999 through 2015, the MSCI EAFE Index returned 4.1 percent, while the MSCI EAFE Small Cap Index returned 8.4 percent. Additionally, DFA's 2015 research report "Dimensions of Equity Returns in Europe" covered 15 European markets for the 33-year period from 1982 through 2014. It found evidence of a small-cap premium overall, as well as in each country but one (Finland, where data were only available beginning in 1990).

Thanks to the availability of Fama-French indices, we can also look at emerging markets. From 1989 through 2015, the Fama-French Emerging Markets Index returned 10.4 percent and the Fama-French Emerging Markets Small Cap Index returned 11.7 percent. Hence we see a size premium not just domestically, but also in developed and emerging equity markets around the world.

INVESTABLE

A logical question regarding the size premium is: Given that small-cap stocks are less liquid and thus potentially more expensive to trade, is the size premium realizable — or, does it just exist on paper? We can answer this question by examining the returns of live mutual funds to see if they have been successful at capturing the returns of the small-cap stock asset class. We will begin by looking at the returns of the Bridgeway Ultra-Small Company Market Fund (BRSIX). We chose this fund because it is passively managed and invests in the smallest of small-cap stocks (called microcap stocks), where trading costs are potentially a significant hurdle. The fund's inception date was July 31, 1997. For the period from August 1997 through December 2015, the fund returned 10.3 percent and outperformed the CRSP 9–10 Index (the bottom 20 percent of stocks ranked by market capitalization), which returned 9.5 percent. And it matched the return of the CRSP 10 Index (the smallest 10 percent of stocks). Keep in mind that indices have no costs. It is also worth noting that the Fama-French U.S. Small Cap Index returned 8.5 percent, and the Russell 2000 Index, which also tracks small stocks, returned 7.0 percent.

As further evidence that returns to small-cap stocks can be captured by well-structured, passively managed funds, we can look at the returns of the DFA U.S. Micro Cap Portfolio fund (DFSCX), with a current expense ratio of 0.52 percent, and the DFA Small Cap Portfolio fund (DFSTX), with a current expense ratio of 0.37 percent. From its inception in January 1982 through December 2015, DFSCX returned 11.8 percent, outperforming the Fama-French U.S. Small Cap Index by 0.2 percent, both the CRSP 9–10 and CRSP 10 indices by 0.8 percent, and the Russell 2000 Index by 1.7 percent. From its inception in April 1992 through December 2015, DFSTX returned 10.4 percent, underperforming the Fama-French U.S. Small Cap Index by just 0.05 percent and outperforming the Russell 2000 Index by 1.4 percent. Both funds were able to capture the returns of their asset classes.

Vanguard also has a small-cap index fund with performance we can examine. NAESX, which currently has an expense ratio of 0.20 percent (their lower-cost Admiral Shares mutual fund version currently has an expense ratio of just 0.08 percent), became an index fund in September 1989. The original benchmark index for the fund was the Russell 2000 Index. Due to issues with that index (which led to relatively poor performance as compared to other small-cap indices), Vanguard eventually changed its benchmark, first to an MSCI index, then eventually to a CRSP index. For the period from September 1989 through December 2015, the fund returned 9.6 percent, outperforming the Russell 2000 Index (which returned 8.9 percent) but underperforming the CRSP 6–10 Index (which returned 10.5 percent).

We can also examine the live returns of DFA's international and emerging market small-cap funds in relation to the returns of comparable small-cap indices. From its inception in October 1996 through 2015, the DFA International Small Company Portfolio Institutional Class fund (DFISX), with a current expense ratio of 0.54 percent, returned 6.7 percent. It did underperform the Dimensional International Small Cap Index, which returned 7.7 percent. However, when we compare its return to the MSCI EAFE Small Cap Index, which began in January 1999, we find that DFISX outperformed the MSCI index, 9.1 percent versus 8.0 percent. Looking at emerging markets, we find that from its inception in April 1998 through 2015, the DFA Emerging Markets Small Cap Portfolio fund (DEMSX), with a current expense ratio of 0.72 percent, returned 10.8 percent and outperformed both the MSCI Emerging Markets Small Cap Index, which returned 6.7 percent, and the Fama-French Emerging Markets Small Cap Index, which returned 9.2 percent.

The body of evidence demonstrates that, in answer to our question, the size premium can indeed be captured by live funds.

INTUITIVE

As is the case with the equity premium, there are clear and simple risk-based explanations for the size premium. Relative to large companies, small companies typically are characterized by:

- greater leverage;
- a smaller capital base, reducing their ability to deal with economic adversity;
- greater vulnerability to variations in credit conditions due to more restrictive access to capital;
- higher volatility of earnings;
- lower levels of profitability;
- greater uncertainty of cash flow; and
- less liquidity, which therefore makes their stocks more expensive to trade.

Other explanations might include:

- a less-proven, or even unproven, track record for the business model; and
- less depth of management.

Furthermore, small-cap stocks are more volatile than large-cap stocks. From 1927 through 2015, the annual standard deviation of small-cap stocks has been about 30 percent versus about 20 percent for large-cap stocks. That is a relative difference of 50 percent. Additionally, smaller companies tend to perform relatively poorly in bad times, and assets that do poorly in bad times should require a risk premium. For example, in the Great Depression year of 1931, the single worst calendar year for U.S.

stocks, the CRSP 1–5 Index of large-cap stocks lost 43.3 percent while the CRSP 6–10 Index of small-cap stocks lost 50.2 percent. In the recession and bear market of 1973 through 1974, large-cap stocks lost 39.2 percent and small-cap stocks lost 53.1 percent. And in 2008, large-cap stocks lost 36.5 percent, while small-cap stocks lost 38.7 percent.

Gerald Jensen and Jeffrey Mercer, authors of the 2002 paper "Monetary Policy and the Cross-Section of Expected Stock Returns," examined the relationship between economic-cycle risk and the size effect. They found that when size is isolated, there is a significant small-firm premium only in periods of expansionary monetary policy. In restrictive periods, the size effect is not statistically significant. They concluded that monetary policy has a significant impact on the size effect. Good economic times generally occur when the Federal Reserve is either expansionist in its policy or simply "leaning against the wind," and bad times occur when the Fed is being restrictive in its policy.

Moon K. Kim and David A. Burnie, authors of the 2002 paper "The Firm Size Effect and the Economic Cycle," also examined the relationship between firm size and performance across the economic cycle. They found that small companies grow faster than large companies in good economic times (their risk is rewarded) but do poorly in the worst of times (their risk materializes, frequently ending in bankruptcy). Thus, it is logical that the size premium should vary across economic cycles. The authors concluded that the size effect is really compensation for economic cycle risk.

This is consistent with findings from Motohiro Yogo in his 2006 study, "A Consumption-Based Explanation of Expected Stock Returns." Yogo found that small-cap stocks deliver low returns during recessions, when the marginal utility of consumption is highest. In other words, the returns of small-cap stocks are more pro-cyclical than the returns of large-cap stocks. Thus, investors must be rewarded with high expected returns to hold these risky equities.

Before concluding, any discussion of the size factor would not be complete without addressing the anomaly of the poor returns to small-cap growth stocks, particularly the stocks of firms that make relatively large investments and have poor profitability.

THE SMALL-CAP GROWTH ANOMALY

While small-cap stocks as a whole have provided higher returns (the size premium), small-cap growth stocks have produced below-market returns. Using the Fama-French indices, from 1927 through 2015, the annualized return for U.S. large-cap stocks was 9.8 percent, 2 percent below the 11.8 percent return of U.S. small-cap stocks. However, over the same period, U.S. small-cap growth stocks returned just 8.7 percent.

At the same time they earned lower annualized returns, small-cap growth stocks exhibited higher volatility. Their annualized standard deviation of returns was 32 percent compared to a standard deviation of 30 percent for small-cap stocks as a whole. Their tendency to produce lower returns while exhibiting higher volatility is why small-cap growth stocks have been referred to as the "black hole" of investing — and why they present an anomaly.

BEHAVIORAL EXPLANATION

The field of behavioral finance provides an explanation for this anomaly. It exists because investors have a preference for "lottery tickets." Nicholas Barberis and Ming Huang, authors of the 2008 study "Stocks as Lotteries: The Implications of Probability Weighting for Security Prices," found that:

- Investors have a preference for securities that exhibit positive skewness, in which returns to the right of (more than) the mean are fewer but farther from it than returns to the left of (less than) the mean. Such investments provide the small chance of a huge payoff (winning the lottery). Investors find this small possibility attractive. The result is that positively skewed securities tend to be "overpriced" and thus subsequently earn negative average excess returns.

- The preference for positively skewed assets explains the existence of several anomalies (deviations from the norm) to the efficient market hypothesis (EMH), including the low average return on initial public offerings (IPOs), private equity, and distressed stocks, despite their high risks.

In theory, we would expect anomalies to be arbitraged away by investors who do not have this same preference for positive skewness. They should be willing to accept the risks of a large loss in exchange for the higher expected return that shorting overvalued assets can provide. However, in the real world, anomalies can persist because there are limits to arbitrage. First, many institutional investors (such as pension plans, endowments, and mutual funds) are prohibited by their charters from taking short positions.

Second, the cost of borrowing a stock in order to short it can be expensive, and there can also be a limited supply of stocks available to borrow for the purpose of shorting. This can be especially true for small growth stocks.

Third, investors are unwilling to accept the risks of shorting because of the potential for unlimited losses. This is prospect theory at work, where the pain of a loss is much larger than the joy of an equal gain.

Fourth, short-sellers run the risk that their borrowed securities are recalled before the strategy pays off. They also run the risk that the strategy performs poorly in the short run, triggering an early liquidation.

Taken together, these factors suggest that investors may be unwilling to trade against the overpricing of skewed securities, allowing the anomaly to persist.

CONTROLLING FOR JUNK

Some researchers have questioned the robustness of the size premium, noting that it has declined since its initial publication. We cover the topic of post-publication decay more generally in Chapter 8, and conclude that size is still a factor worth using. Furthermore, while size is powerful on its own, its merits further increase when considered in combination with other factors. For example, both the value and momentum factors (covered in the next two chapters) are stronger for small stocks than for large stocks. Clifford Asness, Andrea Frazzini, Ronen Israel, Tobias Moskowitz, and Lasse Pedersen further contributed to our understanding of the size premium with their 2015 study "Size Matters, If You Control Your Junk." They examined the size premium while controlling for the quality factor (see Chapter 5).

Asness and his colleagues noted: "Stocks with very poor quality (i.e., "junk") are typically very small, have low average returns, and are typically distressed and illiquid securities. These characteristics drive the strong negative relation between size and quality and the returns of these junk stocks chiefly explain the sporadic performance of the size premium and the challenges that have been hurled at it."

We will discuss the characteristics of high-quality stocks in detail in Chapter 5. But briefly, the research shows that these types of stocks, the kind Benjamin Graham and Warren Buffett have long advocated buying, outperform low-quality stocks with the opposite characteristics (those "lottery-ticket" equities). The authors additionally found that "small quality stocks outperform large quality stocks and small junk stocks outperform large junk stocks, but the standard size effect suffers from a size-quality composition effect."

In other words, the returns to small stocks would be notably higher except that they tend to be of lower quality. The authors concluded that after controlling for quality, a significant size premium emerges. This premium:

- is stable through time;
- is robust to its specification;
- is more consistent across seasons and markets, for example, making the "January effect" of high size returns more smoothly distributed throughout the year;
- is not concentrated in microcaps;
- is not captured by an illiquidity premium;
- explains interactions between size and other return characteristics, such as value and momentum; and
- results in an almost perfect monotonic relationship between size deciles and excess returns (as we move from small-cap to large-cap stocks, excess returns steadily decline and eventually become negative for the largest equities).

Another important finding was that higher-quality stocks were more liquid, which has important implications for portfolio construction and implementation.

Asness, Frazzini, Israel, Moskowitz, and Pedersen found similar results when, instead of controlling for the quality factor, they controlled for the low-beta factor (discussed in Appendix D). High-beta stocks tend to be more speculative (again, those lottery tickets) and have very poor historical returns. What is more, high-beta stocks tend to be the very same stocks as those with low-quality attributes. In addition, they found that small-cap stocks have negative exposure to two relatively new factors, the profitability factor (referred to as RMW, or robust minus weak; see Chapter 5) and the investment factor (referred to as CMA, or conservative minus aggressive). High-profitability firms outperform low-profitability ones, and low-investment firms outperform high-investment ones. So again, controlling for these factors further improves the performance of size.

Recognizing the negative premium provided by "black hole" small-cap growth stocks, certain mutual fund families run structured, passively managed funds that, in their fund construction rules, create screens to eliminate stocks that have negative characteristics from being considered. Among the funds in this group are those managed by AQR Funds, Bridgeway Capital Management, and Dimensional Fund Advisors.

The bottom line, however, is that, even without these refinements, the size factor clearly meets all of our criteria for considering an allocation to it.

Table 2.2 provides a summary of the data on the two equity premiums we have covered so far.

TABLE 2.2 MARKET BETA AND SIZE (1927–2015)

	MARKET BETA	SIZE
ANNUAL PREMIUM (%)	8.3	3.3
SHARPE RATIO	0.40	0.24
1-YEAR ODDS OF OUTPERFORMANCE (%)	66	59
3-YEAR ODDS OF OUTPERFORMANCE (%)	76	66
5-YEAR ODDS OF OUTPERFORMANCE (%)	82	70
10-YEAR ODDS OF OUTPERFORMANCE (%)	90	77
20-YEAR ODDS OF OUTPERFORMANCE (%)	96	86

We now turn to the value factor and our evaluation of it against the established criteria.

CHAPTER 3
THE VALUE FACTOR

As we discussed, Eugene Fama and Kenneth French's 1992 paper "The Cross-Section of Expected Stock Returns" resulted in the development of the Fama–French three-factor model. This model added the size and value factors to the market beta factor. A benefit of adding the value factor — the tendency for relatively cheap assets to outperform relatively expensive ones — was that its inclusion went a long way toward explaining the superior performance of superstar investors from the value school of Benjamin Graham and David Dodd. The anomaly these investors presented diminished as alpha was transformed into beta (loading on factors). Of course, this hindsight should not detract from how we should view the ingenuity of their work. After all, they not only employed these factors in strategies before they were added to the model, but they employed them before factor investing was even an academic concept.

Because all factors are long/short portfolios, the value premium is calculated by taking the annual average return of value stocks and subtracting the annual average return of

61

growth stocks. Thus, the value factor is referred to as HML —
the return on high (the "H") book-to-market (BtM) stocks minus
the return on low (the "L") BtM stocks. While there are various
metrics for determining value, the most commonly used
academically is the BtM ratio. Value stocks are then defined as
the 30 percent of stocks with the highest BtM ratio and growth
stocks are defined as the 30 percent of stocks with the lowest
BtM ratio. The middle 40 percent are considered core stocks.
From 1927 through 2015, the annual U.S. value premium has
been 4.8 percent.

PERSISTENT

Although not as persistent as the market beta premium, the
value premium has been more persistent than the size premium.
Table 3.1 shows the persistence of the value premium over the
period from 1927 through 2015.

TABLE 3.1: ODDS OF OUTPERFORMANCE (%)

	1-YEAR	3-YEAR	5-YEAR	10-YEAR	20-YEAR
VALUE	63	72	78	86	94

The Sharpe ratio of the value premium was 0.34, the fourth-
highest of all the premiums we will discuss. Recall that the
highest Sharpe ratio was 0.61 and the lowest 0.06.

PERVASIVE

To determine if the value premium has been pervasive, we will first compare the returns of the Fama-French International Growth Index to the returns of the Fama-French International Value Index. For the period from 1975 through 2015, the Fama-French International Growth Index returned 8.6 percent and the Fama-French International Value Index returned 13.8 percent, a 5.2 percent advantage for value.

We can also look at emerging markets. From 1989 through 2015, the Fama-French Emerging Markets Growth Index returned 9.3 percent and the Fama-French Emerging Markets Value Index returned 13.0 percent.

Thanks to the research team at DFA, we can also examine the evidence from individual European equity markets. The firm's November 2015 research report "Dimensions of Equity Returns in Europe" covered 15 European markets for the 33-year period from 1982 through 2014. Researchers found that value stocks in Europe showed a sizeable return premium over growth stocks in their data sample. The value premium was 4.9 percent for Europe as a whole. Across the 15 individual markets, the value premium ranged from a low of 1.5 percent in Ireland to 7.3 percent in Sweden. The value premium in Europe was similar to realized value premiums in the United States (4.5 percent) and in international developed markets (6.0 percent) during the period from 1982 through 2014.

The 2013 study from Clifford Asness, Tobias Moskowitz, and Lasse Pedersen, "Value and Momentum Everywhere," provides us with further evidence on the pervasiveness of the value premium. The authors examined the value factor across 18 developed market countries, including the United States, the United Kingdom, continental Europe, and Japan, and found a significant return premium to value in every stock market, with the strongest performance in Japan.

INVESTABLE

Over sufficiently long time periods, value index funds have typically outperformed their growth counterparts around the world. To further determine if live funds can capture the returns of the value factor, we will compare the returns of DFA's value funds with the returns of appropriate value indices.

From inception in March 1993 through December 2015, the DFA U.S. Large Cap Value Portfolio Institutional Class fund (DFLVX), with a current expense ratio of 0.27 percent, returned 9.8 percent. It outperformed the MSCI US Prime Market Value Index, which returned 9.3 percent, and the Russell 1000 Value Index, which returned 9.4 percent.

From inception in April 1993 through December 2015, the DFA U.S. Small Cap Value Portfolio Institutional Class fund (DFSVX), with a current expense ratio of 0.52 percent, returned 11.6 percent. It outperformed the MSCI US Small

Cap Value Index, which returned 10.6 percent, and the Russell 2000 Value Index, which returned 9.7 percent.[1]

From June 1994 (the start-date of the MSCI EAFE Value Index) through December 2015, the DFA International Value III Portfolio fund (DFVIX), with a current expense ratio of 0.25 percent, returned 5.9 percent and outperformed the MSCI EAFE Value Index, which returned 5.1 percent.

From inception in January 1995 through December 2015, the DFA International Small Cap Value Portfolio I fund (DISVX), with a current expense ratio of 0.69 percent, returned 7.4 percent, matching the return of the MSCI EAFE Small Cap Value Index.

From January 1997 (the start-date of the MSCI Emerging Markets Value Index) through December 2015, the DFA Emerging Markets Value Portfolio Institutional Class fund (DFEVX), with a current expense ratio of 0.56 percent, returned 9.8 percent and outperformed the MSCI Emerging Markets Value Index, which returned 5.7 percent.

The body of evidence demonstrates that the value premium certainly can be captured by live funds and that the deeper the value exposure, the higher the return.

---

1   The MSCI index returns that we report throughout this book are gross returns. Net returns include a reduction for the impact of international taxes on dividends. We use the gross returns mainly because they often have a longer history. Additionally, gross returns present a higher hurdle. If a fund compares favorably against gross returns, it will look even better against net returns. For example, the MSCI Emerging Markets Value Index had net returns of 7.0 percent for this period.

INTUITIVE

While there has been little controversy over the source of the size premium (it is generally accepted that small-cap stocks are riskier than large-cap stocks), there has been great debate as to the source of the value premium. There is a belief among many academics that the value premium is actually an anomaly (in contradiction to the EMH) and the result of persistent pricing errors made by investors. For example, those from the "behavioral school" of finance believe investors naively extrapolate past growth when evaluating a company and thus overreact to that information, resulting in a situation where growth companies are persistently overpriced and value companies are persistently underpriced. Behavioralists also find that investors confuse familiarity with safety. Because they tend to be more familiar with popular growth stocks, those stocks tend to be overvalued.

The debate rages on among financial economists over whether the value premium is risk-based or behavioral-based, with supporting evidence on both sides. And it is certainly possible that both the mispricing and risk explanations play a role in the premium. We will first look at the academic evidence supporting the risk-based explanation for the value premium, beginning with the 1998 paper "Risk and Return of Value Stocks." The authors Nai-fu Chen and Feng Zhang make the case that value stocks do contain a distress (risk) factor. They examined three intuitive measures of distress present in value companies:

cutting dividends by at least 25 percent, a high ratio of debt to equity, and a high standard deviation of earnings.

Chen and Zhang found that the three measures all captured the returns information (produced high correlations) contained in portfolios as ranked by BtM. When these three metrics were present, returns were greater. Because all three measures have simple, intuitive risk interpretations by being associated with firms in distress, the authors state that it is not surprising the risk factors they studied were both highly correlated and were also highly correlated with BtM rankings. Their conclusion was that value stocks are cheap because they tend to be firms in distress, with high leverage, and that face substantial earnings risk. They therefore provide higher returns due to the greater risks facing value investors.

Next, we look at the 2005 study by Lu Zhang, "The Value Premium." He concluded that the value premium could be explained by the asymmetric risk of value stocks. Value stocks are much riskier than growth stocks in bad economic times and only moderately less risky than growth stocks in good times. Zhang explains that the asymmetric risk of value companies exists because value stocks are typically companies with unproductive capital. Asymmetric risk is important because of the following:

- Investment is irreversible. Once production capacity is put in place, it is very hard to reduce. Value companies carry more nonproductive capacity than growth companies.

- In periods of low economic activity, companies with

nonproductive capacity (value companies) suffer a greater negative impact in earnings because the burden of nonproductive capacity increases, and they find it more difficult than growth companies to adjust capacity.

- In periods of high economic activity, the previously nonproductive assets of value companies become productive, while growth companies find it harder to increase capacity.
- In good times, capital stock is easily expanded. In bad times, adjusting the level of capital is an extremely difficult task — especially so for value companies.

When these facts are combined with a high aversion to risk (especially when that risk can be expected to show up in difficult economic times, when investors' employment prospects are more likely to be in jeopardy), the result is a large and persistent value premium. This is consistent with the results of Motohiro Yogo's 2006 study "A Consumption-Based Explanation of Expected Stock Returns." Similar to his results for small-cap stocks, Yogo found that value stocks deliver low returns during recessions, when the marginal utility of consumption is highest. In other words, the returns of value stocks are more pro-cyclical than growth stocks. Thus, investors must be rewarded with high expected returns to hold these risky stocks.

We next examine a 2005 study, "Is the Book-to-Market Ratio a Measure of Risk?" The authors, Robert F. Peterkort and James

F. Nielsen, developed a leverage-based approach to investigate the BtM effect. Because leverage is risky, it is not surprising that they found a positive relationship between higher stock returns and market leverage. Their regression results also showed that when compared with market leverage, the BtM ratio added a small amount of explanatory power for stock returns. They wrote that they believe the incremental power of the BtM ratio is due to additional information about the riskiness of the firm's assets. Thus, they concluded that BtM effect is mostly a leverage (risk) effect. The authors had another interesting finding. When they considered only companies that they called "all-equity" firms (those with minimal amounts of mostly current debt, as opposed to long-term liabilities), there was no BtM effect at all. If the value premium is an anomaly, the mispricing should show up in all high-BtM firms, not just those with high leverage. These findings are consistent with those of Ralitsa Petkova's 2006 study "Do the Fama-French Factors Proxy for Innovations in Predictive Variables?"

Petkova found that value companies tend to be firms under distress, with high leverage and high uncertainty of cash flow. Therefore, shocks to the default spread (the spread between bonds of higher-rated credit and lower-rated credit) explain the cross-section of returns and is consistent with value being a measure of distress risk. In addition, growth stocks are high-duration assets (much of their value comes from expected future growth), making them similar to long-term bonds. Value stocks, on the other hand, are low-duration assets, making them more similar to short-term bonds. Thus, shocks to the term spread (the difference between short-term bonds and long-term bonds) also explain the cross-section of returns and is further consistent with value being a measure of distress risk.

Next, we look at the 2014 study "Value Premium and Default Risk," which covered the period from 1927 through 2011. The authors, Mohammed Elgammal and David G. McMillan, found that there was a "positive relationship between default risk and the value premium for both large and small firms together with a leverage effect." They concluded: "The results show a positive association between the default premium and the value premium accompanied with evidence for a leverage effect on the value premium. This lends support to the risk-based explanation for the source of value premium. That is, where the default premium captures systematic risk in the macroeconomy and that the value premium is associated with rational decision making on the part of investors. Value stocks characterized by poor performance, earnings and profitability compared with growth stocks are more vulnerable to the risk of default and lead the investors to require a higher return on value stocks as leverage increases."

These papers demonstrate the link between value stocks and financial distress at the asset level. Value stocks are not simply great bargains waiting to be scooped up as free money. Rather, they are cheap for a reason — a reason related to their riskiness.

And finally, we have the study "The Value Premium and Economic Activity: Long-Run Evidence from the United States."

To test the validity of the risk explanation, the authors, Angela J. Black, Bin Mao, and David G. McMillan, examined the relationship between the value premium and macroeconomic variables, such as industrial production, inflation, money supply, and interest rates. Their study covered the period from 1959 through 2005. The following is a summary of their findings.

First, in times of economic expansion, when industrial production rises, value stocks become less risky relative to growth stocks. Thus, the prices of value stocks increase more than the prices of growth stocks. The result is that the spread between the high book-to-market and low book-to-market stocks narrows and the value premium declines. In bad times, value stocks become riskier relative to growth stocks. The result is that the prices of value stocks decrease faster than growth stocks, and the value premium increases (a sign of increased risk). Therefore, there is a negative relationship between the value premium and industrial production. This certainly was the case in the most recent recession, which lasted from December 2007 through June 2009, when the value premium was –0.44 percent per month.

Second, a similar, negative relationship exists between the value premium and the money supply. Following an increase in the money supply, stock prices increase. The prices of value stocks tend to increase more than growth stocks, and the value premium shrinks. When money supply decreases, stock prices decrease, with the prices of value stocks decreasing more than growth stocks, and the value premium increases.

Third, there is a positive relationship between the value premium and interest rates. As long-run interest rates rise, stocks become less attractive than bonds and stock prices decrease, with the prices of value stocks decreasing faster than the prices of growth stocks. That leads to an increasing value premium. When interest rates fall, the prices of value stocks increase faster than the prices of growth stocks. This leads to a decreasing value premium.

Overall, Black, Mao, and McMillan found that value stocks are more sensitive to bad economic news, whereas growth stocks are more sensitive to good economic conditions. They reached the conclusion that the value premium is largely based on fundamental risk factors within the economy and arises through macroeconomic risk.[2]

The bottom line is that there are very simple and logical risk-based explanations for the existence of a value premium. We will add one final intuitive explanation. Value stocks have been more volatile than the market. From 1927 through 2015, the annual standard deviation of the Fama-French Large Cap Index was 19.7 percent. The annual standard deviation of the Fama-French Large Cap Value Index (ex-utilities) was much higher at 26.8 percent. The Fama-French Large Cap Growth Index (ex-utilities)

2 These paragraphs might tempt one to try and time their value exposure, for example by selling value stocks when adverse economic conditions arise. We strongly caution against this. Not only can trading costs and taxes increase, but getting the timing right is problematic for many reasons too lengthy to go into here. Suffice it to quote Harvard professor John Kenneth Galbraith: "The only function of economic forecasting is to make astrology look respectable."

had an annual standard deviation of 21.5 percent. We see the same pattern in small stocks. The annual standard deviation of the Fama-French Small Cap Index was 30.1 percent. It was 33.4 percent for both their Small Cap Value Index (ex-utilities) and Small Cap Growth Index (ex-utilities).

In summary, the academic research demonstrates that value firms have poorer earnings and profitability compared to growth firms. And value firms' greater leverage increases their risks in times of financial distress. Stocks that do poorly in bad times should command large premiums. Thus, investors demand a higher return on value stocks than on growth stocks as compensation for higher vulnerability due to financial distress. With that said, there are behavioral explanations for the premium as well.

BEHAVIORAL EXPLANATIONS (MISPRICINGS)

One behavioral explanation for the value premium is that investors are systematically too optimistic in their expectations for the performance of growth companies and too pessimistic in their expectations for value companies. Ultimately, prices correct when expectations are not met. An early well-known study of this reasoning is the 1994 paper "Contrarian Investment, Extrapolation, and Risk" by Josef Lakonishok, Andrei Shleifer, and Robert W. Vishny. Another behavioral explanation is that investors confuse familiarity with safety. Because they tend to be more familiar with popular growth stocks, those stocks tend to be overvalued.

Joseph D. Piotroski and Eric C. So, authors of the study "Identifying Expectation Errors in Value/Glamour Strategies: A Fundamental Analysis Approach," which covered the period from 1972 through 2010, tested the mispricing hypothesis by identifying potential ex-ante biases and comparing expectations implied by pricing multiples against the strength of firms' fundamentals. Value strategies would be successful if prices do not accurately reflect the future cash flow implications of historical information in a timely manner, resulting in equity prices that temporarily drift away from their fundamental values.

Piotroski and So classified and allocated observations into value and glamour (growth) portfolios on the basis of each firm's BtM ratio. A firm's BtM ratio reflects the market's expectations about future performance. Firms with higher expectations will have higher prices and a lower BtM ratio, while, conversely, firms with weak expectations will have lower prices and a higher BtM ratio. Thus, the book-to-market ratio serves as a proxy for the relative strength of the market's expectations about a firm's future performance.

The authors classified a firm's recent financial strength by utilizing the aggregate statistic FSCORE, which is based on nine financial signals designed to measure three different dimensions of a firm's financial condition: profitability, change in financial leverage/liquidity, and change in operational efficiency. The FSCORE is an early example of a composite quality factor, which we discuss more fully in Chapter 5. Firms with the poorest signals have the greatest deterioration in fundamentals and are classified as low FSCORE firms. Firms receiving the highest score have the greatest improvement in fundamentals and are classified as high FSCORE firms. Prior research has demonstrated that the FSCORE is positively correlated with future earnings growth and future profitability levels. Low FSCORE firms experience continued deterioration in future profitability and high FSCORE firms experience overall improvement in profitability.

The following is a summary of Piotroski and So's findings:

- Among firms where the expectations implied by their current value/glamour classification were consistent with the strength of their fundamentals, the value/glamour effect in realized returns is statistically and economically indistinguishable from zero.

- The returns to traditional value/glamour strategies are concentrated among those firms where the expectations implied by their current value/glamour classification are incongruent ex-ante with the strength of their fundamentals.

- Returns to this "incongruent value/glamour strategy" are robust and significantly larger than the average return generated by a traditional value/glamour strategy.

In the academic literature, the explanation for the mispricing of value stocks relative to growth stocks is that behavioral errors, such as optimism, anchoring, and confirmation biases, cause investors to underweight or ignore contrarian information. As Piotroski and So noted, "Investors in glamour stocks are likely to under-react to information that contradict their beliefs about firms' growth prospects or reflect the effects of mean reversion in performance. Similarly, value stocks, being inherently more distressed than glamour stocks, tend to be neglected by investors; as a result, performance expectations for value firms may be too pessimistic and reflect improvements in fundamentals too slowly."

Piotroski and So's findings were consistent with the mispricing explanations for the value premium. They found that the value/glamour effect was concentrated among the subset of firms where expectations implied by book-to-market ratios were not aligned with the strength of the firms' fundamentals (FSCORE). And, more importantly, the value/glamour effect was nonexistent among firms where expectations in price *were* aligned with the strength of the firm's recent fundamentals. They concluded that firms with low book-to-market ratios and low FSCOREs (weak fundamentals) were persistently overvalued, and firms with high book-to-market ratios and high FSCOREs (strong fundamentals) were persistently undervalued. It was in these subsets that the pricing errors were strongest. The authors also noted that while both the traditional value/glamour strategy (relying solely on BtM rankings) and the incongruent value/

glamour strategy produce consistently positive annual returns, the frequency of positive returns was higher for the incongruent value/glamour strategy. It generated positive returns in 35 out of 39 years over the sample period (versus 27 out of 39 years for the traditional value/glamour strategy). They also found that annual returns to the incongruent value/glamour strategy were larger than the traditional value/glamour strategy in all but six years, with an average annual portfolio return of 20.8 percent versus 10.5 percent for the traditional value/glamour strategy.

Another behavioral error that has been shown to lead to mispricing of stocks is the problem known as "anchoring."

ANCHORING

Keith Anderson and Tomasz Zastawniak contributed to the literature that demonstrates the persistent overvaluation of the earnings prospects for growth stocks with their 2016 study "Glamour, Value and Anchoring on the Changing P/E." Their working hypothesis was that the differing experiences of glamour and value investors can be explained by the well-documented behavior of anchoring.

Anchoring is a form of cognitive bias in which people place an inordinate amount of importance on certain values or attributes, which then act as a reference point, and inappropriately weight the influence of subsequent data to support their initial assessment. For example, some investors will tend to hang on to a losing investment because they are waiting for it to at least break even, anchoring their investment's present value to the value it once had.

Anchoring is such a powerful force that, even in experiments when subjects could plainly see the anchor and that it could not possibly be any sort of guide to an answer, the bias continued to play a role. For example, in a famous experiment, Daniel Kahneman and Amos Tversky asked subjects to spin a roulette wheel rigged to stop at 10 or 65, and then asked that they estimate the percentage of countries in the United Nations that are African. Subjects who saw a spin of 10 guessed 25 percent, while those who spun 65 guessed 45 percent.

ANCHORING ON THE P/E RATIO

Anderson and Zastawniak hypothesized that investors may anchor on the price-to-earnings (P/E) ratio of a stock when they initially invest in it. They write: "Given an observed high P/E of 25 [investors] may think (consciously or not), 'Thousands of investors, some of whom are better informed than I am, are already paying $25 for each $1 of current earnings. This must be a valuable, high growth company to justify that.'"

The authors then posit that such investors "fail to adjust their future expectations sufficiently according to mean reversion." Thus, having now bought the stock, investors "expect the P/E to change slowly, if at all. As time goes on, the P/E decile changes, and different prospects for returns attach to each decile. If there is a differential drift in the P/E and hence returns between value and glamour stocks that are not expected by investors, this could account for why glamour investors end up disappointed." In other words, investors expect stocks with high valuations to remain that way, even though the evidence suggests that results are likely to disappoint.

Anderson and Zastawniak's study covered the period from 1983 through 2010. They ranked stocks by P/E, putting them into 15 bins, five of which had negative earnings. On average, about one-third of stocks in their sample had losses in a given year. They then tracked the movement of each stock into a bin the next year and examined the equal-weighted returns of all these transitions. They reported the following results:

- Examining the two extremes of stocks with positive earnings, value stocks outperformed glamour stocks by an annual average of 7.5 percent. Furthermore, the value bin's standard deviation of returns is only slightly greater than that of the glamour bin's and not enough to account for the higher returns.

- The returns for glamour investors are relatively poor, whatever their time horizon. However, value investors can expect superior returns if they hold for two to three years (not just for one year), as recommended by Benjamin Graham. The returns to value stocks, while just 5 percent for the first year, were 21 percent for the second year, and 15 percent for the third year. After that, returns declined to little more than the returns on glamour shares.

- A glamour company has a 34 percent chance of becoming a loss-maker next year, compared to just 25 percent for a value company.

- Extreme loss-makers and value companies are most likely to remain in their same bins the following year, at 32 percent and 34 percent, respectively. Companies in the bins between the extremes are much more likely to move, with the probability of remaining in the same bin only 15–20 percent. But glamour investors appear to underestimate the tendency of their preferred stocks to change bins.

- Extreme loss-makers find it particularly difficult to break out of the spiral. They have only a one-in-six chance of turning a profit in the next year, compared to a 27 percent chance of being delisted. Recall that this is in line with the lottery effect and the underperformance of small growth stocks we examined in the last chapter.

- Glamour stocks that remain in the same bin provide three times the rate of return of value stocks that remain in the same bin (36 percent versus 12 percent, respectively). This could help explain the preference for glamour stocks.

However, few companies stay in the same bin the following year, and glamour stocks have a greater tendency to move (roughly five-sixths of the time) and then give very poor returns. In addition, if glamour stocks start making losses, they suffer greatly. For example, those extreme glamour stocks that move from slightly positive earnings to the most negative earnings lose on average 41 percent. On the other hand, value shares are much more likely to remain in or near the value P/E range.

• Smaller companies are much more likely than large companies to move from the glamour bins to the value bins. In other words, the small high-flyers have a greater tendency to see their shares come tumbling down, moving from lofty valuations to being more reasonably priced. These are exactly the sort of stocks most likely to be dominated by retail investors more prone to behavioral biases. These also are exactly the type of stocks most difficult for arbitrageurs to short, thereby correcting mispricings.

• Shares in the extreme-loser bins have respectable mean returns, but the median returns are very poor and the standard deviation of returns is double what it is for the glamour and value bins. Any good returns from an extreme-loser stock depend on the firm becoming profitable, or at least halting such heavy losses. Each year, however, there is an almost 60 percent chance of an extreme-loser firm either ceasing to be quoted or remaining an extreme loser stock.

When considered together, the findings support Anderson and Zastawniak's thesis that glamour investors anchor on the high P/E value of growth shares, while ignoring the high likelihood that this P/E ratio will change in the future.

Another mispricing explanation relates to the behavior of loss aversion.

LOSS AVERSION

Loss aversion is the tendency to be more sensitive (place greater utility) on losses than on gains. For instance, the pain of a $1,000 loss is much greater than the pleasure received from a $1,000 gain. Loss aversion leads individuals to require more than even-money odds to accept even-money bets. An example would be that the average individual would not be willing to bet on the outcome of a coin flip unless they received odds of greater than 2:1 to make the bet. And the larger the amount involved, the greater the odds they would need. Note that the reverse is true, even when the odds on winning are very poor but losses are small and the payoff is great, like in a lottery. Individuals then become risk lovers, as we saw in the section on small growth stocks in Chapter 2.

Nicholas Barberis and Ming Huang, authors of the 2001 study "Mental Accounting, Loss Aversion, and Individual Stock Returns," explain that the size of investor loss aversion depends on whether the individual has recently experienced gains or losses. They write: "A loss that comes after prior gains is less painful than usual, because it is cushioned by those earlier gains." In other words, risk aversion decreases because the investor is now playing with the house's money. The authors continue: "On the other hand, a loss that comes after other losses is more painful than usual: After being burned by the first loss, people become more sensitive to additional setbacks."

Growth stocks are generally companies that have performed well recently, as evidenced by their current high price. Investors, therefore, become less concerned about future losses, being cushioned by the gains from recent performance. They thus apply a lower risk premium (as they are now willing to accept more risk) to growth stocks. This might also help explain the momentum effect (see Chapter 4) because the now low required risk premium drives prices up even further and, of course, future expected returns lower. On the other hand, value stocks are generally associated with companies that have performed poorly in the recent past, as evidenced by their current low prices. The pain of the recent loss causes investors to perceive these stocks as even riskier. They therefore raise the required risk premium, driving prices even lower and expected future returns even higher.

There is one other behavioral explanation we need to cover. As we discussed in the section on the small-cap growth anomaly, many investors have a preference for "lottery ticket" investments that provide the small chance of a huge payoff. Investors find this small possibility attractive. The result is that positively skewed securities (small-cap growth stocks) tend to be "overpriced," meaning that they earn negative average excess returns. The poor returns to these stocks are reflected in the value premium.

Summarizing, the behavior patterns we have discussed help explain why the value premium has been so large, larger indeed than most financial economists believe is justified based solely on risk characteristics. It also explains why these patterns are likely to continue to persist — unless, of course, investors stop acting like human beings.

ROBUST TO VARIOUS DEFINITIONS

While the most common value metric is the BtM ratio, there are other metrics that can be used to separate cheap from expensive stocks. Thus, if BtM was the only metric that delivered a value premium, we would be suspicious that the finding was simply the result of researchers engaging in a data mining exercise, in which they torment the data until it confesses. However, this is not the case. For example, in the United States for the period from 1952 through 2015, the annualized value premium as measured by BtM was 4.1 percent (t-stat[3] = 2.4), 4.7 percent (t-stat = 2.9) as measured by the cash flow-to-price ratio, and 6.3 percent (t-stat = 3.4) as measured by the earnings-to-price ratio. Not only do we see a value premium despite the various definitions, many of these alternates have even higher returns.

As further evidence of the robustness of the value premium, the research report "Value vs. Glamour: A Long-Term Worldwide Perspective" by The Brandes Institute, which covered developed markets for the period from January 1980 through June 2014, found a similar value premium no matter the metric used. Using the BtM metric, the premium was 6.1 percent. Using the earnings-to-price metric, it was 7.3 percent. And using the cash flow-to-price metric, it was 8.0 percent. The value premium was there across all market capitalizations (although it has been greater in small-cap stocks than in large-cap stocks), in the non-U.S. developed markets, and in emerging markets as well (where the value premium was the largest). These findings give us confidence that these results for value are not just random outcomes.

The bottom line is that the value factor clearly meets all of our criteria for considering an allocation to it.

Table 3.2 provides a summary of the data on the equity factors we have covered so far.

---

3   A t-statistic (or t-stat) is a measure of statistical significance. A value greater than about 2 is generally considered meaningfully different from random noise, with a higher number indicating even greater confidence.

TABLE 3.2: MARKET BETA, SIZE, AND VALUE (1927–2015)

	MARKET BETA	SIZE	VALUE
ANNUAL PREMIUM (%)	8.3	3.3	4.8
SHARPE RATIO	0.40	0.24	0.34
1-YEAR ODDS OF OUTPERFORMANCE (%)	66	59	63
3-YEAR ODDS OF OUTPERFORMANCE (%)	76	66	72
5-YEAR ODDS OF OUTPERFORMANCE (%)	82	70	78
10-YEAR ODDS OF OUTPERFORMANCE (%)	90	77	86
20-YEAR ODDS OF OUTPERFORMANCE (%)	96	86	94

We now turn to the momentum factor and, as we have done before, will evaluate it against our established criteria.

CHAPTER 4
THE MOMENTUM FACTOR

Momentum is the tendency for assets that have performed well (poorly) in the recent past to continue to perform well (poorly) in the future, at least for a short period of time. In 1997, Mark Carhart, in his study "On Persistence in Mutual Fund Performance," was the first to use momentum, together with the three Fama–French factors (market beta, size, and value), to explain mutual fund returns. Initial research on momentum was published by Narasimhan Jegadeesh and Sheridan Titman, authors of the 1993 study "Returns to Buying Winners and Selling Losers: Implications for Stock Market Efficiency."

Here we define momentum as the last 12 months of returns excluding the most recent month (in other words, months 2–12). The most recent month is excluded as it tends to show a reversal, which some have attributed to microstructure (trading) effects. The momentum factor is the average return of the top 30 percent of stocks minus the average return of the bottom 30 percent as ranked by this measure. The momentum factor is referred to as UMD, or up minus down.

The addition of the momentum factor made another significant contribution to the explanatory power of asset pricing models. Whereas the three-factor model explained about 90 percent of the differences in returns of diversified portfolios, that explanatory power was now increased by about 5 percentage points, into the mid-90s. And with that, the four-factor model became the workhorse model in finance, used to analyze and explain the performance of investment managers and their strategies. For the period from 1927 through 2015, the annual average return to the momentum factor was 9.6 percent.

Before beginning our analysis, we need to explain that the academic literature has investigated the existence and performance of two different types of momentum. The first is what is called cross-sectional momentum. This is the type of momentum that Jegadeesh and Titman, as well as Carhart, studied and is used in the four-factor model. Cross-sectional momentum measures *relative* performance, comparing the return of an asset relative to the returns of other assets within the same asset class. Thus, in a given asset class, a cross-sectional momentum strategy might buy the 30 percent of assets with the best relative performance and short sell those with the worst relative performance. Even if all the assets had risen in value, a cross-sectional momentum strategy would still short the assets with the lowest returns.

The other type of momentum is called time-series momentum. It is also referred to as trend-following because it measures the trend of an asset with respect to its own performance. Thus, unlike cross-sectional momentum, time-series momentum is defined by *absolute* performance. It buys assets that have been rising in value and short sells assets that have been falling. In contrast to cross-sectional momentum, if all assets rise in value, then none of them would be shorted.

The following discussion is focused on the cross-sectional momentum factor. We look at the evidence on time-series momentum in Appendix F.

PERSISTENT

Over the period from 1927 through 2015, not only has the momentum premium been larger than the United States' equity premium (9.6 percent versus 8.3 percent), it has also been more persistent.

TABLE 4.1: ODDS OF OUTPERFORMANCE (%)

	1-YEAR	3-YEAR	5-YEAR	10-YEAR	20-YEAR
MOMENTUM	73	86	91	97	100

It is important to note that the momentum premium has also been persistent over the more than 20 years since the publication of the aforementioned 1993 paper by Jegadeesh and Titman. Though smaller than the 9.6 percent premium for the full period from 1927 through 2015, from 1994 through 2015 the momentum premium was still 6.3 percent. And finally, its Sharpe ratio was

0.61 — by far the highest of all the premiums we will discuss. The next closest Sharpe ratios were the 0.40 ratio for the market beta factor and the 0.38 ratio for the quality factor.

PERVASIVE

The size of the premium and its persistence provides strong empirical evidence for the momentum premium. Further, it has been quite pervasive. In his 2010 white paper "Explanations for the Momentum Premium," Tobias Moskowitz found that it has been present in 40 other countries, and in more than a dozen other asset classes. And the 2013 study "Value and Momentum Everywhere" by Clifford Asness, Tobias Moskowitz, and Lasse Pedersen examined the value and momentum factors across eight different markets and asset classes (individual stocks in the United States, the United Kingdom, continental Europe, and Japan, as well as country equity index futures, government bonds, currencies, and commodity futures). The authors found that not only was there a positive momentum premium in every asset class and market (especially in Europe), it was also statistically significant everywhere except Japan.

We also have evidence from the 2012 study "Size, Value, and Momentum in International Stock Returns." Eugene Fama and Kenneth French examined international stock returns for 23 countries for the period from November 1989 through March 2011. They split these 23 markets into four regions: North America (which includes the United States and Canada);

Japan; Asia Pacific (which includes Australia, New Zealand, Hong Kong, and Singapore, but not Japan); and Europe (which includes Austria, Belgium, Denmark, Finland, France, Germany, Greece, Ireland, Italy, the Netherlands, Norway, Portugal, Spain, Sweden, Switzerland, and the United Kingdom). They found that momentum returns were strong everywhere except Japan, with the premium ranging from 0.64 percent per month (t-stat = 1.9) for North America to 0.92 percent per month (t-stat = 3.4) for Europe. The authors also found that while there is a momentum premium in all size groups, the effect is stronger for small stocks, especially microcaps. The average global momentum premium was 0.62 percent per month (t-stat = 2.3), the result of a 0.82 percent per month premium for small-cap stocks (t-stat = 3.1) and a 0.41 percent per month premium for large-cap stocks (t-stat = 1.4). Japan exhibited no momentum premium for either small- or large-cap stocks — this exception could easily be explained by a chance result. It could also be explained by the fact that value has worked so strongly in Japan during this period, and value and momentum tend to be negatively correlated. The interaction of value and momentum in Japan was studied in detail by Clifford Asness in his 2011 paper "Momentum in Japan: The Exception That Proves the Rule."

The study covering the longest period is the 2015 paper by Christopher C. Geczy and Mikhail Samonov, "215 Years of Global Multi-Asset Momentum: 1800–2014 (Equities, Sectors, Currencies, Bonds, Commodities and Stocks)." Using Global Financial Data databases and additional data available through Bloomberg, the authors created an expanded dataset going back to 1800. It included 47 country equity indices, 48 currencies (including the euro), 43 government bond indices, 76 commodities, 301 global sectors, and 34,795 U.S. stocks. They found that over this 215-year history, the momentum return is consistently significant within each asset class and across six of them (country equities, currencies, country government bonds, commodities, global sectors, and U.S. stocks). Country equity momentum (using price-only data, as older dividend information was not always available) had the largest long/short spread at 0.88 percent per month (t-stat = 10.6). Using the total return definition of momentum, the premium is smaller, but still 0.57 percent per month (t-stat = 6.8). Tied for the second-largest momentum premium were currencies, with a spread of 0.51 percent per month (t-stat = 9.6), and U.S. stocks with a premium of 0.51 percent per month (t-stat = 6.0). Global sector momentum generated a premium of 0.36 percent per month (t-stat = 6.6), and global country bond momentum averaged a premium of 0.13 percent per month (t-stat = 2.3). This is the longest backtest of any sort we are aware of. It clearly establishes momentum as a persistent and pervasive empirical fact.

INVESTABLE

Despite this long history, some have questioned the usefulness of momentum in practical money management because its higher turnover could lead to excessive transaction costs. Yet, one can always use momentum to provide information on which assets to avoid and which to hold longer, thereby avoiding an increase in turnover. And while trading was certainly more difficult and expensive in the 1800s, markets today are far more liquid. Momentum is currently utilized by many institutional investors.

Using nearly $1 trillion of live trading data from a large institutional money manager across 19 developed equity markets over the period from 1998 to 2011, Andrea Frazzini, Ronen Israel, and Tobias Moskowitz, authors of the paper "Trading Costs of Asset Pricing Anomalies," measured the real-world transaction costs facing an arbitrageur and applied them to the momentum strategy. The following is a summary of their findings:

- Actual trading costs are low enough to allow for the potential scale of these strategies to be much larger than previous studies would indicate. The reason is that prior studies computed trading costs for average investors, which are about 10 times higher than the costs estimated for a large arbitrageur using more sophisticated strategies, such as algorithmic trading programs.
- Strategies designed to reduce transaction costs can substantially increase net returns and capacity, without incurring significant style drift. The institutional money manager in the study had been running long-only momentum indices since

July 2009. The actual realized price impact costs in these funds had been just 8.0, 18.2, and 5.9 basis points in large-cap, small-cap, and international momentum funds, respectively. This is in line with, but slightly lower than, the estimates from historical trading data. Based on the data, the authors estimated that capacity for long/short strategies of size, value, and momentum are $103 billion, $83 billion, and $52 billion among U.S. securities, respectively, and $156 billion, $190 billion, and $89 billion, respectively, for global securities.

Frazzini, Israel, and Moskowitz concluded that these strategies are robust, implementable, and sizeable. We additionally note that momentum becomes even easier to implement in combination with lower turnover factors, such as value.

CRITIQUES ABOUT MOMENTUM

One of the persistent myths about momentum is that it cannot be captured by long-only investors because momentum can only be exploited on the short side. And the short side is more expensive to trade, because in order to sell short, shares must be borrowed and a lending fee is incurred. With that said, Clifford Asness, Andrea Frazzini, Ronen Israel, and Tobias Moskowitz, authors of the 2014 paper "Fact, Fiction and Momentum

Investing," found that only slightly more than half (52 percent) of the U.S. momentum premium in stocks actually comes from the long side. They also found no evidence that the short side dominated the momentum premium in either international markets or any of the five asset classes they examined. Even if it were true that momentum cannot be captured on the short side, the authors observed that "for a long-only investor, being underweight a security relative to the market is economically similar to being short the security (albeit with the constraint that your largest underweight can only be as large as a stock's weight in the benchmark or market)."

Asness, Frazzini, Israel, and Moskowitz also addressed a second myth about momentum, specifically that it exists only in small-cap stocks where trading costs are higher. They found that while there is some evidence that the momentum premium is stronger in small-cap stocks, there is still a notable momentum premium in large-cap stocks. From 1927 through 2013, the U.S. momentum premium was 9.8 percent per year in small-cap stocks, and 6.8 percent per year in large-cap stocks — and both were highly statistically significant. The international data are similar.

We also note the results of a 2016 study by Robert Novy-Marx and Mihail Velikov, "A Taxonomy of Anomalies and Their Trading Costs." Novy-Marx and Velikov examined the performance of 23 anomalies after accounting for estimated transaction costs. They also examined the effectiveness of three strategies designed to mitigate transaction costs. The first strategy calls for limiting trading to stocks with low expected transaction costs. The second is to reduce rebalancing frequencies (at the expense of some staleness in the signals on which the strategies are based). The authors note that this technique is popular among large institutional money managers. For example, the AQR Momentum indices from AQR Capital Management LLC, which are designed to track the momentum strategy with limited trading costs, are rebalanced quarterly instead of monthly. The third strategy is to lower turnover by introducing a buy/hold range, holding stocks that would no longer be bought. This strategy has long been used by Dimensional Fund Advisors (among others) for its small-cap funds and is also used now in MSCI indices.

Novy-Marx and Velikov divided their 23 anomalies into three groups according to these strategies' turnover. These three groups correspond roughly to strategies where the long and short sides, on average, each turn over less than once per year, between one and five times per year, and more than five times per year. Among the mid-turnover strategies were momentum, combining value and momentum, and combining value, momentum, and profitability. Of the anomalies they considered, the authors found that most of those with one-sided monthly turnover lower than 50 percent continued to remain significantly profitable, at least when designed to mitigate transaction costs. Well-designed momentum-based funds have turnover much lower than this. For example, both AQR's Large Cap Momentum Style Fund Class I (AMOMX) and its Small Cap

Momentum Style Fund Class I (ASMOX) have an annual turnover of about 80 percent. Novy-Marx and Velikov concluded that well-designed momentum strategies do survive transactions costs.

The bottom line is that the key to a successful momentum strategy is to not simply rebalance as automatons, ignoring costs. Trading patiently — by breaking up orders into smaller sizes and setting limit order prices that provide, not demand, liquidity — and allowing some tracking error to a theoretical style portfolio can significantly reduce trading costs and increase capacity without changing the nature of the strategy.

INTUITIVE

While there are a few papers putting forth a risk-based story, most of the literature on the momentum premium favors a behavioral explanation, generally either investor underreaction or overreaction. In his paper "Explanations for the Momentum Premium," Yale University professor Tobias Moskowitz points out: "Underreaction results from information travelling slowly into prices. That causes momentum. For example, there is ample evidence that investors underreact to corporate earnings and dividend announcements. Delayed overreaction results from investors who chase returns providing a feedback mechanism that drives prices further away from fundamentals, causing momentum in the short term that is eventually reversed when prices correct themselves in the long-term." In their 2014 study "Frog in the Pan: Continuous Information and Momentum,"

Zhi Da, Umit G. Gurun, and Mitch Warachka used the analogy of the "frog in the pan" to explain the momentum phenomenon.

According to the frog-in-the-pan anecdote, a frog placed into a pan containing boiling water will immediately jump out, since the dramatic temperature change induces an immediate reaction. Conversely, if the frog is placed in a pan of water which is then slowly raised to a boil, the frog will underreact and perish. (Note that while the analogy may serve its purpose, it is not scientifically accurate. Furthermore, no frogs were harmed in the making of this book.) When it comes to humans, there is evidence that we react differently to a series of small, gradual changes than we do to dramatic ones, even when the sum of the small changes has the same cumulative impact as the large change. For example, the way consumers respond to small, continuous price increases is noticeably different than their reaction to large, one-time price jumps. That is why companies typically institute small, continuous price increases that are not as discernible to consumers, but large, dramatic price decreases (sales) that are. This behavior is explained by what is referred to as "limited attention bias." Similarly, limited attention can be used to explain large inflows into mutual funds with extraordinarily high recent returns.

The limited attention literature implicitly assumes the existence of an upper attention threshold constraining the maximum amount of information on all firms that investors can process in a single period. For example, there is greater post-earnings announcement drift following days with a large number of earnings announcements because investors are overwhelmed by the copious amounts of information released on these days. If investors react differently to small bits of information in a persistent stream than they do to discrete chunks of information, this would provide a behavioral explanation for momentum.

In their aforementioned paper, Da, Gurun, and Warachka postulated the existence of a lower attention threshold for firm-specific information. Specifically, their hypothesis predicts investor underreaction to information that arrives continuously in small amounts. Using price changes as a measure of continuous information, they did indeed find that the momentum profit following continuous information persists for eight months while the momentum profit following discrete information is insignificant after only two months. The authors also found that, consistent with their hypothesis, security analyst forecast errors are larger following continuous information. Continuous information fails to attract analyst attention and that affects asset prices, inducing strong and persistent momentum. Over a six-month holding period, returns to momentum decreased monotonically from 8.9 percent for stocks with continuous information during their formation period to 2.9 percent for stocks with discrete information but similar cumulative formation-period returns. Finally, higher media coverage and higher analyst coverage are associated with discrete and continuous information, respectively, while management press releases coincide with continuous good information. In other words, managers tend to release good information as soon as it is available, but delay the release of bad news.

Another behavioral explanation arises from what is called the disposition effect. Investors tend to sell winning investments prematurely to lock in gains and hold on to losing investments too long in the hope of breaking even. Moskowitz explains: "The disposition effect creates an artificial headwind: when good news is announced, the price of an asset does not immediately rise to its value because of premature selling or lack of buying. Similarly, when bad news is announced, the price falls less because investors are reluctant to sell."

Markus Baltzer, Stephan Jank, and Esad Smajlbegovic contribute to the literature on momentum, as well as the tendency for momentum to experience crashes, with their 2015 study, "Who Trades on Momentum?" The authors use a unique dataset of holdings information for all stocks in the German equity market (the seventh largest in the world) covering the period from 2006 through 2012. The authors studied the investment decisions of various investor types before, during, and after the 2008–2009 financial crisis. By observing the entire ownership structure of the market, they were able to determine who trades on momentum and which investors are on the other side. The following is a summary of their findings:

- Financial institutions, in particular mutual funds and foreign investors (which generally are also institutional investors), are momentum traders, while private households are instead contrarians taking the other side. The data were statistically significant at the 1 percent confidence level.

- When looking at winner and loser stocks separately, momentum trading is particularly strong among losers.

- The degree of contrarian trading is negatively correlated with the level of sophistication of individual investors, as proxied by investors' average financial wealth and home-country bias, two metrics common in the literature. The more sophisticated the investor, the less contrarian the behavior exhibited. In other words, lack of financial sophistication is costly.

- Aggregate momentum trading increases during market downturns and in high-volatility phases.

- When separating winner and loser stocks, only the sale of losers increases during bad economic states, while the purchase of winners is largely unrelated to the business cycle, the state of the market, or volatility.

- Strong (increased) previous momentum trading negatively predicts future momentum profits. Excessive selling of loser stocks by institutions predicts reversals of the momentum strategy.

The authors noted that their results are consistent with prior research, which has found that private investors are strongly contrarian. They write: "Investors prone to the disposition effect (private investors) generate price distortions, underpricing winners and overpricing losers, which in turn are exploited by rational investors (institutional and foreign investors)." Rational investors exploit this mispricing, but because of limits to arbitrage, the prices only converge slowly, giving rise to momentum profits.

The authors also cited prior research showing that "arbitrageurs try to exploit underreactions to news by other investors. However, excessive momentum trading in the market can lead to an overreaction of arbitrageurs, pushing prices above/below their fundamental values and leading to a (long-term) reversal of returns." Their evidence regarding the excessive sales of loser stocks by institutional investors followed by the momentum reversal in 2009 is consistent with prior research. Baltzer, Jank, and Smajlbegovic write: "Particularly, we find that the sale of loser stocks by institutions and foreign investors in bad economic states forecasts reversals in the momentum strategy." They concluded: "Our findings that momentum trading in the loser portfolio increases during market downturns and volatile times and also forecasts momentum returns thus contributes to research into time-varying momentum profits." This also is consistent with prior research showing that the profitability of momentum strategies is time-varying — periods of high volatility tend to lead to crashes (on the short side of momentum).

All of these explanations seem intuitive. On the other hand, the risk-based explanations academics have offered seem counterintuitive — the risk of an asset would have to increase after positive returns. Yet, there are several papers positing the risk story. Moskowitz summarized the risk story from this research: "Past winners face greater risk going forward either because their growth prospects have now been identified as more risky or they face greater beta (market) risk than before because their investment opportunities have been adjusted. In either case, a firm that has recently experienced a huge rise (fall) in returns over the past year will now face a higher (lower) cost of capital because their cash flow risks and/or risk exposures have increased (decreased)."

One intuitive risk-based explanation, however, is from a 1997 study by Clifford Asness, "The Interaction of Value and Momentum Strategies," which continued his doctoral research on momentum.[4] Asness found that momentum is stronger among stocks with large growth opportunities and risky cash flows. These stocks would then run the risk that actual growth does not materialize and cash flows disappoint. Other papers have found that liquidity risk can explain at least part of the momentum phenomenon. Recent winners have greater exposure to liquidity risk than recent losers and therefore command a return premium going forward. Another explanation related to liquidity risk that might explain at least part of the momentum premium is that mutual funds experiencing large outflows

---

4   Asness's thesis advisor was Eugene Fama, of the Fama–French three-factor model discussed earlier.

engage in distressed selling of their stock portfolios, and mutual funds experiencing inflows might engage in "window dressing," buying recent winners.

In the end, it is much harder to tell a story in which risk increases after prices go up, as you would have to do for momentum. However, as we discuss in Chapter 8, behavioral explanations can be sufficient because human behavior tends to persist, and there are limits to arbitrage that prevent "rational" investors from correcting mispricings. And, as we noted, there has continued to be a large momentum premium well after the publication of findings on it made the investing public aware of the anomaly.

ROBUST TO VARIOUS DEFINITIONS

While the most commonly used metric for determining momentum uses the returns of the past 12 months excluding the most recent month, there has been a momentum premium with other time periods, such as six and nine months. Using variations such as residual returns (after accounting for other factors) also produces a momentum effect. In addition, it has been shown that other measures of what is referred to as fundamental momentum, such as earnings momentum, changes in profit margins, and changes in analysts' forecasts, produce premiums.

Given the evidence, we conclude that the momentum factor clearly meets all of our criteria for considering an allocation to it. However, before closing this chapter, we have an important issue to cover related to using long/short momentum strategies.

IMPLEMENTING MOMENTUM STRATEGIES

While momentum has offered investors the highest risk-adjusted return of all the factors we have discussed, it also has a "dark side" — it has experienced the worst crashes. Using annual data, we see that its large gains come at the expense of a very high excess kurtosis (a fat tail) of 13.0 percent combined with a pronounced left-skew of –2.5 percent. In other words, the returns smaller than the mean are fewer but farther from it, compared to returns greater than the mean. These two features of the momentum strategy mean it runs the risk of a large loss. Said another way, the apparent "free lunch" of momentum returns can very rapidly turn into a "free fall," wiping out many years of excess returns. This feature makes the strategy unappealing to investors with strong risk aversion (and is a possible risk story to explain momentum's existence). With that said, it is important to note that momentum crashes result from the short side, occurring during reversals such as the one we experienced starting in March 2009. In the reversal that occurred, with the market bouncing back from large losses, low-momentum stocks produced the largest gains. While high-momentum stocks still rose, their gains were of much lower magnitude. Thus, investors using long-only momentum strategies have to worry less about momentum crashes. Long/ short momentum strategies, however, are more exposed to such crashes.

Pedro Barroso and Pedro Santa-Clara, authors of the 2015 study "Momentum Has Its Moments," found that the risk of momentum is highly variable over time and claim it is quite predictable. They found that the major source of its predictability does not come from a systematic risk, but instead from a specific, time-varying risk. And while returns are difficult to forecast, volatility is less so. The reason is that this month's volatility provides information about next month's volatility, making volatility a useful risk management input that can greatly reduce the impact of crashes in long/short momentum strategies.

The way to mitigate the risk of crashes is to vary exposure to momentum over time. The authors found that if they scaled exposure to momentum (using the realized variance of the daily returns in the previous six months), the risk-managed momentum strategy achieves a higher cumulative return with less risk. The weights of the scaled momentum strategy over time ranged between the values of 0.13 and 2.00, reaching the most significant lows in the early 1930s, in 2000–2002, and in 2008–2009. On average, the weight was 0.90, slightly less than full exposure to momentum. Barroso and Santa-Clara concluded: "Risk-managed momentum depends only on ex ante information, so this strategy could be implemented in real time." They show how a scaled strategy reduces the crash risk of momentum, dramatically lowering the kurtosis and reducing the left skew. The benefit of this risk management is especially important in turbulent times. The authors added: "The risk-managed strategy no longer has variable and persistent risk, so risk management indeed works."

By targeting a specific level of volatility, a long/short momentum strategy would invest fewer dollars (by reducing the amount of leverage used) when markets are more volatile and more dollars (by increasing the amount of leverage used) when markets are less volatile. Such an approach historically has dampened volatility without negatively impacting returns. AQR Capital Management uses the volatility-targeting approach in their Style Premia Alternative Fund Class I (QSPIX).

While many investors believe that highly volatile markets occur as a result of large losses (in which case volatility-targeting would sell after a drop in prices has already occurred), AQR's research has found that empirically this is not the case. In fact, the firm found the opposite holds true more often than not, as increased volatility generally precedes large drawdowns. In a study of more than 70 liquid investments in several asset classes between 2000 and 2011, AQR analyzed how constant volatility-targeting (using rolling 21-day volatilities) changed risk and performance statistics compared to constant, nominal holdings. They found that kurtosis declined in about 80 percent of cases. In addition, the Sharpe ratio increased in about 70 percent of cases, with the average across all assets rising from 0.32 to 0.40.

In addition, by reducing the risk of large losses, volatility-targeting can also provide the benefit of increasing investor discipline, lowering the risk that stressed investors will abandon their financial plans and engage in panic selling.

Another way to reduce the risk of momentum crashes is presented in the 2016 paper "Idiosyncratic Momentum: U.S. and International Evidence" by Denis B. Chaves. He utilized a regression approach to remove the return component due to market beta and thus produced a new definition of momentum with reduced volatility. His results held over a sample of 21 countries as well as in the United States. Interestingly, this new version of momentum also works in Japan, where, as noted earlier, the traditional definition is weak. Bridgeway's Small-Cap Momentum Fund Class N (BRSMX) makes use of a similar risk-adjusted approach.

There is one last point we need to cover. Diversification across different factors is a good way to mitigate momentum crashes. For example, because momentum and value are negatively correlated, combining momentum with a value-oriented portfolio has been an effective strategy. Unfortunately, many people have a tendency to look at the performance of individual strategies or factors in isolation, when it is really a strategy's impact on the overall portfolio that ultimately matters. We will cover the topic of combining factors in further detail in Chapter 9.

Table 4.2 provides a summary of the data on the equity factors we have covered thus far.

TABLE 4.2: MARKET BETA, SIZE, VALUE, AND MOMENTUM (1927–2015)

	MARKET BETA	SIZE	VALUE	MOMENTUM
ANNUAL PREMIUM (%)	8.3	3.3	4.8	9.6
SHARPE RATIO	0.40	0.24	0.34	0.61
1-YEAR ODDS OF OUTPERFORMANCE (%)	66	59	63	73
3-YEAR ODDS OF OUTPERFORMANCE (%)	76	66	72	86
5-YEAR ODDS OF OUTPERFORMANCE (%)	82	70	78	91
10-YEAR ODDS OF OUTPERFORMANCE (%)	90	77	86	97
20-YEAR ODDS OF OUTPERFORMANCE (%)	96	86	94	100

We now turn to the related, and more recently "discovered," factors of profitability and quality, evaluating them against our established criteria.

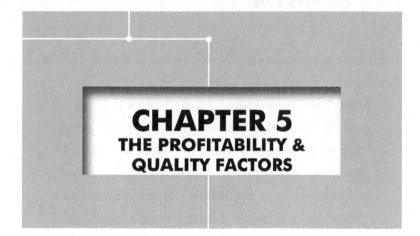

CHAPTER 5
THE PROFITABILITY & QUALITY FACTORS

As we have discussed, the 1997 publication of Mark Carhart's paper "On Persistence in Mutual Fund Performance" led to the four-factor model, which added momentum to market beta, size, and value, becoming the workhorse model in finance. The next major contribution came from Robert Novy-Marx. His 2013 paper "The Other Side of Value: The Gross Profitability Premium" not only provided investors with new insights into the cross-section of stock returns, but also helped further explain some of Warren Buffett's superior performance.

Novy-Marx's study built upon a 2006 paper, "Profitability, Investment and Average Returns," by Eugene Fama and Kenneth French, who showed that firms with high profitability measured by earnings have high subsequent returns after controlling for book-to-market ratio and investment. And as is the case with other factors, profitability had been used for decades by practitioners such as Benjamin Graham and David L. Dodd. Novy-Marx's work investigated gross profits, defined as sales minus the cost of goods sold, over the period from 1962 through 2010. The following is a summary of his findings:

- Profitability, as measured by the ratio of gross profits to assets, has roughly the same power as book-to-market ratio (a value measure) in predicting the cross-section of average returns.

- Surprisingly, profitable firms generated significantly higher returns than unprofitable firms, despite having significantly higher valuation ratios (for instance, higher price-to-book ratios).

- Profitable firms tend to be growth firms, meaning they expand comparatively quickly. Gross profitability is a powerful predictor of future growth as well as of earnings, free cash flow, and payouts.

- The most profitable firms earn returns 0.31 percent per month higher on average than the least profitable firms. The data are statistically significant, with a t-statistic of 2.49.

- The abnormal return (alpha) of the profitable-minus-unprofitable return spread relative to the Fama–French three-factor model is 0.52 percent per month, with a t-statistic of 4.49.

- The returns data are economically significant, even among the largest, most liquid stocks.

- Gross profitability has far more power in predicting

the cross-section of returns than earnings-based measures of profitability.

- High asset turnover (defined as sales divided by assets, an accounting measure of operating efficiency) primarily drives the high average returns of profitable firms, while high gross margins are the distinguishing characteristic of "good growth" stocks.

- Controlling for profitability dramatically raises the performance of value strategies, especially among the largest, most liquid stocks. Controlling for book-to-market ratio improves the performance of profitability strategies.

- While the more profitable growth firms tend to be larger than less profitable growth firms, the more profitable value firms tend to be smaller than less profitable value firms.

- Strategies based on gross profitability generate value-like average excess returns, even though they are actually growth strategies.

- Because both gross profits-to-assets and book-to-market ratios are highly persistent, the turnover of both the profitability and value strategies is relatively low.

- Strategies built on profitability are growth strategies, so they provide an excellent hedge for value strategies. Adding profitability on top of a value strategy reduces the strategy's overall volatility.

This last point provided insight into a strategic way to implement a value strategy. The monthly average returns for the profitability and value strategies were 0.31 percent and 0.41 percent per month, respectively, with standard deviations of 2.94 percent and 3.27 percent, respectively. However, an investor running the two strategies together would capture both strategies' returns, 0.71 percent per month, but would face no additional volatility risk. The monthly standard deviation of the joint strategy, despite having long/short positions twice as large as those of the individual strategies, is only 2.89 percent because the two strategies' returns have a correlation of –0.57 over the sample. While both factors add to returns, this negative correlation means the two factors tend to work at different times, producing the lower volatility. The t-statistic on the average monthly returns for the mixed profitability/value strategy is 5.87, and its realized annual Sharpe ratio is 0.85 — two-and-a-half times the 0.34 Sharpe ratio of the overall market.

As further evidence that the two strategies combine well, consider the following: While both the profitability and value strategies generally performed well over the full sample period, both had significant periods in which they lost money. Profitability performed poorly from the mid-1970s to the early 1980s and over the mid-2000s, while value performed poorly over the 1990s. However, profitability generally performed well in the periods when value performed poorly and vice versa. As a result, the mixed profitability/value strategy never experienced a losing five-year period.

Ray Ball, Joseph Gerakos, Juhani Linnainmaa, and Valeri Nikolaev, authors of the 2016 paper "Accruals, Cash Flows, and Operating Profitability in the Cross Section of Stock Returns," provide additional, and important, insights into the profitability factor. They observe that profitability includes accruals (adjustments that accountants make to operating cash flows in order to measure earnings) which, when added to cash flows, provide a better measure of current-period performance. This improved measure works because, as the research shows, there is a strong negative relationship between accruals and the cross-section of expected returns. This relationship is known as the "accrual anomaly." It is an anomaly because none of the current factor models can explain it. The authors' paper covers the period from July 1963 through December 2013. The following is a summary of their findings:

- Cash-based operating profitability devoid of any accounting accrual adjustments outperforms other profitability measures, including operating profitability (which excludes accruals), gross profitability, and net income-based profitability measures.

- Cash-based operating profitability produces an average annualized return of 4.8 percent compared to 3.5 percent for operating profitability. The t-statistics were 6.3 versus 4.0, respectively.

- Any increase in profitability solely due to accruals has no relation with the cross-section of expected returns.
- Cash-based operating profitability performs so well in explaining the cross-section of expected returns that it subsumes the accrual anomaly. Investors are served better by adding only cash-based operating profitability to their investment opportunity set than they are by adding both accrual and profitability strategies.
- Cash-based operating profitability explains expected returns as far as 10 years ahead, suggesting that the anomaly is not due to initial earnings mispricing or its two components: cash flows and accruals.

Ball and colleagues concluded: "Taken together, our results provide a simple and compelling explanation for the accrual anomaly. Firms with high accruals today earn lower future returns because they are less profitable on a cash basis."

As we have discussed, because all factors are long/short portfolios, the profitability factor is calculated by taking the annual average return of the top 30 percent of firms with high profitability minus the returns of the bottom 30 percent of firms with low profitability. It is referred to in the literature as RMW, or robust-minus-weak.

PERSISTENT

Again, defining profitability as revenue minus cost of goods sold, for the period from 1927 through 2015, the most profitable firms earned average returns that were 3.1 percent per year higher than the least profitable firms. Table 5.1 shows the persistence of the premium over the same period.

TABLE 5.1: ODDS OF OUTPERFORMANCE (%)

	1-YEAR	3-YEAR	5-YEAR	10-YEAR	20-YEAR
PROFITABILITY	63	72	77	85	93

The Sharpe ratio of the profitability premium was 0.33, the third smallest of the premiums we will review.

PERVASIVE

In his 2013 study, Novy-Marx tested the profitability strategy in international markets and found similar results, demonstrating the pervasiveness of the premium. The study covered the period from July 1990 through October 2009 and included the major developed markets of Australia, Austria, Belgium, Canada, Denmark, Finland, France, Germany, Great Britain, Hong Kong, Italy, Japan, The Netherlands, New Zealand, Norway, Singapore, Spain, Sweden, and Switzerland.

As further evidence, in the 2015 research report "Dimensions of Equity Returns in Europe," which covered 15 European markets and the 33-year period from 1982 through 2014, Dimensional Fund Advisors found that the average annual profitability premium in Europe was 3.6 percent and greater than 2 percent in 11 of the 15 countries. It was negative in two — Belgium and Finland. Once again we see the benefits of diversification. During the same period, the profitability premium in the United States was 4.4 percent.

Thanks to a 2013 research report by Masha Gordon, "The Profitability Premium in EM Markets," we also have evidence of a profitability premium in emerging markets. In her study, which covered the period from January 1998 through September 2013, she found the annual return on an equal-weighted strategy that went long high return on equity (ROE) and short low ROE was 5.1 percent, and it was statistically significant at the 10 percent level (t-stat = 1.7). Note that the relatively short time span available for emerging markets data makes it difficult to achieve high t-statistics. On a return on invested capital (ROIC) basis, the annual premium was 3.6 percent with a t-statistic of 1.2. In terms of gross profitability (revenues minus cost of goods sold), which research suggests may be the best measure of quality, the premium was a statistically significant 9.0 percent (t-stat = 2.79). These results are similar to the United States, where gross profitability outperforms ROE and ROIC. Note that the emerging market equity premium during the period was 6.7 percent. Thus, we have three profitability metrics, ROE,

ROIC, and gross profitability, which all show large premiums in emerging markets, though only the latter was statistically significant at the 5 percent confidence level. Specifically, in the case of gross profitability, which research suggests may be the best measure of quality (as we will discuss later in this chapter), the premium was even larger than the equity premium.

INTUITIVE

The academic research provides at least some support for both risk-based and behavioral explanations for the profitability premium. A problem, however, for risk-based explanations is that, intuitively, more profitable firms are less prone to distress and have lower operating leverage than unprofitable firms. These characteristics suggest that they are less risky. On the other hand, more profitable firms tend to be growth firms, which have more of their cash flow in the distant future. More distant cash flows are more uncertain and should require a risk premium. Another risk-based explanation is that higher profitability should attract more competition, threatening profit margins (and thus making future cash flows less certain). And that, too, creates more risk and should require a risk premium.

Ryan Liu contributed to the literature with his 2015 study "Profitability Premium: Risk or Mispricing?" Consistent with prior research, Liu found that, over the period from July 1963 through 2013, profitable firms have quite consistently outperformed unprofitable firms (in 73 percent of the years in his sample) and have done so with lower return volatility, resulting in a higher Sharpe ratio.

While profitable firms have higher unconditional returns, investors might still avoid them if their returns are the lowest during bad times. Investors tend to care the most about returns during bad times, when their marginal utility of wealth is high. However, Liu found that the premium is actually higher during economic downturns. Profitable firms do even better than unprofitable firms during bad times, which, as we mentioned previously, is when marginal utility (the benefit of incremental income or wealth) is the highest. Thus, profitable companies are less susceptible to negative macroeconomic conditions, and the profitability premium increases in recessions and when the stock market is doing poorly.

For example, Liu found that the worst one-year drawdown for the least profitable firms was –74 percent, nearly 30 percent worse than that of the most profitable firms. He concluded that the evidence makes it hard to reconcile the profitability premium with a risk-based explanation, although it is consistent with persistent behavioral errors related to expectations.

Liu then investigated the mispricing hypothesis. Specifically, he examined the difference between earnings forecasted by sell-side analysts[5] and actual earnings realized across profitability-

---

5   A sell-side analyst works for a brokerage or firm that manages individual accounts and makes recommendations to the clients of the firm. Sell-side analysts issue the often-heard recommendations of "strong buy," "outperform," "neutral," or "sell."

sorted portfolios. If the low return of the unprofitable firms relative to profitable firms was due to investors being too optimistic about future performance, the difference between forecasted and actual earnings (the expectation error) should be larger for unprofitable firms. He found a monotonically decreasing relationship across the 10 deciles of profitability from low to high. The expectation error was not only larger for unprofitable firms, but it was persistent for up to five years. His investigation of the data led him to conclude that investors expect the performance of profitable firms to mean-revert faster than they actually do, and they are willing to bet on the revival of the unprofitable firms despite low net income and poor current performance.

This is somewhat different from the more typical glamour story, in which naive investors become overly optimistic about the stocks in favor at the time because of good news or good past performance, resulting in the overvaluation of glamour stocks. But in this case, the excessive optimism is about the potential for mean-reversion of unprofitable companies, which tend to be newer, smaller firms in distress. Thus, these stocks tend to be overvalued. Due to limits to arbitrage, as well as the costs and risks of shorting, overvaluation is harder to correct than undervaluation.

Liu's findings are consistent with those of the 2016 paper "The Excess Returns of "Quality" Stocks: A Behavioral Anomaly" by Jean-Philippe Bouchaud, Ciliberti Stefano, Augustin Landier, Guillaume Simon, and David Thesmar. They described potential risk explanations, such as firms choosing more risky projects only if those projects are potentially more profitable. However, they also note that "while well-known risk premia strategies are indeed rewarding investors for carrying a significant negative skewness risk, quality strategies are in fact found to have a positive skewness and a very small propensity to crash."

The authors then investigate behavioral explanations, using analysts' price forecasts to study how their errors vary with several different profitability measures. They confirm that analysts as a whole are overly optimistic, a well-known result. However, the greater the profitability of a firm, the less optimistic analysts become. They found that "analysts are clearly under-weighting operating cash-flows; in fact they even seem to be putting a slightly negative weight on that variable, even though it is a strong positive predictor of future returns. These last results strongly suggest that the quality anomaly is likely due to a significant underweighting of quality in price forecasts."

F.Y. Eric C. Lam, Shujing Wang, and K.C. John Wei authored the 2016 study "The Profitability Premium: Macroeconomic Risks or Expectation Errors?" and also explored our two alternative explanations for the profitability premium: the rational explanation based on macroeconomic risks and the mispricing explanation attributed to expectation errors. The macroeconomic risk measures were related to industrial production, inflation, the term premium, and default risk. The measure of expectation errors was based on an investment sentiment index that includes the average closed-end fund discount, the number and first-day returns of IPOs, NYSE turnover, the equity share of total new issues, and the dividend premium (the natural log of the difference in the average market-to-book ratio between dividend-paying stocks and nonpayers). The authors found that both explanations play a role, with macroeconomic risks explaining about one-third of the profitability premium. The remainder was explained by a misvaluation factor based on investor sentiment. Their findings were consistent with those of Huijun Wang and Jianfeng Yu, authors of the 2013 study "Dissecting the Profitability Premium," which focused on ROE.

In examining behavioral explanations, Wang and Yu hypothesized that to the extent the profitability premium reflects mispricing, it should be larger among firms that are more difficult to arbitrage and have greater information uncertainty. In other words, the greater the level of uncertainty, the greater we should expect the impact of investor overconfidence to be on prices. And where there are higher limits to arbitrage, the mispricing is more likely to be sustained. In addition, with greater information uncertainty, psychological biases are increased and information is more asymmetric among investors, leaving more room for mispricing. Using a large set of standard proxies in the literature for limits to arbitrage and information uncertainty, the authors found the profitability premium is substantially stronger among firms more difficult to arbitrage or that have greater information uncertainty. Specifically, they found:

- The profitability premium is insignificant or only marginally significant among firms that have low information uncertainty and are easy to arbitrage.

- The profitability premium is about 1 percent higher per month among firms with smaller capitalization, higher return volatility, higher cash flow volatility, less analyst coverage, larger analyst forecast dispersion, fewer institutional holdings, higher idiosyncratic return volatility, lower dollar trading volume, higher bid-offer spread, lower credit rating, higher illiquidity, and that are younger.

- The majority of the ROE (a measure of profitability) premium is derived from the subsequent low returns of the low-ROE firms. This is consistent with the notion that overpricing is harder than underpricing for arbitrageurs to correct due to greater shorting impediments.

- The profitability premium is not driven by ex-post overreaction (there is no evidence of long- term reversion), but by ex-ante underreaction. Investors underreact to the current profitability news, and hence high-profitability (low-profitability) firms are relatively underpriced (overpriced).

Wang and Yu concluded that the profitability premium persists because of limits to arbitrage, which prevent mispricings from being corrected. The fact that pricing errors — instead of rational, risk-based explanations — may be responsible for the majority of the premium does not mean that the profitability premium is doomed to disappear. A good example, as we have discussed, is that the momentum premium has persisted for more than 20 years since the publication of the first paper addressing it.

INVESTABLE

Profitability is a low-turnover strategy. In addition, it persists across size deciles. And mutual funds implementing long-only strategies avoid the higher transaction costs of shorting the less-liquid, low-profitability small-cap companies where the premium is negative. Thus, investors should be able to capture the premium. In the aforementioned study, "A Taxonomy of Anomalies and Their Trading Costs," authors Robert Novy-Marx and Mihail Velikov found this to be the case, even for long/short portfolios. It was especially true for strategies that focus on minimizing trading costs by, for example, employing patient trading strategies through the use of algorithmic programs.

An important point to consider is that the research shows that strategies built on profitability are growth strategies, and so provide an excellent hedge for value strategies. Adding profitability on top of a value strategy reduces overall volatility. Thus, one way to implement the strategy is to incorporate profitability into the construction rules of value funds. This is what research-oriented firms, such as Dimensional Fund Advisors and AQR Capital Management, often do.

ROBUST TO VARIOUS DEFINITIONS

A pair of studies mentioned earlier in this chapter, authored by Novy-Marx and Ball and colleagues, investigated a variety of profitability measures and generally found good results. And research by AQR Capital Management found that three different measures of profitability all provide a premium: total profits-to-assets, total profits-to-sales, and free cash flow-to-assets. The firm uses these three metrics to determine a profitability score, which then determines the allocation to specific stocks within its multi-style funds.

Another example of the robustness of the profitability premium is provided by Kewei Hou, Chen Xue, and Lu Zhang, authors of the 2014 paper "Digesting Anomalies: An Investment Approach." They proposed a new four-factor model that went a long way toward explaining many of the anomalies that neither the Fama–French three-factor model nor the Carhart four-factor model (which added momentum as the fourth factor) can explain. In the new model, which they call the q-factor model, the expected return of an asset in excess of the riskless rate is described by the sensitivity of its return to the returns of four factors: market beta, size, investment (the difference between the return on a portfolio of low-investment stocks and the return on a portfolio of high-investment stocks), and profitability (the difference between the return on a portfolio of high return on equity stocks and the return on a portfolio of low return on equity stocks). Using return on equity (ROE) as the profitability metric, they found the ROE factor earns an average return of 0.60 percent per month and is statistically significant.

Before moving on, we will discuss the quality factor, which is related to the profitability factor because one characteristic of quality companies is that they are more profitable.

THE QUALITY FACTOR

The profitability factor we have been discussing has been extended to a broader quality factor, the returns of high-quality companies minus the returns of low-quality companies, which captures a larger set of quality characteristics. High-quality companies have the following traits: low earnings volatility, high margins, high asset turnover (indicating efficient use of assets), low financial leverage, low operating leverage (indicating a strong balance sheet and low macroeconomic risk), and low stock-specific risk (volatility that is unexplained by macroeconomic activity). Companies with these attributes historically have provided higher returns, especially in down markets. In particular, high-quality stocks that are profitable, stable, growing, and have a high payout ratio outperform low-quality stocks with the opposite characteristics.

The quality factor is referred to as QMJ, or quality minus junk. For the period from 1927 through 2015, the quality premium had an annual average return of 3.8 percent. In addition, it was slightly more persistent than the value premium, and only slightly less persistent than the market beta premium.

TABLE 5.2: ODDS OF OUTPERFORMANCE (%)

	1-YEAR	3-YEAR	5-YEAR	10-YEAR	20-YEAR
QUALITY	65	75	80	89	96

The Sharpe ratio of the quality premium was 0.38, higher than the 0.33 ratio for the profitability factor and very close to the market beta premium's 0.40 Sharpe ratio. That the consistency and Sharpe ratio of quality are higher than for profitability should be no surprise, as quality encompasses profitability plus other characteristics. Also of interest is that the quality premium, along with the value premium, goes a very long way toward explaining Warren Buffett's legendary success.

EXPLAINING BUFFETT'S ALPHA

The "conventional wisdom" has always been that Warren Buffett's success can be explained by his stock-picking skills and his discipline — his ability to keep his head while others are losing theirs. However, the 2013 study "Buffett's Alpha," authored by Andrea Frazzini, David Kabiller, and Lasse H. Pedersen, provides an interesting and unconventional alternative account. The authors found that, in addition to benefiting from the use of cheap leverage provided by Berkshire Hathaway's insurance operations, Buffett bought stocks that are safe, cheap, high-quality, and large. The most interesting finding in the study was that stocks with these characteristics tend to perform well in general, *not just the stocks with these characteristics that Buffett buys.*

In other words, it is Buffett's strategy, or exposure to factors, that explains his success, not his stock-picking skills. Frazzini and Pedersen, also the authors of the 2014 study "Betting Against Beta," found that once all the factors — market beta, size, value, momentum, betting against beta (a strategy that takes leveraged long positions in low-beta assets and short positions in high-beta assets), quality, and leverage — are accounted for, a large part of Buffett's performance is explained, and his alpha is statistically insignificant.[6]

With this in mind, it is important to understand that this finding does not detract in any way from Buffett's performance. As discussed in the introduction, it took decades for modern financial theory to catch up with him and discover his "secret sauce." And being the first, or among the first, to discover a strategy that beats the market is what allows you to pick the juiciest, low-hanging fruit and will buy you that yacht.

6   A 2014 article by John Alberg and Michael Seckler questioned some of these conclusions, noting, for example, that Buffett looked at different value metrics than book-to-market, avoided leverage and didn't even have the insurance part of the business until later years. These are valid points, and we are firm believers in using other value metrics, such as price relative to earnings and cash flow. But the main point that Buffett uses certain factors still holds, regardless of specific definitions.

With that said, the study's findings do provide insight into why Buffett was so successful. His genius appears to be in recognizing long ago that these factors work. He applied leverage without ever resorting to a fire sale and stuck to his principles. Buffett himself stated in Berkshire Hathaway's 1994 annual report: "Ben Graham taught me 45 years ago that in investing it is not necessary to do extraordinary things to get extraordinary results."

In recent years, Buffett has bought more foreign companies, presumably applying his time-tested criteria. Thus, we next provide evidence of the pervasiveness of the quality factor.

PERVASIVE

Max Kozlov and Antti Petajisto, authors of the 2013 study "Global Return Premiums on Earnings Quality, Value, and Size," provide us with an out-of-sample test on the existence of a return premium for stocks with high earnings quality using a broad and recent global dataset, which covered developed markets from July 1988 through June 2012. High-quality firms are characterized by high cash flows (relative to reported earnings), while low-quality firms are characterized by high reported earnings (relative to cash flow). This definition is a variation of the quality factor. The following is a summary of the authors' findings:

- A simple strategy that is long stocks with high

earnings quality and short stocks with low earnings quality produces a higher Sharpe ratio than the overall market or similar strategies betting on value or small-cap stocks.

• The value premium was the largest at 4.9 percent, followed by the market beta premium at 4.0 percent, and the quality premium at 2.8 percent. The size factor was slightly negative for the period at –0.5 percent. The positive excess returns are statistically significant for quality (t-stat = 3.38) and value (t-stat = 2.73), but not the overall market.

• The market beta factor was the most volatile with 16 percent annual volatility, followed by size and value at 8 percent and 9 percent annual volatility, respectively. Quality is by far the least volatile, with only 4 percent annual volatility.

• While the market beta and value factors had the largest premiums, because they also had the largest volatilities, the highest Sharpe ratio of 0.69 was earned by the quality factor, followed by value at 0.56 and market beta at 0.25.

• Simple capitalization-weighted, long-only strategies combined with a value/quality tilt have beaten the broad market by 3.9 percent per year among large-cap stocks and 5.8 percent among small-cap stocks.

- The result holds both in the overall sample as well as in the more recent time period since 2005.
- Because the global earnings quality portfolio has a negative correlation with a value portfolio, an investor wishing to invest in both factors can achieve significant diversification benefits. The Sharpe ratios were much higher for the combined strategies.

Kozlov and Petajisto also tested for various measures of quality, including factors based on ROE, cash flow to assets, and debt to assets (financial leverage). Low leverage (either financial or operating) leads to more stable earnings and less dependence on current financing conditions in the economy. They found comparable results with all of these variations, as well as with a mix of them.

The bottom line is that given the evidence, we conclude that the profitability factor, as well as the quality factor, clearly meets all of our criteria for considering an allocation to it.

Table 5.3 provides a summary of the data on the equity factors we have discussed to this point.

TABLE 5.3: MARKET BETA, SIZE, VALUE, MOMENTUM,
PROFITABILITY, AND QUALITY (1927–2015)

	MB	SIZE	VAL.	MOM.	PROF.	QUAL.
ANNUAL PREMIUM (%)	8.3	3.3	4.8	9.6	3.1	3.8
SHARPE RATIO	0.40	0.24	0.34	0.61	0.33	0.38
1-YEAR ODDS OF OUTPERFORMANCE (%)	66	59	63	73	63	65
3-YEAR ODDS OF OUTPERFORMANCE (%)	76	66	72	86	72	75
5-YEAR ODDS OF OUTPERFORMANCE (%)	82	70	78	91	77	80
10-YEAR ODDS OF OUTPERFORMANCE (%)	90	77	86	97	85	89
20-YEAR ODDS OF OUTPERFORMANCE (%)	96	86	94	100	93	96

We next turn our attention to the bond market, and
specifically, the term factor.

CHAPTER 6
THE TERM FACTOR

Just as they have for stocks, academics have created an asset pricing model for bonds. In this case, however, the model is much simpler because we only need two factors to explain the vast majority of the differences in returns among bond portfolios: term risk (otherwise known as duration) and default risk (credit). The term premium is referred to by those clever financial economists as TERM.

For the period from 1927 through 2015, the term premium, defined as the annual average return on long-term (20-year) U.S. government bonds minus the annual average return on one-month U.S. Treasury bills, was 2.5 percent.

PERSISTENT

The term premium has been as persistent as the value, profitability, and quality factors, more persistent than the size factor, and almost as persistent as the market beta premium. Table 6.1 shows its persistence over the period from 1927 through 2015.

TABLE 6.1: ODDS OF OUTPERFORMANCE (%)

	1-YEAR	3-YEAR	5-YEAR	10-YEAR	20-YEAR
TERM	64	74	80	88	95

The Sharpe ratio of the term premium was 0.25, smaller than the Sharpe ratio for all the factors we've examined, except for the 0.24 ratio for the size premium.

PERVASIVE

While the period for which we have data is relatively short, we do have evidence of a global term premium as measured by the annual average difference in returns between the Barclays Global Treasury Index and one-month U.S. Treasury bills. For the period from 2001 to 2015, the global term premium was 3.2 percent.

INVESTABLE

The market for U.S. government instruments is the most liquid market in the world. Thus, trading costs are very low.

INTUITIVE

The simple, risk-based explanation for the term premium is that investors demand a premium for accepting the risk of unexpected inflation (the longer the term, the greater the risk). In addition, the longer the maturity/duration of a bond, the greater its volatility becomes.

ROBUST TO VARIOUS DEFINITIONS

While there has been a term premium of 2.5 percent based on the difference in the annual average return of long-term (20-year) U.S. government bonds and the annual average return of one-month U.S. Treasury bills, there has been a term premium regardless of the bond maturity chosen. What is more, the longer the maturity, the higher the premium. For example, relative to the five-year U.S. Treasury note, the term premium was 1.8 percent.

DIVERSIFICATION BENEFIT

Not only has there been a term premium, but given its historically low to negative correlation with other factors, the term premium has provided diversification benefits. For the period from 1964 through 2015, its correlation to the other factors has been: market beta: 0.12; size: –0.12; value: 0.01; momentum: 0.08; profitability: 0.06; and default: –0.42.

The takeaway is that the term premium meets all of the criteria we have established.

As we mentioned at the beginning of this chapter, there is a second factor that explains bond returns — default.

Because we have chosen to relegate to the appendices factors not recommended for inclusion in portfolio construction, the default factor is covered in Appendix E.

CHAPTER 7
THE CARRY FACTOR

The carry factor is the tendency for higher-yielding assets to provide higher returns than lower-yielding assets. It is a cousin to the value factor, which, if you recall, is the tendency for relatively cheap assets to outperform relatively expensive ones. A simplified description of carry is the return an investor receives (net of financing) if an asset's price remains the same. The classic application is in currencies, specifically, in going long currencies of countries with the highest interest rates and shorting those with the lowest. Currency carry has been both a well-known and a profitable strategy over several decades. However, the carry trade is a general phenomenon, having been profitable across asset classes.

At the retail level, carry has been particularly popular in Japan, with the typical investor fictionalized as the housewife Mrs. Watanabe. She would borrow the low-yielding yen and buy a higher-yielding currency, such as the Australian dollar, benefitting from the interest rate spread. This works as long as the borrowed currency remains stable, depreciates, or does not appreciate by more than the interest rate differential. But as the financial crisis hit in 2007, the yen was perceived to be a safe-haven currency and surged 20 percent against the U.S. dollar and 47 percent against the Australian dollar. Small investors like Mrs. Watanabe — as well as large institutions — suffered severe losses. Carry can be like picking up nickels in front of a steam roller. It has been profitable over the long term, but one must be sure they can handle being run over every so often.

PERVASIVE

Carry can be defined as the expected return on an asset assuming its price does not change — that is, for example, if stock prices do not change, currency yields do not change, bond yields do not change, and spot commodity prices remain unchanged. Thus, for equities, the carry trade is defined by the dividend yield (the strategy of going long stocks with high dividend yield and short stocks with low dividend yield). For bonds, it is determined by the term structure of interest rates (and thus, related to the term premium). And for commodities, it is determined by the roll return (the difference between spot rates and future rates).

Ralph Koijen, Tobias Moskowitz, Lasse Pedersen, and Evert Vrugt, authors of the 2015 study "Carry," found that a carry trade that takes long positions in high-carry assets and short positions in low-carry assets earns significant returns in each asset class, with an annualized Sharpe ratio of 0.7 on average. Further, a diversified portfolio of carry strategies across all asset classes earns a Sharpe ratio of 1.2. They also found that carry predicts future returns in every asset class, although the strength of the predictability varies across them.

PERSISTENT

Table 7.1 shows the persistence of the carry premium in stocks, bonds, commodities, and currencies. The source of the data is the aforementioned paper, "Carry." Please note that, due to data availability, the start dates vary for the different asset classes (although in each case, the end date is 2012).

TABLE 7.1: CARRY PREMIUM

	GLOBAL EQUITIES	10-YEAR GLOBAL FIXED INCOME	COMMODITIES	CURRENCIES
ANNUAL PREMIUM (%)	9.1	3.9	11.2	5.3
SHARPE RATIO	0.88	0.52	0.60	0.68
1-YEAR ODDS OF OUTPERFORMANCE (%)	81	70	72	75
3-YEAR ODDS OF OUTPERFORMANCE (%)	94	81	85	88
5-YEAR ODDS OF OUTPERFORMANCE (%)	98	88	91	94
10-YEAR ODDS OF OUTPERFORMANCE (%)	100	95	97	98
20-YEAR ODDS OF OUTPERFORMANCE (%)	100	99	100	100
SAMPLE START DATE	MARCH 1988	NOVEMBER 1983	FEBRUARY 1980	NOVEMBER 1983

In each of the four asset classes, the carry trade has basically been at least as persistent as any of the premiums we have examined thus far, regardless of the time horizon. In addition, the Sharpe ratios are among the highest (our other top finisher — momentum — posted a ratio of 0.61).

INVESTABLE

The markets in which the carry trade invests are among the most liquid in the world, including foreign exchange markets, government bond markets, and commodities futures. To implement the carry trade, investors do not need to venture into thinly traded, illiquid markets such as microcap stocks or emerging market currencies. Thus, trading costs can be low. Importantly, the correlations of carry strategies across asset classes are low. This substantially reduces the volatility of a diversified carry strategy and mitigates the fat-tail risks associated with all carry trades, such as we saw in the case of Mrs. Watanabe at the start of this chapter. The result is that while all individual carry strategies do have excess kurtosis (fat tails), an across-all-asset-classes diversified carry strategy has a skewness close to zero and thinner tails than diversified, passive exposure to the global market portfolio. The carry trade can also be implemented in conjunction with investments in foreign equities; an example would be the decision to hedge currency exposure.

INTUITIVE

Carry has a simple, intuitive rationale arising from the long-established concept that prices balance out the supply and demand for capital across markets. High interest rates can signal an excess demand for capital not met by local savings, while low rates suggest an excess supply. In traditional economic theory, what is known as uncovered interest parity (UIP) states that there should be an equality of expected returns on otherwise comparable financial assets denominated in two different currencies. Rate differentials would be offset by currency appreciation or depreciation such that investor returns would be the same across markets. However, there is overwhelming empirical evidence contradicting the UIP theory, resulting in what is known as the UIP puzzle.

The UIP anomaly may be due to the presence of non-profit-seeking market participants, such as central banks (who may try to counter the impact of capital flows and even impede the flow of capital) and corporate hedgers (companies that must convert currencies in order to conduct business abroad), introducing behavior-related inefficiencies to currency markets and interest rates.

The carry strategy is not without risk, as there can be instances when capital flees to low-yielding "safe havens." This provides a simple risk-based explanation for the carry premium in which positive performance over the long term is compensation for potential losses in bad economic environments. In other words, currencies that appreciate when the stock market falls might be a good investment because they provide valuable insurance against unfavorable fluctuations in equity markets. On the other hand, currencies that depreciate in times of poor stock market performance tend to further destabilize investors' positions, and should therefore offer a premium for that risk. With this in mind, we will now examine the evidence from the literature.

Victoria Atanasov and Thomas Nitschka, authors of the 2015 paper "Foreign Currency Returns and Systematic Risks," found "a strong relation between currencies' average returns and their sensitivities to cash-flow shocks in equity markets. High forward-discount currencies (currencies in which the futures trade at a large discount to the spot rate) react strongly to stock-market cash flows while low forward-discount currencies are much more resilient in this regard."

Atanasov and Nitschka explain: "Basic finance theory suggests that high forward-discount currencies depreciate when the 'home' stock market receives bad cash-flow news that is associated with capital losses, whereas low forward-discount currencies appreciate under the same conditions. Thus, holding high forward-discount currencies is risky for a stockholder, while investing in low forward-discount currencies can provide him a hedge."

The authors found that their model "can explain between 81% and 87% in total variation in average returns on foreign-currency portfolios." They concluded: "The free-lunch hypothesis on foreign-exchange markets is strongly rejected by the data. We argue that making money on currency investments is tightly linked to bad news about future dividend payments on stock markets: high forward-discount currencies load more on cash-flow risk than their low forward-discount counterparts."

Martin Lettau, Matteo Maggiori, and Michael Weber, authors of the 2014 study "Conditional Risk Premia in Currency Markets and Other Asset Classes," also provide a risk-based explanation for the success of the carry trade. Their study covered the period from January 1974 through March 2010 and more than 50 currencies. The authors found that "while high yield currencies have higher betas [exposure to equity market risk] than lower yield currencies, the difference in betas is too small to account for the observed spread in currency returns." However, because investors are known to exhibit downside risk aversion, they extended their research to include a downside risk capital asset pricing model, which they call DR-CAPM. They found that the DR-CAPM does price the cross-section of currency returns. Specifically, they found that while the overall correlation of the carry trade to market beta is 0.14, and is statistically significant, most of the unconditional correlation is due to the downstate. Conditional on the downstate, the correlation between the carry trade and market beta increases to 0.33, while it is only 0.03 in the upstate. In other words, when the equity market rises, the carry trade is quite uncorrelated. But when the equity market falls, the correlation of returns with the carry trade tends to turn highly positive, resulting in losses. The authors also found that while the correlation of high-yield currencies with market returns is a decreasing function of market returns, the opposite is true for low-yield currencies (low-yielding currencies benefit from a flight to quality in bad times). They found that the DR-CAPM explained about 85 percent of the cross-section of returns.

Lettau and colleagues concluded that "high yield currencies earn higher excess returns than low yield currencies because their co-movement with aggregate market returns is stronger conditional on bad market returns than it is conditional on good market returns." They also found that this downside risk premium is a feature not only of currencies, but also of equities, commodities, and sovereign bonds. Their findings are aligned with standard asset pricing theory, which posits that assets tending to perform poorly in bad times should carry risk premiums.

These risk-based findings are consistent with other research. The following studies come to similar conclusions:

- Charlotte Christiansen, Angelo Ranaldo, and Paul Söderlind, in their 2011 study "The Time-Varying Systematic Risk of Carry Trade Strategies," found that while the carry trade strategy has been quite successful, it has a high exposure to the stock market and is mean-reverting in regimes of high foreign exchange volatility. In addition, the carry strategy experiences what can be called crashes — it comes with the risk of large losses (so-called fat tails) that tend to occur at the same time equity markets are crashing.

- Lucio Sarno, Paul Schneider, and Christian Wagner, in their 2012 study "Properties of Foreign Exchange Risk Premiums," found that the time-varying excess returns to carry provide compensation for both currency and interest rate risk. Financial and macroeconomic variables are important drivers of the foreign exchange risk premium, and the expected excess returns are related to global risk aversion. This supports flight-to-quality and flight-to-liquidity arguments for the risk premium in the carry trade. The authors concluded that "foreign exchange risk premiums are driven by global risk perception and macroeconomic variables in a way that is consistent with economic intuition."

- Hanno Lustig, Nikolai Roussanov, and Adrien Verdelhan, in their 2011 study "Common Risk Factors in Currency Markets," also found that the carry trade premium is related to changes in global equity market volatility. High-interest-rate currencies (conversely, low-interest-rate currencies) tend to depreciate (appreciate) when global equity volatility is high. They concluded that the price of volatility is negative (and statistically significant). In other words, by investing in high-interest-rate currencies and borrowing low-interest-rate currencies, U.S. investors are loading up on global risk.

- Lukas Menkhoff, Lucio Sarno, Maik Schmeling, and Andreas Schrimpf, in their 2012 study "Carry Trades and Global Foreign Exchange Volatility," found that more than 90 percent of cross-sectional excess returns from the carry trade were explained by foreign exchange volatility, evidence that the excess return is a result of an economically meaningful risk–return relationship. In times of heightened volatility, lower interest rate currencies offer insurance because their exchange rate appreciates in response to an adverse global shock. Thus, these "safe havens" (such as the Swiss franc) earn a lower risk premium than other currencies perceived as riskier.

- The aforementioned 2015 study, "Carry," found that individual carry strategies have excess kurtosis (fat tails) and exhibit sizeable declines for extended periods of time coinciding with bad economic states, such as recessions and liquidity crises. However, an exception is the carry trade across U.S. Treasuries of different maturities, which has opposite loadings than other carry strategies on liquidity and volatility risks, thus making it a hedge against them and dampening the risk of a diversified carry strategy. Indeed,

Koijen and colleagues noted that the risks of carry can be mitigated in a portfolio where carry is applied across many asset groups, thus providing a clear example of how diversified style investing can potentially generate more attractive risk and return characteristics.

IMPLEMENTING CARRY

The academic literature provides an important insight to consider when constructing your portfolio.

Vineer Bhansali, Joshua Davis, Matt Dorsten, and Graham Rennison, authors of the 2015 paper "Carry and Trend in Lots of Places," studied four asset classes (stocks, bonds, commodities, and currencies) across five different major country markets (for a total of 20 sets of data) and an extended sample period from 1960 to 2014. For each market, they categorized assets into one of four groups: (1) positive carry and positive trend, (2) positive carry and negative trend, (3) negative carry and positive trend, or (4) negative carry and negative trend. (We discuss trend-following, also referred to as time-series momentum, in Appendix F.) Their results show that "combining positive carry and positive trend positions has high positive risk-adjusted expected return."

The following example from their study is based on results for the 10-year U.S. Treasury note and demonstrates how having both factors in your favor improves results. Bhansali and colleagues found that "over the full sample, the average excess return were [sic] 2.9% per year, but in periods when both trend and carry were in favor (i.e., positive), the average annualized excess return was almost double the average, at 5.2% per year. Conversely, when both trend and carry were against the position, the average return was −4.2%. The mixed categories, with one of trend and carry against, and one in favor, the returns were in between, at 1.6% and 3.2%, respectively."

The authors also found that this result appears robust across samples, including the period of rising interest rates from 1960 to 1982. In particular, they found that while carry predicts returns almost unconditionally, trend-following works just as well. But the two strategies work far better when they are in agreement. They added: "The results are striking and intuitive. In all but one case ([German] Bund futures), the positive carry, positive trend buckets significantly outperform the negative trend, negative carry positions."

These findings were consistent with those of Andrew Clare, James Seaton, Peter Smith, and Stephen Thomas, authors of the 2015 paper "Carry and Trend Following Returns in the Foreign Exchange Market," which also studied the carry trade in combination with trend-following. Their research, which covered 39 currencies measured against the U.S. dollar and the period from January 1981 through December 2012, focused on the issue of market liquidity, which has been identified as a source of risk in all financial markets. The following is a summary of their findings:

- Equity market betas conditional on market liquidity help determine a cross-section of currency returns and provide an explanation for the excess return to the carry trade. The high but negatively skewed returns of the carry trade are compensation for increased exposure to market risk due to reduced market liquidity.

- While a strategy of buying any currency that shows positive carry against the U.S. dollar provides a positive average return, a strategy focusing on currencies with the highest (and lowest) carry generates the highest average return and Sharpe ratio.

- When measuring the return to the carry trade, by taking the average returns from the quintile with the highest forward premium (the largest difference between the spot rate and future rates) and subtracting the average returns of the lowest quintile, the average carry trade return is 0.62 percent per month.

- Trend-following (adopting long positions when the trend is positive and short positions, or cash, when the trend is negative) can provide a successful hedge against the risks of the carry trade while generating a significant, unexplained average return in an order of magnitude similar to that offered by a carry strategy. Results based on moving averages (the average stock price over a certain period) between four and 12 months were similar.

- When combined with a trend-following overlay, the combined strategy generates an average return well above that earned by the two components separately. The increased average return also has desirable characteristics. It offers a higher Sharpe ratio and positive skewness, as well as a smaller maximum drawdown than the individual components or alternative strategies.

The important implication for portfolio construction is that the research shows both carry and trend-following can be linked to liquidity, but they tend to hedge each other at different times. When trend-following produces large losses, carry tends to produce large gains, and vice versa. This is another reason why combining investment styles can be an excellent way to diversify.

Another important point to consider is that carry has relatively low correlations to the other factors we recommend. In developing their Style Premia funds, AQR Capital examined the correlations of returns of a broad, multi-asset class carry strategy with the returns of a global 60/40 portfolio, equities, stocks, bonds, commodities, momentum, and value. In each case, they found carry had low correlations, ranging from about −0.1 for value to only as high as 0.2 in three other cases.

Before concluding, there is one more issue we need to address with regard to carry trade implementation. Klaus

Grobys and Jari-Pekka Heinonen authored the 2016 study "Is There a Credit Risk Anomaly in FX Markets?" and contributed to the literature by exploring whether a link exists between sovereign credit ratings and currency returns.

The availability of credit rating data dictated the sample period, which was the relatively short time frame from January 1998 through December 2010. Grobys and Heinonen divided a sample of 39 currencies into three portfolios by sorting on the previous month's Oxford Economics sovereign credit rating. Portfolios were formed by going long the one-third of currencies with the lowest credit rating and going short the one-third of currencies with the highest credit rating. The following is a summary of their surprising findings:

- While premiums were found for the carry trade, volatility (long high-volatility and short low-volatility; see Appendix D), and momentum, there was a negative premium of 0.30 percent per month for the credit strategy. And importantly, the data were statistically significant at the 1 percent level.
- Average portfolio returns sorted by credit risk decrease linearly as they move from the low- to the high-credit-risk portfolio. This suggests that higher credit risk is associated with lower returns. In addition to negative returns, the long low-credit-quality and short high-credit-quality portfolio has a non-normal distribution: There is negative

skewness (–0.5) and excess kurtosis (2.9), or a fat tail.

Grobys and Heinonen concluded: "Even though risk-based asset pricing theory suggests that riskier assets should generate higher payoffs than less risky assets, our results suggest that currencies of countries with a high credit risk tend to generate lower returns than currencies of less risky countries." An important implication is that investors should account for credit risk when implementing a carry strategy. For example, one can pursue carry only in currencies of countries with high-quality sovereign debt, or avoid going long low-quality sovereign debt. The authors' findings also add to the evidence demonstrating that credit risk has not been well rewarded (see Appendix E).

What is perhaps surprising about these results is that this anomaly exists despite the fact that there are not the same constraints against shorting in currency markets that there are in equity markets — constraints that can allow anomalies to persist.

Summarizing the literature discussed in this chapter, there are logical, risk-based explanations for the carry premium. These explanations also provide a logical resolution to the uncovered interest parity puzzle.

To conclude, not only has carry met all of the established criteria, it provides a diversification benefit as well.

CHAPTER 8
DOES PUBLICATION REDUCE
THE SIZE OF PREMIUMS?

As we have been discussing, financial research has uncovered many relationships between investment factors and security returns. For investors, an important question is whether the relationship will continue after the research has been published. Said another way, if everyone knows about it, should we expect the premium to continue outside of the sample period? In the introduction, we provided five criteria a factor should be required to meet before that relationship can be expected to continue: The premium should be persistent, pervasive, robust, investable, and have logical, risk-based and/ or behavioral-based explanations.

Chapters 1 through 7 provided evidence and explanations for why we believe the premiums for each factor addressed therein should be expected to continue. However, this conclusion says nothing about the size of the premiums, provoking the question: Does the publication of research impact the future size of premiums? The question is important on two fronts.

First, if anomalies are the result of behavioral errors —
or even investor preferences — and publication draws the
attention of sophisticated investors, it is possible that post-
publication arbitrage would cause the premiums to disappear.
Investors seeking to capture the identified premiums could
quickly move prices in a manner that reduces the return
spread between assets with high and low factor exposure.
However, limits to arbitrage (such as aversion to shorting and
its high cost) can prevent arbitrageurs from correcting pricing
mistakes. And the research shows that this tends to be the case
when mispricings exist in less-liquid stocks where trading
costs are high.

Second, even if the premium is fully explained by economic
risks, as more cash flows into funds acting to capture the
premium, the size of the premium will be affected. At first,
publication will trigger inflows of capital, which drives prices
higher and thus generates higher returns. However, these
higher returns are temporary because subsequent future
returns will be lower.

Again we turn to the academic literature. Paul Calluzzo,
Fabio Moneta, and Selim Topaloglu contribute to our
understanding of how markets work and become more
efficient over time (the adaptive markets hypothesis) with their
2015 study "Anomalies Are Publicized Broadly, Institutions
Trade Accordingly, and Returns Decay Correspondingly." They
hypothesized: "Institutions can act as arbitrageurs and correct
anomaly mispricing, but they need to know about the anomaly

and have the incentives to act on the information to fulfill this role."

To test their hypothesis, Calluzzo and colleagues studied the trading behavior of institutional investors in 14 well-documented anomalies. Note that many of these anomalies are either specific examples of factors we have discussed in the preceding chapters or are explained by those factors. The 14 anomalies are the following:

1. Net Stock Issues: Net stock issuance and stock returns are negatively correlated. It has been shown that smart company management issues shares when sentiment-driven traders push prices to overvalued levels.

2. Composite Equity Issues: Issuers underperform non-issuers with "composite equity issuance," defined as the growth in a firm's total market value of equity minus the stock's rate of return. It is computed by subtracting the 12-month cumulative stock return from the 12-month growth in equity market capitalization.

3. Accruals: Firms with high accruals earn abnormally lower average returns than firms with low accruals. Investors overestimate the persistence of the accrual component of earnings when forming earnings expectations.

4. Net Operating Assets: The difference on a firm's balance sheet between all operating assets and

all operating liabilities, scaled by total assets, is a strong negative predictor of long-run stock returns. Investors tend to focus on accounting profitability, neglecting information about cash profitability, in which case net operating assets (equivalently measured as the cumulative difference between operating income and free cash flow) captures such a bias.

5. Asset Growth: Companies that grow their total assets more earn lower subsequent returns. Investors overreact to changes in future business prospects implied by asset expansions.

6. Investment-to-Assets: Higher past corporate investment predicts abnormally lower future returns.

7. Distress: Firms with high failure probabilities have lower, rather than higher, subsequent returns.

8. Momentum: High (low) recent past returns forecast high (low) future returns.

9. Gross Profitability: More profitable firms have higher expected returns than less profitable firms.

10. Return on Assets: More profitable firms have higher expected returns than less profitable firms.

11. Book-to-Market: Firms with high book-to-market ratios have higher expected returns than firms with low book-to-market ratios.

12. Ohlson O-Score: Stocks with a high risk of

bankruptcy have lower returns than stocks with a low risk of bankruptcy.

13. Post-Earnings Announcement Drift: This "drift" is the tendency for a stock's cumulative abnormal returns to drift for several weeks (or even several months) following a positive earnings announcement.

14. Capital Investment: Firms that substantially increase their capital investments subsequently achieve negative benchmark-adjusted returns.

To determine if investors exploit these anomalies and help bring stock prices closer to efficient levels, Calluzzo and colleagues built portfolios that were long stocks with positive expected returns and short those with negative expected returns. Their study covered the period from January 1982 through June 2014. The following is a summary of their findings:

- For both the annual and quarterly versions of the anomalies, trading with the anomaly was profitable during the original in-sample period. The alpha of the equally weighted (across each of the anomalies) portfolio was 1.54 percent per quarter.

- Raw returns in the period after publication decay to an average of 1.05 percent — a 32 percent relative reduction. Using the Fama–French three-factor model, there is a reduction in nine of the 14 anomalies.

- During the in-sample, prior-to-publication period, institutional investors did not take advantage of stock return anomalies.
- In the post-publication period, institutions traded to exploit the anomalies. The net change in aggregate holdings (the change in the long leg minus the change in the short leg) is positive.
- Partitioning institutional investors into hedge funds, mutual funds, and others, the results are strongest among hedge funds, and then among actively managed mutual funds with high turnover.
- There is a significant negative relationship between institutional trading and future anomaly returns in the ex-post portfolio. Institutional trading after anomaly publication is related to the post-publication decay in anomaly returns.
- There is a significant increase in trading by hedge funds in the period just before publication, suggesting that hedge funds have knowledge about the anomalies prior to journal publication (likely through presentations at conferences or from postings on the Social Science Research Network [SSRN]; www.ssrn.com).

Calluzzo and colleagues concluded: "Institutional trading and anomaly publication are integral to the arbitrage process which helps bring prices to a more efficient level." Their findings demonstrate the important role that both academic research and hedge funds (through their role as arbitrageurs) play in making markets more efficient.

These findings are consistent with those of R. David McLean and Jeffrey Pontiff, authors of the 2016 study "Does Academic Research Destroy Stock Return Predictability?"

McLean and Pontiff re-examined 97 factors published in tier-one academic journals and were able to replicate the reported results for only 85 of them. That the remaining 12 factors were no longer significant may be due to a variety of reasons, such as incomplete details in the original paper or changes in databases. They also found that, following publication, the average factor's return decays by about 32 percent (note the agreement of that figure with the one in the Calluzzo, Moneta, and Topaloglu paper just discussed) and that returns do not decay to zero, but remain positive.

In addition, McLean and Pontiff found that factor-based portfolios containing stocks that are more costly to arbitrage decline less post-publication. This is consistent with the idea that costs limit arbitrage and protect mispricing. As the authors note: "Decay, as opposed to disappearance, will occur if frictions prevent arbitrage from fully eliminating mispricing." They also found that "strategies concentrated in stocks that are more costly to arbitrage have higher expected returns post-publication. Arbitrageurs should pursue trading strategies with the highest after-cost returns, so these results are consistent with the idea that publication attracts sophisticated investors."

We draw two conclusions from the research. First, anomalies can persist even when they become well known. As McLean and Pontiff remark: "We can reject the hypothesis that return predictability disappears entirely, and we can also reject the hypothesis that post-publication return predictability does not change." Second, research does appear to lead to increased cash flows from investors seeking to gain exposure to the premiums, which in turn leads to lower future realized returns. However, we note that where logical, risk-based explanations exist, premiums should never disappear. For example, no one expects the market beta premium to disappear even though it has been well known for decades. However, we do caution investors not to automatically assume that future premiums will be as large as the historical record.[7]

The preceding research examines the United States. What happens in international markets? Heiko Jacobs and Sebastian Müller provide an initial and intriguing answer to that question with their 2016 paper, "Anomalies Across the Globe: Once Public, No Longer Existent?" Their study covered the pre- and post-publication return predictability of 138 anomalies in 39

7 There is no definitive method to estimate what future premiums might actually be, and any discussion would be too lengthy and take us too far off topic to include here. But we will caution investors not to infer premiums from very recent returns. As we have repeatedly seen in the previous chapters, no factor works all the time, and there are environments where any given factor tends to be weak. Basing expected future returns on recent results may lead investors to abandon a factor just before it is poised to rebound. To effectively harvest these premiums, one must be in it for the long run.

stock markets that account, on average, for almost 60 percent of global equity market capitalization and more than 70 percent of global gross domestic product. The data covered the period from January 1981 to December 2013.

While their findings for the United States were similar to those of McLean and Pontiff, showing declining premiums, none of the 38 international markets yielded a significant post-publication decline in anomaly returns. In fact, Jacobs and Müller found that returns to anomalies in international markets actually had increased. Equally weighted (value-weighted) monthly returns increased from 34 (28) basis points between 1981 and 1990 to 56 (40) basis points between 2001 and 2013. The following is a summary of their findings:

- Averaged over the sample period, long/short anomaly returns in various subsets of international markets turn out to be similar in magnitude to the estimates for the U.S. market.
- Many anomalies tend to be a global phenomenon and thus are unlikely to be driven mainly by data mining. This, of course, aligns with pervasiveness, a characteristic we have stressed.
- In almost every country, equally weighted portfolios generate larger returns than value-weighted portfolios. This is consistent with the notion that both mispricing and limits to arbitrage tend to be stronger for smaller stocks.
- For the majority of countries, pooled long/short

returns are statistically significantly positive at the 1 percent level.

• There are large differences between the United States and international markets with respect to subperiods in both calendar time (i.e., time trends) and in event time (i.e., publication effects).

Jacobs and Müller concluded that, while their findings point to a strong negative time trend and increased post-publication arbitrage trading in the United States, they did not find reliable evidence for an arbitrage-driven decrease in anomaly profitability in international markets. In addition, the authors found that differences in standard arbitrage costs "seem to explain at best a fraction of the large differences in post-publication." They did add that they explored "several possible mechanisms behind the surprisingly large differences between the return dynamics in the U.S. and international markets" but were "unable to fully explain the results" and that their findings were "consistent with the idea that sophisticated investors learn about mispricing from academic studies, but then focus mainly on the U.S. market." They end with the following: "Our results may thus be interpreted as a puzzle that calls for further theoretical and empirical investigation."

We certainly agree that the difference in decay between the U.S. market and the rest of the world is surprising and worthy of further study. As in the United States, we would have expected some increased attention and, thus, decay of returns. But for the investor, the message remains the same, if not stronger: Factor returns certainly can persist after their discovery.

We next review the pre- and post-publication returns to the size, value, and momentum equity factors that we discussed in earlier chapters. We will show that while the returns have lessened, they certainly still exist. We did not include the profitability/quality factor because only recently has research been published on this topic.

In 1981, Rolf Banz's paper "The Relationship between Return and Market Value of Common Stocks" found that market beta did not explain the higher average return of small-cap stocks. From 1927 through 1981, the annual size premium was 4.7 percent. In the post-publication period, from 1982 through 2015, the premium was only 1.0 percent. A reduction in the premium is logical if for no other reason than trading costs have decreased substantially since Banz's paper was published (the elimination of fixed commissions led to a dramatic fall in their cost). The decimalization of prices led to narrower bid-offer spreads. And the presence of high-frequency traders has also led to smaller spreads. Because implementation costs have fallen, investors can capture more of the size premium. Thus, the premium itself should be expected to shrink. However, before you draw too strong a conclusion about how much the premium has diminished, consider that for the nine-year period from 1975 through 1983, the size premium was 13.8 percent, quite a bit larger than even the market beta premium, which was 9.8 percent. That "run" (or what some would call a "bubble") for small stocks drove valuations way up, virtually dooming future returns to be smaller. In fact, from 1984 through 1990, the size premium was –7.1 percent. From 1991 through 2015, the premium was once again positive at 2.5 percent. And from 2000 through 2015, it was an even greater 3.7 percent, although still below the pre-publication figure of 4.7 percent.

Of course, a picture is worth a thousand words, so in Figure 8.1 we show the rolling 10-year annualized returns to the size factor (SMB).[8] The top plot gives compounded returns, which is what an investor would experience. The bottom plot gives the arithmetic average, which is how most financial economists measure factor premiums. Note that while the numbers can differ in times of extreme returns, generally they are comparable. For example, our first data point in the top figure is the 10 years from 1927 through 1936, for which SMB had an average compound return of 5.5 percent per year. In the bottom figure, the number for the corresponding period is a simple arithmetic average of 7.3 percent. The weak returns immediately post-publication in 1981 are clearly observable, but the size premium bounced back nicely subsequently. Indeed, the whole post-publication period does not look too different from the returns of the mid-1940s through the 1960s.

8   All data plotted here use returns from Ken French's data library.

FIGURE 8.1: RETURN TO THE SIZE PREMIUM (1927–2015)

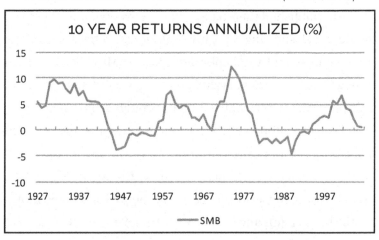

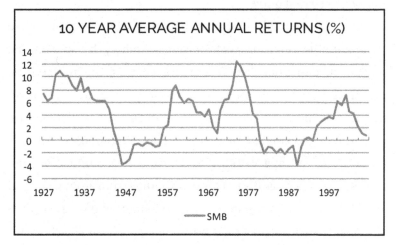

In 1985, Barr Rosenberg, Kenneth Reid, and Ronald Lanstein published their paper "Persuasive Evidence of Market Inefficiency," showing a positive relationship between average stock returns and the book-to-market (BtM) ratio. From 1927 through 1985, the annual value premium was 5.8 percent. In the post-publication period, from 1986 through 2015, the premium was a smaller 2.8 percent. Figure 8.2 shows a couple dips into negative territory post-publication, but they are of comparable magnitude to a dip in the early period of the series. These latter periods of underperformance correspond to the technology bubble in the 1990s and the more recent period starting with the financial crisis of 2007.

In 1993, the study "Returns to Buying Winners and Selling Losers: Implications for Stock Market Efficiency" by Narasimhan Jegadeesh and Sheridan Titman found that the momentum premium from 1927 through 1993 was 10.9 percent. In the post-publication period, from 1994 through 2015, the momentum premium was a smaller 5.5 percent. Figure 8.3 (page 171) shows momentum initially working quite well post-publication, but then suffering a huge drop. This drop comes from a –82.9 percent shortfall in momentum in 2009 as the stock market recovered and beaten-down stocks rose dramatically. As noted earlier, this crash risk is one potential explanation for the existence of the momentum premium.

In each case, we see evidence that post-publication factor premiums have fallen. However, they certainly have not disappeared. The premiums, along with their diversification

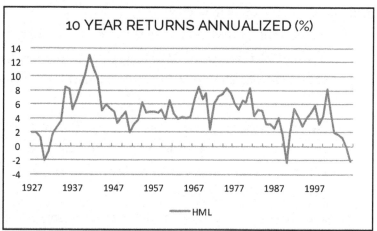

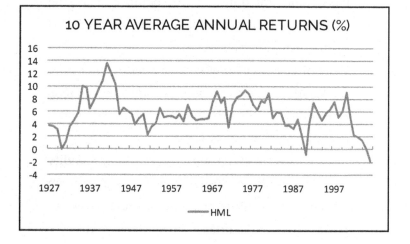

benefits, provide the rationale for investors to consider including exposure to them in portfolios.

It is important to understand that there are reasons for premiums to shrink that have nothing to do with the publication of academic research. The following are explanations for why the U.S. equity risk premium has shrunk over time:

- The Securities Exchange Commission (SEC) has strengthened investor protections, reducing the risk of investing in stocks and thus justifying a lower equity risk premium.
- Since the Great Depression, the Federal Reserve has demonstrated its ability to dampen economic volatility, reducing the risk of equity investing and justifying higher valuations.
- The United States has become a wealthier country. As wealth increases, capital becomes less scarce. Less-scarce assets should become less expensive, leading to higher equity valuations.
- Investors demand a premium for taking liquidity risk (less-liquid investments tend to outperform more-liquid investments). All else equal, investors prefer greater liquidity. Thus, they demand a risk premium to hold less-liquid assets. Over time, the cost of liquidity, in the form of bid-offer spreads, has decreased. There are several reasons for this, including the decimalization of stock prices and the provision of additional liquidity by

FIGURE 8.3: RETURN TO THE MOMENTUM PREMIUM (1927–2015)

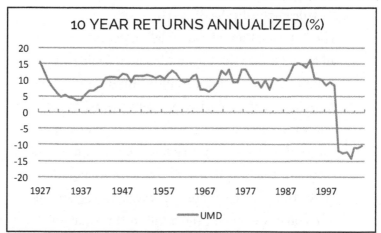

10 YEAR RETURNS ANNUALIZED (%)

UMD

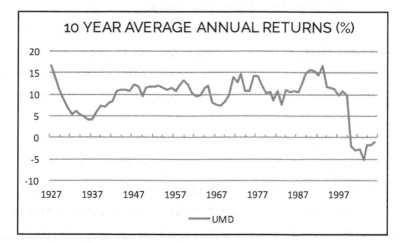

10 YEAR AVERAGE ANNUAL RETURNS (%)

UMD

high-frequency traders. In addition, commissions have dramatically decreased in price.

- The introduction of financial instruments that allow investors to buy and sell illiquid assets indirectly (such as futures, index funds, and ETFs) work to lower the sensitivity of returns to liquidity. These instruments enable investors to hold illiquid stocks indirectly with very low transaction costs, reducing the sensitivity of returns to liquidity. With these innovations in markets, again all else equal, we should see a fall in the equity risk premium demanded by investors.

These points demonstrate that as the implementation costs of equity strategies fall, investors are able to capture more of the gross equity premium. This increased liquidity, combined with greater investor protections, leads to a shrinking of the premium itself.

In their 2014 paper "Have Capital Market Anomalies Attenuated in the Recent Era of High Liquidity and Trading Activity," Tarun Chordia, Avanidhar Subrahmanyam, and Qing Tong conducted an interesting study of the effects of increased liquidity on various factors. They used the January 2001 switch from fractional pricing to decimal pricing in the United States to demarcate eras of lower and higher liquidity and study the returns to 12 factors or anomalies during these two eras. The 12 anomalies were size, BtM, share turnover, prior one-month return, momentum, the Amihud illiquidity measure, accounting accruals, asset growth, stock issuance, idiosyncratic volatility, profitability, and unexpected earnings. Many of these are, of course, factors we have studied in the preceding chapters.

The authors found that after decimalization, all 12 factors or anomalies had a decline in their excess returns, and for five of the 12, the attenuation was statistically significant. They also tested for the effects of greater attention by arbitrageurs to these factors by examining the impact of increased hedge fund assets and short interest (the quantity of shares that investors have sold short but not yet covered or closed out), as well as of decimalization and higher share turnover. They found that both improvements in liquidity and increased arbitrage activity have led to a decline in the excess returns of these strategies. But they also note that while profits have declined, they still remain statistically significant for a comprehensive portfolio.

WHY DO ANOMALIES PERSIST?

As we have just explained, factor returns can remain strong despite publication making them known and enhanced liquidity making them easier to trade — which raises the question: What allows their higher returns to continue? The financial theory for why anomalies can persist long after they become well known is that limits to arbitrage prevent rational investors from exploiting them. For example:

- Many institutional investors (such as pension plans, endowments, and mutual funds) are prohibited by their charters from taking short positions.

- Shorting can be expensive. It requires borrowing shares to take a short position, and many stocks are costly to borrow because the supply of equities available from institutional investors is low (they tend to underweight these stocks). The largest anomalies tend to occur in small-cap stocks, which are costly to trade in large quantity — both long and (especially) short. Also, the volume of shares available to borrow is limited, and borrowing costs are often high.

- Investors are unwilling to accept the risks of shorting because of the potential for unlimited losses. Even traders who believe a stock's price is too high know that, even though they might be correct and the price may eventually fall, they still face the risk that the price will go up before it goes down. Such a price move, which would require additional capital, can force traders to liquidate at a loss.

- There are other limits, including leverage (ability to borrow), transaction costs, and (for taxable investors) taxes.

These limits to arbitrage allow mispricings to persist and, in turn, delay the flow of wealth from irrational investors (generally thought of as "dumb" money) to sophisticated investors. That is the theory, anyway. Yongqiang Chu, David Hirshleifer, and Liang Ma, authors of the 2016 paper "The Causal Effect of Limits to Arbitrage on Asset Pricing Anomalies," contribute to the literature by studying the causal effect of limits to arbitrage on 10 anomalies: momentum, gross profitability, asset growth, investment to assets, return on assets, net operating assets, accruals, net stocks issues, composite equity issues, and financial distress.

Their study makes use of an SEC experiment, Regulation SHO, to identify the causal effect of limits to arbitrage (short-sale constraints in particular) on asset pricing anomalies. Regulation SHO was adopted by the SEC in July 2004. The Regulation SHO pilot program removed short-sale restrictions on a randomly selected group of stocks. For stocks within the Russell 3000 Index as of June 2004, Regulation SHO removed the "uptick rule" (which prevented a short sale on a stock when the price was declining) for a subset of NYSE/AMEX equities. Regulation SHO designated every third stock ranked by trading volume on the NYSE and AMEX stock markets (as well as the Nasdaq) as pilot stocks. Pilot stocks were exempted from the uptick rule or similarly motivated bid price test from May 2, 2005, to August 6, 2007. The program made it easier to short-sell pilot stocks relative to non-pilot stocks. This period thus provided an ideal setting to examine the causal effect of short-sale constraints on asset pricing anomalies, which can be quite powerful.

To test the limits-to-arbitrage hypothesis, Chu and colleagues constructed long/short portfolios with pilot and non-pilot stocks for each asset pricing anomaly.

Specifically, they sorted pilot firms into deciles according to variables that predicted cross-sectional returns, and then calculated the anomaly returns as the return differences between the highest-performing decile (the long legs) and the lowest-performing decile (the short legs). They then applied the same methodology to all non-pilot stocks. The following is a summary of their findings:

- The anomalies were much weaker in long/short portfolios constructed using pilot stocks during the pilot period.
- The effect was statistically significant in four of the 10 anomalies. When the 10 anomalies were combined in a joint test, the effect was both statistically and economically significant.
- Regulation SHO reduced the anomaly returns in the joint test by 77 basis points per month, or 9.2 percent per year. The results were highly statistically significant.
- The returns of short-leg portfolios constructed with pilot stocks were significantly higher during the pilot period, meaning short strategies became less profitable. In contrast, there was no significant effect of the pilot program on long-leg portfolios. This is consistent with the existence of limits to arbitrage. It is also consistent with other research that found most of the anomalies are explained by the short side. However, we note that the factors

we advocate in the main chapters of this book all have higher returns on the long side, in addition to lower returns on the short side. Recall as well that in the "Investable" section of these chapters we demonstrated how the premiums could be captured, often citing live mutual fund results. Further support for the ability to capture factor premiums on the long side is found in the 2013 paper "The Role of Shorting, Firm Size, and Time on Market Anomalies" by Ronen Israel and Tobias Moskowitz.

- The difference in short-sale restrictions between pilot and non-pilot stocks disappeared after Regulation SHO ended in August 2007, and the difference in anomaly returns between pilot and non-pilot portfolios also vanished.
- The effect of easier short-selling on anomalies was more pronounced among small-cap and less-liquid stocks, a finding that is consistent with the limits-to-arbitrage hypothesis.
- The results remained intact after adjusting for the CAPM and Fama–French three-factor model. In both cases, they were economically significant and highly statistically significant.

The results clearly show that the Regulation SHO pilot program, which reduced the impact of limits to arbitrage, also reduced the size of mispricings in hard-to-short stocks. Chu and colleagues concluded: "These results show that limits to arbitrage, and in particular, short-sale constraints play an important role in generating the ten well-known anomalies. These findings therefore suggest that these anomalies are, at a minimum, driven in substantial part by mispricing."

These findings add further weight to an already large body of evidence from the field of behavioral finance showing that short-sale costs/constraints affect asset prices, allowing anomalies to persist. Investors can benefit from this knowledge by directly avoiding the purchase of stocks with well-known, negative anomaly characteristics, or by investing in long-only funds that screen out such stocks.

As a final note on these findings, the SEC adopted amendments to Regulation SHO in March 2011. Among the rule changes was SEC Rule 201 (the alternative uptick rule), a short-sale-related circuit breaker that, when triggered, imposes a restriction on prices at which securities may be sold short. The SEC also issued guidance for broker-dealers wishing to mark certain qualifying orders "short exempt." Again, any constraint on short sales allows anomalies to persist.

The academic research provides another explanation, however, for why anomalies may persist.

BENCHMARKS AS LIMITS TO ARBITRAGE

Malcolm Baker, Brendan Bradley, and Jeffrey Wurgler, authors of the 2011 study "Benchmarks as Limits to Arbitrage:

Understanding the Low-Volatility Anomaly," proposed that an alternate explanation for the persistence of anomalies may be at work: the typical institutional investor's mandate to maximize the ratio of excess returns relative to a fixed benchmark without resorting to leverage. Many institutional investors in a position to offset an irrational demand for risky assets have fixed-benchmark mandates, which are generally capitalization-weighted. Thus, straying from the benchmark to exploit anomalies creates career risk.

The authors explain: "A typical contract for institutional equity management contains an implicit or explicit mandate to maximize the 'information ratio' relative to a specific, fixed capitalization-weighted benchmark without using leverage. For example, if the benchmark is the S&P 500 Index, the numerator of the information ratio (IR) is the expected difference between the return earned by the investment manager and the return on the S&P 500. The denominator is the volatility of this return difference, also called the tracking error. The investment manager is expected to maximize this IR through stock selection and without using leverage."

Baker, Bradley, and Wurgler note that while the investor ultimately cares more about total risk, the use of tracking error has some appealing features. It is potentially easier to evaluate the skill of an investment manager and a portfolio's risk by comparing it to a well-known benchmark. Having each manager stick roughly to a benchmark also helps the investor keep track of overall risk across the entire portfolio.

The authors then note that "these advantages come at a cost." A benchmark makes institutional investment managers less likely to exploit an anomaly. They go on to demonstrate this cost using mathematics. They further show that, in the absence of the ability to use leverage and "in empirically relevant cases, the manager's incentive is to exacerbate [mispricings]." They write that a leverage constraint "is a reasonable assumption for a large portion of the asset management industry" and that the "documented amount of assets under management that can use leverage is small." To further demonstrate that mutual funds generally do not attempt to exploit the low-beta anomaly, the authors observed that the average mutual fund had a market beta of 1.10 over the 10 years prior to writing their paper.

Finally, Baker and colleagues concluded: "The combination of irrational investor demand for high volatility and delegated investment management with fixed benchmarks and no leverage flattens the relationship between risk and return. [...] Yet, sophisticated investors are, to a large extent, sidelined by their mandates to maximize active returns subject to benchmark tracking error." Thus, anomalies persist.

SUMMARY

The academic research has found that, post-publication, institutions do trade to exploit anomalies, with hedge funds and actively managed mutual funds the most aggressive in this pursuit. The research also shows we can reject the hypothesis that return predictability disappears entirely. But, while premiums do not disappear, they do experience a decay in magnitude of about one-third. What is more, portfolios consisting of stocks that are costlier to arbitrage decline less post-publication. This is consistent with the idea that costs limit arbitrage and protect mispricing.

You need to be aware that the publication of research on anomalies does lead to increased cash flows from investors seeking to gain exposure to their premiums, which can then lead to lower future realized returns. Thus, you should not automatically assume that future premiums will be as large as the historical record.

CHAPTER 9
IMPLEMENTING A DIVERSIFIED FACTOR PORTFOLIO

Up to this point, we have discussed investment factors individually, studying whether they meet our criteria (persistent, pervasive, robust, investable, and logically explainable) for an allocation. In this chapter, we address how to actually implement these factors in such a way that optimally harvests their potential rewards, while remaining mindful of their potential risks. We use the word "potential" not just to keep our compliance teams happy — as we have seen, any given factor does not work all the time. Hence, building a portfolio diversified not just across assets, but also by their underlying factors, is a crucial step for investors.

One way to add exposure to the factors we have discussed is to switch from a total market fund (such as DFA's Core Equity Funds: DFEOX, DFQTX, and DFIEX) to one with factor tilts, or by adding "satellite" positions in funds with deep exposure to the factors in which you desire to invest. However, you should not just look at the individual investments in isolation. To build an optimal portfolio that balances risk and return, you should consider how all of its individual pieces fit together. Diversifying a portfolio through factor investing offers an innovative approach to doing just that.

THINKING DIFFERENTLY ABOUT DIVERSIFICATION

Diversification has been called the only free lunch in investing. Despite its obvious benefits, many investors fail to diversify their portfolios. One example of this failure is the well-known "home-country" bias. This bias leads investors to make much higher allocations to their domestic stock market than a global market weighting would call for. The U.S. share of global equity capitalization is only about 50 percent, yet despite this fact, most portfolios are allocated 10 percent or less to international equities.

What we can call modern financial theory has provided investors with a nonconventional way to think about diversification, leading to an approach that can improve risk-adjusted returns. Consider the following example: Investor A, desiring to diversify his portfolio globally and across asset classes, buys the Vanguard Total (U.S.) Stock Market Index Fund Investor Shares (VTSMX) and the Vanguard Total International Stock Index Fund Investor Shares (VGTSX). Because these are total market funds, the investor owns both small- and large-cap stocks, as well as value and growth stocks. This is the conventional way of thinking about diversification.

Modern financial theory suggests a different method. To explain how equity markets work, financial economists have developed what are called factor models. As we have discussed, the five factors that explain the vast majority of the differences in returns of diversified equity portfolios are market beta, size, value, momentum, and profitability/quality. It is important to remember that these factors are all long/short portfolios, and it is exposure to these factors that determines the vast majority of a portfolio's risk.

As we covered in Chapter 1, market beta is the measure of the risk of a portfolio relative to the risk of the stock market, as determined by how much the portfolio and the market as a whole tend to move together. Thus, a total stock market (TSM) fund has, by definition, an exposure to market beta of 1. However, while a TSM fund holds some small-cap stocks, it has no overall exposure at all to the size factor. This seeming contradiction confuses many investors. The confusion generally arises because factors are, if you recall, long/short portfolios. Thus, again by definition, while the small-cap stocks in the TSM fund do provide positive exposure to the size factor, the large-cap stocks in the TSM fund provide an exactly offsetting amount of negative exposure. That puts net exposure to the size factor at zero. The same is true for value stocks. While the value stocks in the TSM fund provide positive exposure to the value effect, the growth stocks in the fund provide an exactly equal amount of negative exposure. The result is that net exposure to the value factor is zero as well. The same is also true for the momentum and profitability/quality factors. Thus, other than market beta, a TSM portfolio is not diversified across the factors that determine the risk and return of a portfolio.

Table 9.1 provides the annual correlations of the factors to each other in the United States for the period from 1964 through 2015. Correlations range from +1 to –1. If two assets are positively correlated, then when one asset produces higher returns relative to its average, the other will also tend to produce higher returns relative to its average. Negative correlation is when one asset produces higher returns relative to its average at the same time the other tends to produce lower returns relative to its average. Thus, the lower the correlation, the stronger the diversification benefits become. Notice in particular the negative correlation of the momentum premium to the market beta, size, and value premiums. This demonstrates the diversification benefit of adding momentum factor exposure to a portfolio that has exposure to these other three factors.

TABLE 9.1: HISTORICAL CORRELATIONS (1964–2015)

FACTOR	MARKET BETA	SIZE	VALUE	MOMENTUM	PROFITABILITY	QUALITY
MARKET BETA	1.00	0.29	–0.27	–0.17	–0.27	–0.52
SIZE	0.29	1.00	0.01	–0.12	–0.22	–0.53
VALUE	–0.27	0.01	1.00	–0.20	0.09	0.04
MOMENTUM	–0.17	–0.12	–0.20	1.00	0.08	0.30
PROFITABILITY	–0.27	–0.22	0.09	0.08	1.00	0.74
QUALITY	–0.52	–0.53	0.04	0.30	0.74	1.00

To diversify a portfolio across the size and value factors, an investor must "tilt" their portfolio so it owns more than the market's share of small-cap and value stocks. Because the size and value factors have provided annual average premiums of 3.3 percent and 4.8 percent, respectively, gaining exposure to this pair of factors provides you with two asset allocation options. The first option, and the "conventional way" to use the factor exposure, is to increase the expected return of the portfolio. And because these factors have very low correlations to each other, tilted portfolios diversified across factors historically have earned higher risk-adjusted returns.

There is, however, a second way to use "tilting." Instead of focusing on increasing expected returns, an investor can focus on reducing risk while holding expected returns about the same. This is accomplished by lowering exposure to market beta while at the same time increasing exposure to the size and value premiums. An investor would need less exposure to market beta to achieve the same expected returns because the equities held have a higher expected return than the market portfolio. The lower exposure to market beta is obtained by owning less in stocks and more in bonds. The result is that the portfolio has now become more diversified in terms of its exposure to factors (exposure to market beta went down, while exposure to the other factors went up). In addition, because the allocation to safe bonds increased, the portfolio's exposure to term risk went up, further diversifying the portfolio across factors.

What most investors fail to understand is that because stocks are so much more volatile than bonds, a typical 60 percent stock/40 percent bond portfolio has much more than 60 percent of its risk concentrated in the stock allocation (i.e., in market beta). Actually, market beta makes up about 85 percent of the risk in a typical 60/40 portfolio, and the portfolio has no exposure to the other equity factors. For portfolios that limit their bond holdings to only safe U.S. Treasury and government agency bonds, FDIC-insured CDs, and the highest-quality municipal bonds (either general obligation or essential service revenue bonds with AAA/AA ratings), term risk more or less makes up the remaining 15 percent or so of overall risk. By tilting the portfolio to other equity factors and lowering market beta at the same time, an investor can reduce the concentration of risk in market beta while spreading it to the other factors, including the term factor. This will create more of what is referred to as a risk-parity portfolio[9] — a portfolio that has more evenly distributed allocations to each factor. You can see the benefits of diversifying across factors in Table 9.2, which covers the period from 1927 to 2015. For each factor, it shows the mean premium, volatility, and the Sharpe ratio. It also provides the same information for three portfolios. Portfolio 1 (P1) is allocated 25 percent to each of four factors: market beta, size, value, and momentum. Portfolio 2 (P2) is allocated 20 percent to each of the same four factors plus a 20

---

9 While risk parity more typically is used to describe allocating between asset classes such as stocks and bonds, it can also be applied to factors.

percent allocation to the profitability factor. Portfolio 3 (P3) is allocated the same way as P2, substituting the quality factor for the profitability factor.

TABLE 9.2: RETURN AND RISK

	MEAN RETURN (%)	STANDARD DEVIATION (%)	SHARPE RATIO
MARKET BETA	8.3	20.6	0.40
SIZE	3.3	13.9	0.24
VALUE	4.8	14.1	0.34
MOMENTUM	9.6	15.7	0.61
PROFITABILITY	3.1	9.3	0.33
QUALITY	3.8	10.0	0.38
P1	6.5	8.8	0.74
P2	5.3	5.5	0.96
P3	5.6	5.6	1.12

The low correlations, with the exception of profitability and quality, among these factors resulted in each of the three portfolios producing a dramatically higher Sharpe ratio than any of the individual factors. We can further see the benefits of diversifying across factors in Table 9.3 (see next page), which shows the odds of underperformance over various time horizons. It, too, covers the period from 1927 to 2015.

As you can see, no matter the time horizon, the odds of underperformance are lower for each of the three portfolios than for any of the factors individually.

Erik Hjalmarsson provided evidence regarding the benefits of diversifying across factors with his 2011 paper "Portfolio Diversification Across Characteristics," in which he studied the performance of long/short portfolio strategies formed on seven different stock characteristics over the period from 1951 through 2008.

TABLE 9.3: ODDS OF UNDERPERFORMANCE (%)

	1-YEAR	3-YEAR	5-YEAR	10-YEAR	20-YEAR
MARKET BETA	34	24	18	10	4
SIZE	41	24	30	23	14
VALUE	37	28	22	14	6
MOMENTUM	27	14	9	3	0
PROFITABILITY	37	28	23	15	7
QUALITY	35	25	19	11	4
P1	23	10	5	1	0
P2	17	5	2	0	0
P3	13	3	1	0	0

Three of the strategies were related to momentum or reversals:

- Short-term reversals, defined as the prior month's $(t-1)$ return
- Medium-term momentum, defined as the returns from month $t-2$ to $t-12$
- Long-term reversals, defined as the returns from

month $t - 13$ to $t - 60$

Three strategies were related to the value factor:

- Book-to-market (BtM) ratio
- Cash flow-to-price (CP) ratio
- Earnings-to-price (EP) ratio

The last strategy was based on the size factor. The performance of the single-characteristic portfolios was then compared to an equal-weighted portfolio made up of the single-characteristic ones. The following is a summary of Hjalmarsson's findings:

- Each individual characteristic resulted in a profitable portfolio strategy.
- The equal-weighted diversified portfolio almost always delivered substantially better Sharpe ratios than any of the single-characteristic portfolios.
- The benefits of diversifying across characteristic-based long/short strategies were substantial and can be attributed to the mostly low, and sometimes substantially negative, correlation between the returns of single-characteristic strategies.
- The three valuation ratios — BtM, CP, and EP — result in portfolio returns that were fairly highly correlated with each other.
- The valuation ratios were mostly negatively correlated with short-term reversals, only weakly correlated with momentum, and generally positively correlated with long-term reversals.

- The size factor was most highly positively correlated with long-term reversals and negatively correlated with momentum.
- Short-term reversals were fairly strongly negatively correlated with momentum and weakly positively correlated with long-term reversals.
- Momentum and long-term reversals exhibited a fairly large negative correlation.
- The results were statistically significant.

Although a full analysis of transaction costs was outside the scope of his study, Hjalmarsson concluded that there were strong reasons to believe the results would remain the same after controlling for them. The results of this study provide further support for the idea that more efficient portfolios can be built by diversifying across multiple factors.

The bottom line is that a TSM portfolio has all of its eggs in one factor (or risk) basket — market beta — while a tilted portfolio diversifies across several risk baskets. And if tilting is used to allow for a lower exposure to market beta, the portfolio will also increase its exposure to the term factor, providing further diversification benefits. Harvesting different risk baskets, each with a premium that has low-to-negative correlations to the others, is a prudent way for investors to diversify their portfolios while improving the risk-adjusted return. Much of the discussion in this chapter has revolved around long/short portfolios to make a general point regarding factor diversification. For a more in-depth discussion of, and demonstration with, long-only portfolios, Larry Swedroe and Kevin Grogan's book "Reducing the Risk of Black Swans: Using the Science of Investing to Capture Returns with Less Volatility," focuses on using a tilted portfolio strategy and shows how investors have been able to reduce the risk of large losses without sacrificing returns.

A brief example, however, may prove illuminating. Consider the period from 1927 to 2015, with annual rebalancing. A portfolio allocated 60 percent to the S&P 500 and 40 percent to five-year U.S. Treasury notes produced an annual return of 8.6 percent with a standard deviation of 12.2 percent. Now, reduce the equity allocation to 40 percent, but place half of it in a strategy with factor tilts (in this case, to size and value). A portfolio allocated 20 percent to the S&P 500, 20 percent to the Fama-French U.S. Small Value Research Index, and 60 percent to five-year U.S. Treasury notes produced an annual return of 8.9 percent with a standard deviation of 10.4 percent. Thus, the second portfolio earned higher returns with notably lower risk.

While diversifying across factors provides several benefits, it also comes with the risk known as "tracking error regret." And that is the subject of Appendix A.

CONCLUSION

While there are more than 600 exhibits in the factor zoo, we have limited your tour to just market beta, size, value, momentum, profitability, quality, term, and carry. If factor investing were compared to the older days of Disneyland, these eight would be the prized E tickets.

We hope we have shown you how using factor tilts, based on evidence from peer-reviewed academic journals, can help today's investors build more efficient portfolios. And given heightened competition among mutual fund providers (which has resulted in a strong downward trend in expense ratios), investors can now do so at much lower costs (which seem likely to go even lower). As evidenced by the recent publication dates of many of the papers we cited, research on the nature of factors that explain asset returns continues at a brisk pace. We cannot hope to predict what future developments might be. But we do hope the framework presented here enables you to better understand them, and to determine whether and how to use these future developments in your portfolios. Additionally, we hope we have brought some clarity to the complex world of factor investing.

We also would like to offer these words of caution. First, as we have discussed, all factors — including the ones we have recommended — have experienced long periods of underperformance. So, before investing, be sure that you believe strongly in the rationale behind the factor and the reasons why you trust it will persist in the long run. Without this strong belief, it is unlikely that you will be able to maintain discipline during the inevitable long periods of underperformance. And discipline is one of the keys to being a successful investor. Finally, because there is no way to know which factors will deliver premiums in the future, we recommend that you build a portfolio broadly diversified across them. Remember, it has been said that diversification is the only free lunch in investing. Thus, we suggest you eat as much of it as you can! With that said, we are not done quite yet, because we have some bonuses for you.

Appendix A is about the dreaded condition known as tracking error regret, which investors who diversify beyond total stock market indices run the risk of catching. Tracking error regret causes investors to make the mistake of confusing ex-ante strategy with ex-post outcomes, which in turn leads to the abandonment of even the most well-thought-out plans.

Appendix B explains that, while there really is in fact such a thing as smart beta, much of it is nothing more than a marketing gimmick — a repackaging of well-known factors.

Appendices C, D, and E explain why you do not need to take a detour and spend time visiting three of the more popular exhibits in the factor zoo: dividends, low volatility (or its relative, low beta), and default (credit).

Appendix F discusses a second momentum factor, known as time-series momentum. It is a kissing cousin of the type of momentum that we discussed in Chapter 4, cross-sectional momentum.

Appendix G shows why, once you have gained exposure to the factors we recommend, there simply is not a great deal of potential to add much, if any, benefit through exposure to additional factors. It also tackles whether to target the factors separately or through a multi-style fund.

Appendix H discusses a fascinating study that examined whether investment factors also work to explain the results of bets on sporting events. If they do, it would provide a unique out-of-sample test of their ability to explain outcomes.

Appendix I takes a new look at the size premium, demonstrating that it is still quite healthy. We also show how looking only at the magnitude of a premium, rather than also considering how much exposure to the premium a fund can capture, may lead investors to make incorrect conclusions.

And, finally, Appendix J provides a short list of the mutual funds and ETFs we believe are worth considering when seeking exposure to the recommended factors.

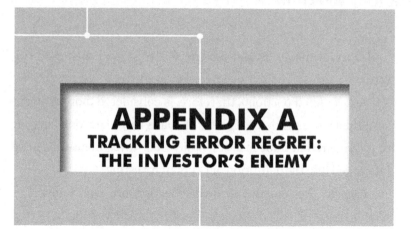

APPENDIX A
TRACKING ERROR REGRET:
THE INVESTOR'S ENEMY

There are several key elements to having a successful investment experience. The first is to create a well-thought-out financial plan. This plan should begin with identifying your ability, willingness, and need to take risk, as well as what it is that you want your money to do for you. Having identified all the appropriate risks and objectives, an overall financial plan can then be developed (one that integrates the investment plan into an estate, tax, and risk management plan). The next step is to decide on the investment strategy most likely to allow you to achieve your goals within the risk parameters acceptable to you.

Two tools that advisors, trustees, and investors can use to help identify the prudent investment strategy are the 1992 Restatement of Trusts (Third), also referred to as the Prudent Investor Rule, and the 1994 Uniform Prudent Investor Act (UPIA). Both of these incorporated modern portfolio theory (MPT) into their writing. Among the fundamental tenets of MPT is that, done properly, diversification reduces the risk of underperformance as well as the volatility and dispersion of returns, without reducing expected returns.

A diversified portfolio, therefore, is considered more efficient (and thus more prudent). The UPIA states that "The long familiar requirement that fiduciaries diversify their investments has been integrated into the definition of prudent investing."

Clearly, the benefits of diversification are well known. In fact, it has been called the only free lunch in investing. It is why we recommend that investors diversify *not only* across domestic equity asset classes (small- and large-cap stocks, value and growth stocks, and real estate) and the other factors we have been discussing, but *also* that they include a significant allocation to international equity asset classes (including emerging markets stocks).

However, investors who adopt the strategy of broad diversification must understand that they are taking on another type of risk: a psychological one known as tracking error regret. Think of tracking error as the risk that a diversified portfolio underperforms a popular benchmark, such as the S&P 500. Regret over tracking error can lead investors to make the mistake of confusing an ex-ante strategy with an ex-post outcome.

CONFUSING STRATEGY WITH OUTCOME

"Fooled by Randomness: The Hidden Role of Chance in Life and in the Markets" author Nassim Nicholas Taleb had the following to say on confusing strategy and outcome: "One cannot judge a performance in any given field (war, politics, medicine, investments) by the results, but by the costs of the alternative (i.e., if history played out in a different way). Such substitute courses of events are called alternative histories. Clearly, the quality of a decision cannot be solely judged based on its outcome, but such a point seems to be voiced only by people who fail (those who succeed attribute their success to the quality of their decision)."

Unfortunately, in investing there are no clear crystal balls. Thus, a strategy should be judged in terms of its quality and prudence *before* its outcome is known, not after.

2008–2015 PROVIDES A TEST

Since 2008, investors have been faced with a significant test of their ability to ignore tracking error regret. From 2008 through 2015, major U.S. asset classes provided fairly similar returns. The S&P 500 Index returned 6.5 percent per year, the MSCI USA Large Cap Value Index returned 5.1 percent, the MSCI US Small Cap 1750 Index returned 7.7 percent, and the MSCI US Small Cap Value Index returned 7.7 percent. The total returns of the four indices were 66 percent, 49 percent, 82 percent, and 70 percent, respectively.

International stocks, however, underperformed by wide margins. Over the same period, the MSCI EAFE Index returned 0 percent per year and the MSCI Emerging Markets Index returned –3 percent per year (with a total return of –21 percent).

Clearly, investors who diversified globally have been disappointed. Unfortunately, that disappointment has led many to consider abandoning their strategy of global diversification. But should we judge the strategy to have been a poor one based on the outcome? Not when we look at the question through the lens provided by Taleb.

To see the wisdom of taking the correct viewpoint (Taleb's), let us consider an investor at the beginning of this period (one who does not have the benefit of a clear crystal ball). How did the world look to that investor? To answer this question, we will look at the returns for the prior five-year period.

THE GOOD SIDE OF TRACKING ERROR

Looking backward, an investor contemplating his or her investment strategy at the start of 2008 would have been reviewing the following returns. For the five-year period from 2003 through 2007, the S&P 500 Index provided a total return of 83 percent. That was less than half the 171 percent total return provided by the MSCI EAFE Index and not much more than one-fifth of the 391 percent total return of the MSCI Emerging Markets Index. Yes, the S&P 500 Index underperformed the MSCI Emerging Markets Index by 308 percentage points over just a five-year period.

If you think that is bad (or impressive, depending on the side of the coin at which you are looking), the DFA Emerging Markets Small Cap Portfolio fund (DEMSX) provided a total return of 430 percent, outperforming the S&P 500 Index by 347 percentage points. And the DFA Emerging Markets Value Portfolio Institutional Class fund (DFEVX) provided a total return of 546 percent, outperforming the S&P 500 Index by 463 percentage points.

Looking at the domestic asset classes, the S&P 500 Index also underperformed the MSCI US Small Cap 1750 Index by a total of 40 percentage points, the MSCI US Small Cap Value Index by a total of 28 percentage points, and the Russell 2000 Value Index by 25 percentage points. It trailed the MSCI US Prime Market Value Index by a total of 14 percentage points and the Russell 1000 Value Index by 15 percentage points.

As you can see, tracking error works both ways. You have to take the positive tracking error with the negative. Importantly, we doubt that any investors looking back at the returns in the period from 2003 through 2007 would have questioned the benefits of building a globally diversified portfolio. Regrettably, the twin problems of "relativism" (how the performance of your portfolio compares to that of your friends and to popular benchmarks) and "recency" conspire to dupe investors into abandoning even well-thought-out plans.

RELATIVISM

Too many investors have entered what Vanguard founder John C. Bogle called the "Age of Investment Relativism." Investor satisfaction or unhappiness (and, by extension, the discipline required to stick with a strategy) seems determined to a great degree by the relative performance of their portfolio to some index (an index that should not even be relevant to an investor who accepts the wisdom of diversification).

Relativism, sadly, can best be described as the triumph of emotion over wisdom and experience. The history of financial markets has demonstrated that today's trends are merely "noise" in the context of the long term. Bogle once quoted an anonymous portfolio manager, who warned: "Relativity worked well for Einstein, but it has no place in investing."

RECENCY

The recency effect — in which the most recent observations have the largest impact on individuals' memory and, consequently, on their perception — is a well-documented cognitive bias. This bias may affect investment behavior if investors focus on the most recent returns and project them into the future. This is a very common mistake, leading investors to buy what has recently done well (at high prices, when expected returns are now lower) and sell what has recently done poorly (at low prices, when expected returns are now higher). Buying high and selling low is not exactly a prescription for investment success. Yet, the research shows that this is exactly what many investors do, partly due to recency bias. And this behavior leads investors to earn lower returns than the very funds in which they invest. A superior approach is to follow a disciplined rebalancing strategy that systematically sells what has performed relatively well recently and buy what has performed relatively poorly.

We have one last problem to discuss.

IMPATIENCE

We have learned that when contemplating investment returns, the typical investor considers three to five years a long time, and 10 years an eternity. When it comes to the returns of risky asset classes, however, periods as short as three to five years should be considered nothing more than noise. And even 10 years is a relatively brief period. No more proof is required than the –1 percent per year return to the S&P 500 Index over the first decade of this century. Investors in stocks should not have lost faith in their belief that stocks should outperform safe U.S. Treasury bills due to the experience of that decade.

Here's an even more striking example. Over the 40-year period ending in 2008, U.S. large-cap and small-cap growth stocks both underperformed long-term U.S. Treasury bonds. We would hope that investors didn't abandon the idea that these risky assets should be expected to outperform in the future just because they had experienced a long period of underperformance. Indeed, the long bull market in bonds has brought yields to historic lows, with more muted potential returns. Similarly, when it comes to international investing, investors are far too willing to abandon well-thought-out strategies involving global diversification (perhaps because of home country bias) when international equities experience inevitable periods of underperformance.

Investors need to understand that when they invest in risky assets and factors, they should expect to experience some long periods in which those assets and factors underperform. In each of this book's chapters on equity factors, we showed that no matter how long the period, there was some chance that a factor — including the equity factor — would produce a negative premium. At the five-year time horizon, the only premium with less than an 18 percent chance of underperformance was the momentum premium. If such potential underperformance were not the case, there would be no risk associated with investing in them, and the premiums would likely disappear.

SUMMARY

Diversification means accepting the fact that parts of your portfolio may behave entirely differently than the portfolio itself. Knowing your level of tolerance for tracking error risk, and investing accordingly, will help keep you disciplined. The less tracking error you are willing to accept, the more the equity portion of your portfolio should look like the S&P 500 Index. On the other hand, if you choose a market-like portfolio, it will not be very diversified by asset class, or by factors, and it will have no international diversification. Between these two choices (avoiding or accepting tracking error) at least, there is no free lunch.

It is almost as important to get this balance right as it is to determine the appropriate equity/fixed-income allocation. If you have the discipline to stick with a globally diversified, passive asset class/factor strategy, you are likely to be rewarded for your discipline.

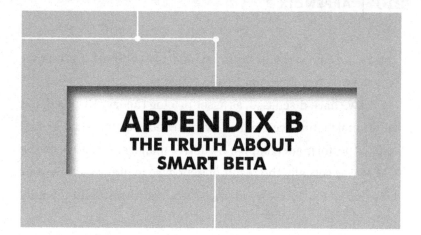

APPENDIX B
THE TRUTH ABOUT
SMART BETA

When Nobel Prize winner William F. Sharpe was asked what he thought about the term "smart beta," he responded that hearing it makes him sick. While our reaction is not as extreme, we do urge caution. The reason is that many of the strategies often referred to as smart beta are mostly marketing gimmicks. They are simply re-packaged, re-branded quantitative management strategies that deliver exposure to the various factors we have discussed. However, the fact that they are marketing gimmicks does not mean they do not work; indeed, we advocate exposure to many of the same factors they target. Thus, we want to be sure that we do not make the mistake of throwing the proverbial baby out with the bathwater.

The argument that there cannot be such a thing as "smart" beta is that beta is just beta, or loading on a factor. William Sharpe coined the term "beta" when he developed the capital asset pricing model (CAPM) of modern portfolio theory. As Sharpe explains, beta (in this case, market beta) is simply a portfolio's sensitivity to movements in the overall market. Which raises the question: So how, then, do you get smart out of that? It is neither smart, nor alternative, nor better. It just is.

As we have discussed, as asset pricing theory advanced and additional factors were added, we learned that what had looked like outperformance (alpha) by active managers relative to the CAPM was actually the result of exposure to other factors — or betas of the size, value, momentum, and profitability/quality factors.

While multifactor models do a much better job of explaining returns than the original CAPM, anomalies (remember, size, value, and momentum were once considered anomalies) that the models cannot explain still remain. Among this group of anomalies is that any asset with a lottery-like distribution has been shown to have poor risk–return characteristics. Exposure to these assets results in negative alphas (below-benchmark returns). This brings us back to the question of whether or not there is such a thing as smart beta. In our view, while it might just be a matter of semantics, the answer is yes. Let us see why this is the case.

FUND CONSTRUCTION RULES

There can be many different portfolios that have the same loading or exposure to the various factors. In other words, their betas are the same. Let us assume that we start with a mutual fund (Fund A) that owns the total U.S. market. By definition, it will have a market beta of 1. The manager of Fund B believes that she can create smarter beta by screening out all the stocks with lottery-like distributions (such as IPOs, "penny stocks," stocks in bankruptcy, and extremely small growth stocks). Fund B will also likely have a market beta of 1, but it can be expected to produce a higher return in the long term. Because the market betas are the same, it seems perfectly appropriate to say that Fund B has smarter beta, or better beta. Or you could say that if Fund B indeed earned a higher return, it has alpha. The difference is just semantics, not a real one.

Creating intelligent construction rules is just one way a fund can create smarter beta. Management of trading costs presents another.

TRADING COSTS

If a fund's sole goal is to replicate an index — which is typically the case for index funds — it must trade when stocks enter or exit that index. This causes the fund to be a demander (buyer) of liquidity. It also forces the fund to demand that liquidity at the same time other index funds are doing so. In addition, the fund must hold the exact weighting of each security in the index. A fund whose goal is instead to earn the return of the asset class (or factor) in which it invests, and is willing to live with some random tracking error, can be more patient in its trading strategy and avoid demanding liquidity. For example, it can use algorithmic trading systems to place market orders, reducing trading costs. It can also use block trading strategies to take advantage of discounts (premiums) offered by active managers that desire to quickly sell (buy) large amounts of stock. Patient trading reduces transaction costs, and block trading can even create negative trading costs in some cases.

There is yet another way in which beta can be made smarter.

MULTI-STYLE VERSUS SINGLE-STYLE FUNDS

We have made the case that investors should at least consider diversifying their portfolios across a broad range of factors. If you decide to do so, your next decision involves whether to invest in a number of single-style funds or in a single fund that provides exposures to multiple factors. Both approaches could provide the same exposure to each factor. However, a well-designed multi-style fund is smarter beta. One reason is that a multi-style approach can net different style signals before trading. Consider an investor who desires exposure to both value and momentum. To gain exposure to both factors, he buys both a value fund and a momentum fund. Stock XYZ has fallen in price and enters the buy range of the value fund. At the same, the recent poor performance of the stock causes the momentum fund to sell it. Multi-style funds avoid needless turnover and its associated costs — and for taxable investors, potentially lower their tax burden. While single-style funds are simpler, there are advantages to multi-style funds.

CHOICE OF INDEX AND
FUND CONSTRUCTION RULES

Yet another example of smarter beta is the choice of benchmark index and the rules used to construct portfolios, including how closely a fund adheres to its underlying benchmark. This can be important because returns can be affected by how often an index reconstitutes. Most indices (such as the Russell and RAFI Fundamental indices) reconstitute annually. The lack of a more frequent reconstitution schedule can create significant style drift. For example, from 1990 through 2006, the percentage of stocks in the Russell 2000 Index in June that would then leave the index when it reconstituted at the end of the month was 20 percent. For the Russell 2000 Value Index, the figure was 28 percent. The result is that a small-cap index fund based on the Russell 2000 would have seen its exposure to the small-cap risk factor drift lower over the course of the year. For small value funds based on the Russell 2000 Value Index, their exposure to both the small and value premiums would have drifted lower. The drift toward lower exposure to these risk factors results in lower expected returns. To avoid this problem, a fund could choose to reconstitute monthly, or quarterly, depending on how it affects turnover and transaction costs.

We hope that the following provides a good example of why smart beta is not entirely a marketing gimmick. Recall that a fund can demonstrate smarter beta in its choice of fund construction rules. This point is best made by performing a regression analysis on the four leading small-cap indices: the Russell 2000, the CRSP 6–10, the S&P 600, and the MSCI US Small Cap 1750. Table B.1 shows the results of a four-factor (market beta, size, value, and momentum) regression using the Fama-French factors, covering the period from 1994 (the inception date of the S&P 600) through December 2015. The *t*-statistics are in parentheses.

TABLE B.1: SMALL-CAP INDICES AND FACTOR EXPOSURES
(1994–2015)

INDEX	ANNUAL ALPHA (%)	MARKET BETA	SIZE	VALUE	MOM.	R² (%)	ANNUALIZED RETURN
CRSP 6–10	0.98 (1.8)	1.01 (90.3)	0.86 (60.3)	0.16 (10.1)	−0.14 (−15.1)	99	10.3
MSCI 1750	−0.01 (0.0)	1.04 (68.1)	0.61 (31.1)	0.26 (12.4)	−0.03 (−2.2)	97	10.3
RUSSELL 2000	−1.96 (−2.9)	1.01 (72.8)	0.79 (44.4)	0.26 (13.3)	0.01 (0.7)	97	8.4
S&P 600	−0.31 (−0.3)	0.98 (47.4)	0.70 (26.5)	0.35 (12.1)	0.01 (0.7)	94	10.2

To begin our analysis, we note that all the R-squared figures are very high, meaning the model is doing a good job of explaining returns. And almost all the loading statistics are highly significant. During the period, using Fama-French data, the market beta premium was 6.3 percent, the size premium was 1.2 percent, the value premium was 1.3 percent, and the momentum premium was 4.4 percent.

As you can see, all four indices had very similar exposure to market beta, ranging from 0.98 to 1.04. However, we see much greater differences in the exposure to the other factors. Exposure to the size factor ranged from 0.86 for the CRSP 6–10 Index to as low as 0.61 for the MSCI US Small Cap 1750 Index. Exposure to the value factor ranged from 0.35 for the S&P 600 Index to 0.16 for the CRSP 6–10 Index. Exposure to the momentum factor ranged from 0.01 for both the Russell 2000 Index and the S&P 600, to –0.14 for the CRSP 6–10 Index.

The CRSP 6–10 Index had the highest exposure to the size factor (providing a relative boost to its return) but the lowest exposure to the value and momentum factors (creating a drag on returns). The negative impact of the lower exposure to value and momentum offset the benefit of its higher exposure to the size premium. And the index did manage to produce an annual alpha of 0.98 percent. What is more, it was close to being statistically significant at the 5 percent level (t-stat = 1.8).

Relative to the CRSP 6–10 Index, the MSCI US Small Cap 1750 Index's lower loading on size was offset by its higher loadings on the other three factors. The result was that it produced the same annualized return of 10.3 percent. The alpha of the index was effectively zero.

A similar story reveals itself when we compare the results of the CRSP 6–10 Index relative to the S&P 600 Index. The latter's higher value and momentum loadings were almost sufficient to offset its lower size loading and slightly lower market beta loading. The result was that the S&P 600 Index underperformed the CRSP 6–10 Index by just 0.1 percent. The S&P 600 did produce a negative annual alpha of –0.31 percent. However, the negative alpha was not close to being statistically significant.

The Russell 2000 Index data tell a very different story. Compared to the CRSP 6–10 Index, it had the same loading on market beta. Its lower loading on the size factor was more than offset by its higher loadings on the value and momentum factors. This should have resulted in a higher return for the Russell 2000 Index. However, the Russell 2000 produced a negative annual alpha of –1.96 percent. And that resulted in it returning just 8.4 percent, 1.9 percent less than the returns of the CRSP 6–10 and the MSCI US Small Cap 1750 indices.[10] As you can see, the index a fund chooses to use to establish its fund construction rules can make a dramatic difference in the return received.

This example demonstrates that it is not only important for investors to make their choice of funds based on the amount of exposure they desire to each of the factors that explain returns, but also to consider how the fund's construction and implementation rules can impact returns — an effect that can be significant.

10 To be fair, the Russell 2000 Index follows a very transparent constitution process, which can be a very useful characteristic for a benchmark, although not necessarily for an index in which to invest. In fact, the Russell 2000 has been by far the most popular small-cap index in terms of assets either indexed or benchmarked to it. This has made it a prime target for front-running, lowering the index's returns. If other small-cap indices become more popular, they too may suffer a similar fate. This is another reason why we consider that a smarter way of obtaining exposure to any type of beta is not strictly adhering to a benchmark.

We are certainly in favor of strategies that provide exposure to the factors we advocate in this book, whether they are dubbed "smart beta" or not. For funds using proprietary, newly minted factors that do not meet our criteria, we do urge caution. Tread carefully and remember that the details of implementation matter quite a bit as well. The bottom line is that the use of intelligent, patient trading strategies and incorporating the findings from academic research can result in the design of portfolios that produce results superior to total market portfolios and pure index funds. In other words, sometimes smart beta is really smarter beta.

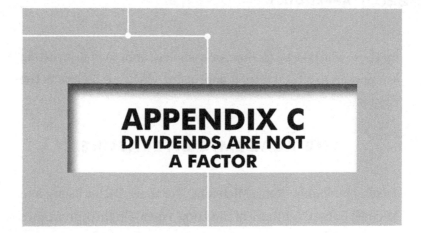

APPENDIX C
DIVIDENDS ARE NOT
A FACTOR

In their 1961 paper "Dividend Policy, Growth, and the Valuation of Shares," Merton Miller and Franco Modigliani famously established that dividend policy should be irrelevant to stock returns. For more than 50 years, this theorem has not faced a challenge in the academic literature. Moreover, the empirical evidence supports the theory, which explains why there are no asset pricing models that include a dividend factor.

Despite this long-held tenet of traditional financial theory, one of the biggest trends to occur in recent years has been a rush to invest in dividend strategies, such as strategies that invest in stocks with relatively high dividends or in stocks with a record of increasing dividends. The heightened interest in these strategies has been fueled both by media hype and the current regime of historically low interest rates.

The low yields generally available on safe bonds since the start of the Great Recession of 2008 has led many once-conservative investors to shift their allocation from safe bonds to riskier dividend-paying stocks. This has been especially true for those who take an income, or cash flow, approach to investing as opposed to a total return approach, which we believe is the right one.

THE ACADEMIC LITERATURE

Jacob Boudoukh, Roni Michaely, Matthew Richardson, and Michael Roberts, authors of the 2007 paper "On the Importance of Measuring Payout Yield: Implications for Empirical Asset Pricing," found that the dividend yield does a poor job predicting future returns in a sample that runs from 1972 through 2003. And Amit Goyal and Ivo Welch, authors of the 2003 paper "Predicting the Equity Premium with Dividend Ratios," found that the dividend yield has little predictive ability out of sample. They concluded: "We find that dividend ratios should have been known to have no predictive ability even prior to the 1990s, and that any seeming ability even then was driven by only two years, 1973 and 1974."

For almost 20 years now, the workhorse model in finance has been the Carhart four-factor model — with the four factors being market beta, size, value, and momentum. The model explains about 95 percent of the differences in returns of diversified portfolios. Newer competing models, such as the q-factor model, which includes profitability and investment (stocks with low investment outperform stocks with high investment), add even further explanatory power and eliminate almost all of the anomalies that exist with earlier models. The important point is that none of the asset pricing models include a dividend factor, just as theory and the research suggest.

If dividends played an important role in determining returns, the current asset pricing models would not work as well as they do. In other words, if dividends added explanatory power beyond that of the factors currently in use, we would have a model that included dividends as one of the factors. No dividend factor exists because stocks with the identical "loading" on (or exposure to) the already well-known factors have the same expected return regardless of their dividend policy. For example, the returns of high-dividend strategies are well explained by their exposure to already common factors, particularly the value factor. The same is true for increasing-dividend strategies, the returns of which are well explained by their factor exposures, particularly to the profitability/quality factors. To demonstrate this point, we will look at Vanguard's highly popular Dividend Appreciation ETF (VIG). Data are available from June 2006. A five-factor regression analysis shows that for the period through February 2016, VIG had exposure to the common factors as follows: market beta (0.93), size (-0.09), value (0.14), momentum (-0.01), and quality (0.34). The market beta of 0.93 shows that the fund had a bit less market risk than the total U.S. stock market (which has a market beta of 1). The small negative loading on the size factor shows that the stocks it held were a bit larger than average. The value loading of 0.14 shows that the stocks the fund holds have some exposure to the value factor. The momentum loading is virtually zero. And VIG has a fairly strong loading on the quality factor.

With the exception of the loading on momentum, the other loadings were all statistically significant. The t-statistic on the value loading was in excess of three, and the t-statistic on the quality factor was in excess of six. Importantly, the R-squared figure was 95 percent, showing that the model did an excellent job of explaining the fund's returns.

These findings have important implications because about 60 percent of U.S. stocks and about 40 percent of international stocks do not pay dividends. Thus, any screen that excludes such equities results in portfolios that are far less diversified than they could be if dividends were included as a factor in the portfolio design. Less-diversified portfolios are less efficient because they have a higher potential dispersion of returns without any compensation in the form of higher expected returns (assuming the exposures to the factors are the same).

Given the theory and evidence against dividends as an explanatory factor, what explains the well-known preference of so many investors for them? From the perspective of classical financial theory, this preference is an anomaly. It is perplexing behavior because, before taking into account what are referred to as "frictions" (such as transaction costs and taxes), dividends and capital gains should be perfect substitutes for each other. Stated simply, a cash dividend results in a drop in the price of the firm's stock by an amount equal to the dividend.[11] This must

---

11 Note that, historically, the drop in the stock price has tended to be slightly less than the amount of the dividend, an effect that many ascribe to taxes.

be the case, unless you believe that $1 is not worth $1. Thus, investors should be indifferent between a cash dividend and a "homemade" dividend created by selling an amount of the company's stock that is equal in value. One is a perfect substitute (not including any frictions) for the other. Thus, without considering frictions, because dividends are neither good nor bad, investors should not have a preference for them.

Warren Buffett made this point in September 2011. After announcing a share buyback program for Berkshire Hathaway, some people went after Buffett for not offering a cash dividend. In his shareholder letter, he explained why he believed the share buyback was in the best interest of shareholders. He also explained that any shareholder who preferred cash can effectively create dividends by selling shares.

Hersh Shefrin and Meir Statman, two of the leaders in the field of behavioral finance, attempted to explain the behavioral anomaly of a preference for cash dividends in their 1984 paper "Explaining Investor Preference for Cash Dividends."

Their first explanation was that, in terms of their ability to control spending, investors may recognize they have problems with the inability to delay gratification. To address the issue, they adopt a "cash flow" approach to spending, limiting it only to the interest and dividends from their investment portfolio. A "total return" approach, using self-created dividends, would not address the conflict created by the individual who wishes to deny himself a present indulgence yet is unable to resist the temptation. While the preference for dividends might not be optimal (for tax reasons), by addressing the behavioral issue, it could be thought of as rational for that individual. In other words, the investor has a desire to defer spending but knows he does not have the will, so he creates a situation that limits his opportunities and, thus, reduces the temptations.

Shefrin and Statman's second explanation was based on prospect theory and loss aversion. Prospect theory states that people value gains and losses differently. As such, they will base decisions on perceived gains rather than perceived losses. Thus, if a person were given two equal choices, one expressed in terms of possible gains and the other in terms of possible losses, that person would choose the former. Loss aversion refers to a person's tendency to prefer avoiding losses more strongly than acquiring gains. Most studies suggest that losses are twice as powerful, psychologically, as gains. Because taking dividends does not involve the sale of stock, it is preferred to a total return approach that may require self-created dividends through sales. Sales might involve the realization of losses, which are too painful for people to accept (they exhibit loss aversion). What they fail to realize is that a cash dividend is the perfect substitute for the sale of an equal amount of stock whether the market is up or down, or whether the stock is sold at a gain or a loss. It makes absolutely no difference. It is just a matter of how the problem is framed. It is form over substance. Whether you take the cash dividend or sell the equivalent dollar amount of the company's stock, you will have the same amount invested in the stock at the end of the day. With the dividend, you own more shares but at a lower price (by the amount of the dividend); with the self-dividend, you own fewer shares but at a higher price (because no dividend was paid). In either case, what you have invested in the stock is, again, the same. The following example provides the mathematics behind the theory.

THE MATHEMATICS OF CASH VERSUS HOMEMADE DIVIDENDS

To demonstrate the point that cash and homemade dividends are equivalent, we will consider two companies identical in all respects but one: Company A pays a dividend and Company B does not. To simplify, we will assume that the stocks of both Company A and Company B trade at their book value (while stocks do not typically do this, the findings would be the same regardless).

The two companies have a beginning book value of $10. They both earn $2 a share. Company A pays a $1 dividend, while Company B pays none. An investor in Company A owns 10,000 shares and takes the $10,000 dividend to meet his spending requirements. At the end of year one, the book value of Company A will be $11 (beginning value of $10 + $2 earnings – $1 dividend). The investor will have an asset allocation of $110,000 in stock ($11 × 10,000 shares) and $10,000 in cash, for a total of $120,000.

Now let us look at the investor in Company B. Because the book value of Company B at the end of year one is now $12 ($10 beginning book value + $2 earnings), his asset allocation is $120,000 in stock and $0 in cash. He must sell shares to generate the $10,000 he needs to meet his spending needs. So he sells 833 shares and generates $9,996. With the sale, he now has just 9,167 shares. However, those shares are worth $12, so his asset allocation is $110,004 in stock and $9,996 in cash, identical to that of the investor in Company A.

Another way to show that the two methods are equivalent is to consider the investor in Company A, who, instead of spending the dividend, reinvests it. With the stock now at $11, his $10,000 dividend allows him to purchase 909.09 shares. Thus, he now has 10,909.09 shares. With the stock at $11, his asset allocation is the same as the asset allocation of the investor in Company B: $120,000 in stock.

It is important to understand that Company B, which retained all of its earnings, should have a somewhat higher expected growth in earnings going forward. The reason is that the company has more capital to invest. And with the assumption being that the market has correctly priced the stock, the additional retained capital will provide additional earnings sufficient to offset the lesser amount of shares owned.

Returning to the paper by Shefrin and Statman, they cite a 1982 manual for stockbrokers to point out: "By purchasing shares that pay good dividends, most investors persuade themselves of their prudence, based on the expected income. They feel the gain potential is a super added benefit. Should the stock fall in value from their purchase level, they console themselves that the dividend provides a return on their cost." The authors do point out that if the sale involves a gain, the investor frames it as a "super added benefit." However, if a loss is incurred, the investor frames it as a "silver lining with which he can 'console himself.'" The fact that losses loom much larger in investors' minds, and that they wish to avoid them, implies they prefer to take the cash dividend, avoiding the realization of a loss.

Shefrin and Statman offered yet a third explanation: regret avoidance. They ask you to consider two cases:

1. You take $600 received as dividends and use it to buy a television set.

2. You sell $600 worth of stock and use it to buy a television set.

After the purchase, the price of the stock increases significantly. Would you feel more regret in case one or in case two? Because cash dividends and self-dividends are substitutes for each other, you should feel no more regret in the second case than in the first case. However, evidence from studies on financial behavior demonstrates that, for many people, the sale of stock causes more regret. Thus, investors who exhibit aversion to regret have a preference for cash dividends.

Shefrin and Statman go on to explain that people suffer more regret when actions are taken than when actions are avoided. In selling stock to create the homemade dividend, a decision must be made to raise the cash. When spending comes from the dividend, no action is taken, thus less regret is felt. Again, this helps explain the preference for cash dividends.

The authors also explain how a preference for dividends might change over an investor's lifecycle. As mentioned earlier, self-control is the behavioral mechanism used to justify the idea of spending only from the cash flow of a portfolio, never touching the principal. Younger investors, generating income from their labor capital, might prefer a portfolio with low dividends because a high dividend strategy might encourage dissavings. On the other hand, retired investors, with no labor income, may prefer a high-dividend strategy for the same reason, to discourage dissavings (spending from capital). A study of brokerage accounts found that there was, in fact, a strong and positive relationship between age and the preference for dividends.

The bottom line is that the preference for cash dividends is an anomaly that cannot be explained by classical economic theory based on investors making "rational" decisions. However, investors who face issues of self-control (such as a weakness for impulse buying) may find that even though there are some incremental costs involved, the benefits provided by avoiding the behavioral problems may make a cash dividend strategy a rational one for them.

IN THE REAL WORLD THERE ARE FRICTIONS

Unfortunately, we do not live in a world without frictions. And where frictions do exist, they can lead us to prefer capital gains over dividends, or vice versa. For example, if dividends are taxed at higher rates than long-term capital gains — as they once were, and still are, for payers of nonqualified dividends such as REITs and business development companies (BDCs) — taxable investors would have a clear preference for capital gains. But even with the current tax regime, taxable investors should prefer capital gains. When creating a self-made dividend, you could sell only the shares that would receive long-term capital gains treatment, and taxes would be due only on the portion that is a gain, not the total amount. With dividends, you are taxed on the full amount. In addition, investors can manage taxes by choosing the highest-cost-basis lot to sell, minimizing taxes. And if there are losses on the sale, the investor gains the benefit of a tax deduction. Even in tax-advantaged accounts, investors diversifying globally (the prudent strategy) should prefer capital gains because in tax-advantaged accounts, the foreign tax credits associated with dividends have no value. And finally, if dividends were throwing off more cash than needed to meet spending requirements, the total return approach would benefit not only from the time value of avoiding taxes on the "excess" amount of dividends, but also from preventing dividends from pushing investors into a higher tax bracket.

Another reason that investors may prefer dividends is transactions costs. Let us assume that all assets are in tax-advantaged accounts and all assets are domestic. In this situation, taxes do not create any frictions. If the creation of self-made dividends does incur transaction fees that could have been avoided by a cash flow approach (with dividends providing the cash flow), those fees could lead to a preference for cash dividends. In today's world, with very low commission rates and with many mutual funds trading at no costs, this is likely to be less of an issue.

Before concluding, we have the findings from a few relatively recent papers to discuss. They have important implications for investors who are considering dividend strategies. The first is the 2014 study "Enhancing the Investment Performance of Yield-Based Strategies," which covers the period from 1972 through 2011. The authors, Wesley Gray and Jack Vogel, found that by expanding the definition of dividend yield to include three alternative measures, the explanatory power of the dividend yield could be improved. The three alternatives were:

- PAY1: dividends plus share repurchases
- PAY2: dividends plus net share repurchases (repurchases less new stock issuance)
- SHYD: shareholder yield that includes net-debt paydown as part of the yield calculation (net-debt paydown yield is measured as the year-over-year difference in the debt load of a firm, scaled by total market capitalization)

The following is a summary of Gray and Vogel's findings:

- The addition of net-debt paydown to the PAY2 yield (dividends plus net share repurchases) improves investment performance.
- There is no evidence that high-dividend strategies

systematically outperform.

- Over the period from 1972 through 2011, firms with the highest SHYD measures earn an average monthly return of 1.3 percent and a statistically significant three-factor alpha of 0.25 percent per month. This compares favorably with the simple dividend yield strategy (DIV), which earns an average 1.2 percent monthly return and has a statistically insignificant alpha of 0.17 percent per month.
- PAY1, PAY2, and SHYD have outperformed the simple dividend yield strategy in three out of the past four decades.
- SHYD is the top performer in virtually all subsample periods.

Gray and Vogel also found that within yield categories, lower-payout-percentage firms outperform higher-percentage-payout firms. They concluded that the addition of net-debt paydown in the yield metric is a robust improvement to high-yield investment strategies. This finding should not come as a surprise, considering that the ability to create an effective yield by combining buybacks and changes in debt with dividends is intuitive. Buying back stock, retiring debt, or paying dividends are all ways to effectively return cash to shareholders. It also demonstrates why dividends alone are not a factor. It is also worth observing that one can think of these metrics as quality, or profitability, indicators. A higher yield with lower payout should lead to sustainable and even increasing payouts.

With that said, it is important to note that the concept of share buybacks being a good thing has been around for a while. However, before 1983, regulatory constraints inhibited firms from aggressively repurchasing shares. With this change, Gustavo Grullon and Roni Michaely, authors of the 2002 paper "Dividends, Share Repurchases, and the Substitution Hypothesis," found that: "Repurchases have not only became [sic] an important form of payout for U.S. corporations, but also that firms finance their share repurchases with funds that otherwise would have been used to increase dividends." They concluded: "Firms have gradually substituted repurchases for dividends."

The last paper we will review addresses the sensitivity of dividend-paying stocks to interest rate risk.

DIVIDEND-PAYING STOCKS AND SENSITIVITY TO INTEREST RATE RISK

Viewed through the lens of traditional financial theory, stocks that pay dividends have less sensitivity to interest rates because the duration of their cash flows is shorter than with non-dividend payers. High-growth firms tend to have lower dividend payouts but higher future growth rates. That skews the distribution of their cash flows toward the most distant future. In contrast, firms with higher dividend payouts tend to have lower retention ratios and lower future growth rates. Thus, the distribution of their cash flows is relatively shorter. As a result, a valuation model predicts that duration tends to be longer for stocks with lower dividend payouts. Thus, we should expect that dividend-paying stocks, especially those paying relatively high dividends, will be less sensitive to interest rate risk. However, Hao Jiang and Zheng Sun, authors of the 2015 study "Equity Duration: A Puzzle on High Dividend Stocks," which covered the period from 1963 through 2014, found that the data told a tale in direct opposition with traditional theory.

They found that "the duration — in terms of sensitivity to interest rates — of the portfolios increases monotonically with the dividend yields. Stocks with high dividends tend to experience decreases in returns when long term bond yields increase, while those with low dividends tend to earn higher returns when interest rates hike up." During the period studied, when interest rates declined by 1 percent, high-dividend stocks tended to experience an increase in returns of 1.35 percent. In contrast, low-dividend stocks tended to have a decrease in returns of 1.12 percent. And both effects were statistically significant at the 1 percent level. This difference in estimated duration between high- and low-dividend stocks of 2.46 percent is highly statistically significant. The authors found the same pattern when they used dividend payout ratios (dividends divided by book equity) as an alternative measure of dividend payments. In addition, they found not only that high-dividend stocks tended to have a long duration that was robust throughout the period, but also that the effect was particularly strong toward the end of the period.

Jiang and Sun found that the results were not caused by higher stock market betas (more exposure to stock risk) among high-dividend-paying stocks. In fact, they found that such stocks tended to have lower stock market betas. And they also found that "despite the highly volatile correlation between aggregate stock market and bond market returns ranging from very negative to very positive the long duration of high dividend stocks remains stable in the past five decades."

There is one other issue related to the dividend discount model and duration that we need to discuss: It does *not* take into account the uncertainty of the cash flows. Risky securities may be less sensitive to interest rate changes and have shorter duration because the relative contribution from distant cash payments to total present value is small as compared to a risk-free security. The link between cash-flow risk and dividends has strong roots in the dividend literature. Studies have found that companies are reluctant to distribute higher dividends if they face high uncertainty and may have to reduce the future dividend payment due to lower earnings. This leads to a negative relationship between dividends and firms' cash-flow risk. If stocks with higher dividends tend to have lower cash-flow risk, then their sensitivity to interest rate changes will be relatively larger. Investors' view that dividend-paying stocks are safer investments lowers the discount rate and increases the duration of the cash flows, increasing the sensitivity to interest rate risk. This understanding helps explain why the data conflict with traditional theory.

Another explanation for Jiang and Sun's findings is that, since 2008, the increased demand from investors seeking cash provided by dividend-paying stocks has driven their valuations higher, lowering the discount rate (and the expected future return) applied to their expected returns, and thus lengthening their duration.

Interestingly, Jiang and Sun found that, in general, there is a tendency for institutional investors to avoid high-dividend stocks. This is consistent with the findings from other studies that indicate individual investors are the ones who have a preference for high-dividend stocks. In fact, Jiang and Sun also found that in high-interest-rate environments (the top 20 percent of quarters with high long-term interest rates), all the types of institutional investors they examined (banks, insurance companies, mutual funds, pension funds, endowments, and investment advisors) tended to underweight high-dividend stocks in their portfolios relative to the market. On the other hand, in low-interest-rate environments (the bottom 20 percent of quarters with low long-term interest rates), the institutional aversion to high-dividend stocks universally shrinks, with mutual funds and insurance companies tending to overweight high-dividend stocks in their portfolios relative to the market. This pattern is particularly pronounced for mutual funds. When interest rates are high, they underweight high-dividend stocks relative to the market portfolio, and when interest rates are low, they overweight high-dividend stocks.

The authors found that the preference for high-dividend stocks by mutual funds appears to be driven by the behavior of equity-income funds. Equity-income funds overweight stocks in the highest-dividend brackets and underweight stocks in the lowest brackets. In addition, they found that the allocation between low- and high-dividend stocks among equity-income funds depends on the level of interest rates. When interest rates are low, income funds exhibit strong preferences for holding high-dividend stocks. However, when interest rates are high, income funds tend to be more reluctant to overweight high-dividend stocks.

Jiang and Sun also found that mutual fund investors send disproportionately more money to income funds when interest rates are low. The time-series correlation between excess flows into income funds over those into all equity funds and long-term interest rates is –50 percent and is statistically significant at the 1 percent level of confidence. Their analysis of flows across income funds indicates that "flows are sensitive not only to net fund returns but also to their dividend yields, and the influence of dividends on fund flows depends crucially on the level of interest rates. In particular, when interest rates are low, the tournament for clients' money among income funds rewards funds' ability to generate income (dividends), incremental to their ability to generate total return. The pressure of competition naturally leads income funds to reach further for dividends in low interest rate environments." The finding that preferences shift has important implications for dividend strategies, as rising interest rates could lead to unexpected, and negative, consequences.

We have one more point to cover. A high-dividend strategy is another form of a value strategy. With that in mind, we can compare the returns of various value strategies to see how well a high-dividend strategy performed. For the period from 1952 through 2015, the dividend-to-price premium was 2.4 percent, compared to a premium of 4.1 percent for book-to-price, 4.7 percent for cash flow-to-price, and 6.3 percent for earnings-to-price. Not only was the dividend-to-price premium the lowest, it was the only one with a t-statistic that failed to show significance. The t-statistic was just 1.2, while the other t-statistics were 2.4, 2.9, and 3.4, respectively. Thus, not only was it the smallest premium, the premium it produced was statistically indifferent from zero.

In summary, neither financial theory nor research evidence provides any support for using dividends as a factor in portfolio construction. Given the negatives of such strategies in terms of the loss of diversification benefits and the tax implications, unless you have a compelling need for the psychological advantages described by Shefrin and Statman, there should be little reason to visit the dividend exhibit in the factor zoo.

APPENDIX D
THE LOW-VOLATILITY FACTOR

One of the big problems for the first formal asset pricing model developed by financial economists, the CAPM, was that it predicts a positive relation between risk and return. But empirical studies have found the actual relation to be flat, or even negative. Over the last 50 years, the most "defensive" (low-volatility, low-risk) stocks have delivered both higher returns and higher risk-adjusted returns than the most "aggressive" (high-volatility, high-risk) stocks. In addition, defensive strategies, at least those based on volatility, have delivered significant Fama–French three-factor and four-factor alphas.

The superior performance of low-volatility stocks was first documented in the literature in the 1970s — by Fischer Black (in 1972) among others — even before the size and value premiums were "discovered." The low-volatility anomaly has been shown to exist in equity markets around the world. Interestingly, this finding is true not only for stocks, but for bonds as well. In other words, it has been pervasive.

While our analysis will focus on low volatility, volatility and market beta are closely related (as we discussed in Chapter 1 on market beta). And the evidence on both is similar, leading us to make the same recommendations for the low-beta factor as we do for low volatility.

EXPLAINING THE ANOMALY

David Blitz, Eric Falkenstein, and Pim van Vliet, authors of the 2014 study "Explanations for the Volatility Effect: An Overview Based on the CAPM Assumptions," provide a broad overview of the literature on explanations for the volatility effect. They begin by explaining that an empirical failure of the CAPM must be attributable to a violation of one or more of the model's underlying assumptions. While models can help us understand how markets work and set prices, by definition, they are flawed or wrong — otherwise, they would be called laws, like we have in physics.

One of the assumptions of the CAPM is that there are no constraints on either leverage or short-selling. In the real world, many investors are either constrained against the use of leverage (by their charters) or have an aversion to its use. The same is true of short-selling, and the borrowing costs for some hard-to-borrow stocks can be quite high. Such limits can prevent arbitrageurs from correcting the pricing mistake. Another assumption of the CAPM is that markets have no frictions, meaning there are neither transaction costs nor taxes.

Of course, in the real world there are costs. And the evidence shows that the most mispriced stocks are the ones with the highest costs of shorting.

The explanation for the low-volatility anomaly, then, is that, faced with constraints and frictions, investors looking to increase their return choose to tilt their portfolios toward high-beta securities to garner more of the equity risk premium. This extra demand for high-beta securities, and reduced demand for low-beta securities, may explain the flat (or even inverted) relationship between risk and expected return relative to the predictions of the CAPM model.

Regulatory constraints can also be a cause of the anomaly. Blitz, Falkenstein, and van Vliet explain: "Regulators typically do not distinguish between different stock types, but merely consider the total amount invested in stocks for determining required solvency buffers. Examples include the standard models in the Basel II and III frameworks (which set a fixed capital charge of 23.2% for equity holdings), Solvency II (which sets a fixed capital charge of 32% for equity holdings) and the FTK for pension funds in the Netherlands (which prescribes a fixed capital buffer of 25% for equity holdings). Investors who wish to maximize equity exposure but minimize the associated capital charge under such regulations are drawn to the high-volatility segment of the equity market, as it effectively gives most equity exposure per unit of capital charge."

The academic literature has long posited that constraints on short-selling can cause stocks to be overpriced. Blitz,

Falkenstein, and van Vliet also explain why high-risk stocks can become so: "In a market with little or no short selling, the demand for a particular security comes from the minority who hold the most optimistic expectations about it. This phenomenon is also referred to as the winner's curse. As divergence of opinion is likely to increase with risk, high-risk stocks are more likely to be overpriced than are low-risk stocks, because their owners have the greatest bias."

Other assumptions under the CAPM are that investors are risk-averse, maximize the expected utility of absolute wealth, and care only about the mean and variance of returns. But we know those assumptions do not hold. In the real world, there are investors with a "taste," or preference, for lottery-like investments — investments that exhibit positive skewness and excess kurtosis. This leads them to "irrationally" invest in high-volatility stocks (which have lottery-like distributions) despite their poor returns. They pay a premium to gamble. Among the stocks that fall into the "lottery ticket" category are IPOs, small-cap growth stocks that are not profitable, penny stocks, and stocks in bankruptcy. Limits to arbitrage and the costs and fear of shorting prevent rational investors from correcting the mispricings.

The CAPM also assumes that investors maximize the expected utility of their own personal wealth. Yet research shows that individuals care more about relative wealth. For example, the authors cite a study that found an "overwhelming majority of people would rather earn $100,000 when others earn $90,000, than earn $110,000 when others earn $200,000. People prefer higher relative wealth over lower absolute wealth." Blitz, Falkenstein, and van Vliet note that the presence of both absolute and relative return-oriented investors implies a partial flattening of the security market line (returns do not increase monotonically as beta increases, and the highest beta stocks have the lowest returns), with the degree of flattening depending on the number of relative-return investors versus the number of absolute-return investors. We note that results for volatility are typically quite similar to those for beta. The CAPM also assumes that agents will maximize option values. But this may not always hold in the real world, which is inhabited by living, breathing investors subject to all sorts of biases. For example, the authors summarize the observations of a 2012 paper by Nardin Baker and Robert Haugen, noting that "a portfolio manager is typically paid a base salary, plus a bonus if performance is sufficiently high. They argue that this compensation arrangement resembles a call option on the portfolio return, the value of which can be increased by creating a more volatile portfolio. In other words, there is a conflict of interest between professional investors, who have an incentive to engage in risk-seeking behavior, and their clients, who are more likely to be risk-averse, as assumed by the CAPM."

Blitz, Falkenstein, and van Vliet explain that the optionality argument can be taken one step further "by arguing that the rewards of being recognized as a top manager are much larger than the rewards for second quintile managers, for instance.

For example, top managers receive a disproportionate share of attention from outside investors, such as making it to the front cover of *Bloomberg Markets* magazine. In order to become a top investment manager, one must generate an extreme, outsized return. This has the additional benefit of signaling to potential future investors and employers that one is truly skilled, as it is virtually impossible to distinguish between skill and luck in a modest outperformance. Delegated portfolio managers focused on realizing an extreme return in the short run may be willing to accept a lower long-term expected return on the high-risk stocks which enable such returns."

The CAPM also assumes that investors have complete information, and that they rationally process the information available. Again, we know this does not hold in the real world. The research demonstrates that both mutual funds and individual investors tend to hold the stocks of firms that are in the news more. In other words, they tend to buy attention-grabbing stocks that experience high abnormal trading volume, as well as stocks with extreme recent returns. Attention-driven buying may result from the difficulty that investors have in searching through the thousands of stocks they can potentially buy. Such purchases can temporarily inflate a stock's price, leading to poor subsequent returns. Attention-grabbing stocks are typically high-volatility stocks, while boring low-volatility stocks suffer from investor neglect. The attention-grabbing phenomenon is therefore another argument supporting the existence of the volatility effect.

The research also shows that investors (including active fund managers) are overconfident. We thus have another violation of the assumptions used by the CAPM, which is predicated on rational information processing. The impact on the volatility effect is that, if an active manager is skilled, it makes sense to be particularly active in the high-volatility segment of the market because that segment offers the largest rewards for skill. However, this results in excess demand for high-volatility stocks.

The literature is filled with a large number of possible explanations. What does seem clear is that many of them come from either constraints and/or agency issues driving managers toward higher-volatility stocks. Given that there does not seem to be anything on the horizon that would have a dampening impact on these issues, it appears likely the anomaly can persist. In addition, human nature does not easily change. So there does not seem to be any reason to believe that investors will abandon their preference for "lottery ticket" investments. And the limits to arbitrage, as well as the fear and costs of margin, make it difficult for arbitrageurs to correct mispricings.

THE EVIDENCE

In his 2016 study "Understanding Defensive Equity," which covered the period from 1968 through 2015, Robert Novy-Marx found that when ranking stocks by quintiles of either volatility or market beta, the highest-quintile stocks dramatically underperform, while the performance of the other four quintiles are very similar and market-like. In fact, the second-highest-volatility quintile (the fourth quintile) had the highest returns, followed by the third, second, and finally the first quintile. This nonlinear relationship is quite different from what we typically find with each of the factors we have recommended, where the returns across deciles, quintiles, or quartiles tend to be linear. Because the sorting is done by volatility or beta, risk-adjusted measures such as Sharpe ratios and CAPM alphas are more monotonic.

Novy-Marx also found that high-volatility and high-market-beta stocks tilt strongly to small-cap, unprofitable, and growth firms. These tilts explain the poor absolute performance of the most aggressive stocks — stocks that are often referred to as "jackpots" or "lottery tickets." It is the underperformance of these high-risk (small, unprofitable, and growth) stocks, which make up a very small percentage of the total market capitalization, that drives the abnormal performance of defensive equity. Novy-Marx also found that a stock's profitability is a significant negative predictor of its volatility, and it is the single most significant predictor of low volatility.

Novy-Marx found that by including profitability as a factor, the defensive strategy (low volatility) performance is well explained by controlling for the common factors of size, profitability, and relative valuations. He also found that defensive strategies tilt strongly toward large-cap stocks (low-volatility stocks are 30 times as large as high-volatility stocks at the end of his sample, and the long/short portfolio has an SMB loading of −1.12), value stocks (the long/short portfolio has an HML loading of 0.42), and profitable stocks. The profitability tilt obscures the extent to which defensive strategies tilt toward value. Because value and profitability tend to be strongly negatively correlated, unless you control for profitability, the value loadings of defensive strategies will be lowered. Novy-Marx also found that five-sixths of the Fama–French three-factor alpha (57 out of 68 basis points per month) was delivered by the aggressive stocks on the short side of the strategy, with only one-sixth (or 12 basis points per month) coming from the actual defensive stocks. And he found similar results when looking at a low-beta strategy.

Novy-Marx's work demonstrates that the anomaly of the poor returns to small-cap growth stocks is driven by unprofitable stocks that tend to have negative book equity. The success of defensive strategies in small-cap stocks is a result of avoiding these high-risk stocks. Unlike other factors, where approximately half the returns come from each of the long and the short sides, the vast majority of the returns from low volatility (and low beta) come from the short side, not because of the low-volatility strategy itself. In other words, accounting for size, relative valuations, and profitability, the performance of defensive strategies is well explained.

To illustrate this point, Novy-Marx showed that $1 invested in the beginning of 1968 in a defensive strategy constructed within small-cap growth stocks (a segment that accounts for on average 37.7 percent of names but only 5.3 percent of the market by capitalization) would have grown to $431, ignoring transaction costs, by the end of 2015. That same dollar invested in defensive strategies constructed in the small-cap value or large-cap growth universes would have grown to only $2.79 or $1.23, respectively. That same dollar invested into a defensive strategy constructed using large-cap value stocks would have left the investor with only $0.27 by the end of 2015, a 73 percent loss of capital over the sample. In contrast, a dollar invested in U.S. Treasury bills grew to $10.30.

Novy-Marx concluded: "While reaffirming the poor absolute performance of the most aggressive stocks, it nevertheless shows that the performance of defensive equity strategies is explained by known drivers of cross-sectional variation in returns." He added: "Defensive strategies are, however, an inefficient way to exploit these premia, which are better accessed directly. The backdoor route defensive strategies provide to an unprofitable small growth exclusion is also transactionally inefficient, entailing significant rebalancing and high transaction costs."

FURTHER EVIDENCE

Novy-Marx's findings add to the research demonstrating that there are problems with implementing a low-volatility strategy. For example, Xi Li, Rodney N. Sullivan, and Luis Garcia-Feijóo, authors of the 2014 study "The Limits to Arbitrage and the Low-Volatility Anomaly," found that the excess return associated with forming the long low-volatility/short high-volatility portfolios are basically present only in the first month after formation, and that they are largely subsumed by high transaction costs associated with low-liquidity stocks (such as low-priced/high-volatility stocks). They also found that the anomalous returns within value-weighted portfolios are largely eliminated when omitting low-priced (less than $5) stocks and are not at all present within equal-weighted portfolios. In fact, the average price of stocks in the highest-volatility quintile was just more than $7, indicating that many, if not most, would be considered "penny stocks." And finally, they found that the low-risk effect has been noticeably weaker since 1990. New regulations were passed in that year, aimed at reducing fraud connected to trading in penny stocks. (We would add that many high-beta stocks simply disappeared after the dot-com crash, and the number of stocks on public U.S. exchanges has decreased dramatically since then.) The authors concluded: "Our findings cast some doubt on the practical profitability of a low risk trading strategy."

The 2016 study by Bradford Jordan and Timothy Riley, "The Long and Short of the Vol Anomaly," which covered the period from July 1991 through December 2012, was motivated by prior research showing that both high-volatility stocks and stocks with high short interest exhibit poor risk-adjusted future performance. (While the "conventional wisdom" is that high short interest is a bullish signal because it predicts future buying from short covering, the reality is that stocks with high short interest perform poorly on average.) However, to date, no one had studied the two together. The authors found that while, on average, stocks with high prior-period volatility underperformed those with low prior-period volatility, the comparison of the two is misleading because, among high-volatility stocks, those with low short interest actually experience extraordinary positive returns. On the other hand, those with high short interest experience equally extraordinary negative returns. The bottom line is that high volatility on its own is not an indicator of poor future returns. In fact, they found that for the period from July 1991 through December 2012, stocks with high volatility and low short interest would have outperformed the CRSP Value-Weighted Index by 7 percent a year with a four-factor alpha of 11 percent a year. In stark contrast, they found that a portfolio long high-volatility and high-short-interest stocks had a four-factor alpha of –9 percent a year.

Another important finding was that high-volatility/low-short-interest stocks outperform the market in turbulent times, such as during the dot-com crash and the Great Recession. During the dot-com "bubble," an equally weighted high-volatility/low-short-interest portfolio had an annualized compound return 3.5 percent greater than that of the CRSP Value-Weighted Index. During the financial crisis, that same gap was 10.8 percent.

Importantly, Jordan and Riley's findings have implications for long-only strategies, as buying high-volatility stocks with low short interest avoids the high costs of shorting strategies and limits to arbitrage. While they did find that high-volatility stocks with low short interest are less liquid than the average stock (thus, execution costs could prevent fully realizing the returns), they found no significant difference in performance between stocks in either the high- or low-liquidity group. And low-short-interest stocks are typically larger stocks with higher trading volumes. High-volatility/high-short-interest stocks have an average size of $556 million, compared to about $2 billion for high-volatility/low-short-interest stocks. Thus, long-only investors can use screens to eliminate stocks with low liquidity, or they can use patient trading strategies to minimize turnover costs.

The authors reached the conclusion that "high volatility is not necessarily a bad thing." Instead, they provide the explanation "that (1) both positive and negative misvaluation exists among hard-to-value, highly volatile stocks and (2) short sellers are adept at identifying and exploiting these valuation errors."

It is also worth noting that DFA and other firms have long used knowledge related to short interest in implementing their structured portfolio strategies. Whenever an individual stock goes on "special" in the securities lending market (meaning the borrowing rate is very high), they suspend the stock from their buy list for a period of up to 15 days. They have found that high borrowing costs, especially in small-cap stocks, predicts poor returns over the near term. Note that this does not mean it pays to short the stock, because the borrowing costs can be sufficiently high that, after all costs are accounted for, there is no alpha generated. However, by avoiding buying more shares, their portfolios do not suffer from the underperformance.

There is yet another issue we need to cover — low-volatility strategies have exposure to the term factor.

TERM RISK

The fact that low-volatility strategies have exposure to term risk (the duration factor) should not be a surprise. Generally speaking, low-volatility/low-beta stocks are more "bond-like." They are typically large stocks, the stocks of profitable and dividend-paying firms, and the stocks of firms with mediocre growth opportunities. In other words, they are stocks with the characteristics of safety as opposed to risk and opportunity. Thus, they show higher correlations with long-term bond returns. Ronnie Shah, author of the 2011 paper "Understanding Low Volatility Strategies: Minimum Variance," found that for the period from 1973 through June 2010, the low-beta strategy has exposure to term risk. The "loading factor" (degree of exposure) was a statistically significant 0.09 (t-stat = 2.6). As further evidence, Tzee-man Chow, Jason C. Hsu, Li-lan Kuo, and Feifei Li, authors of the 2014 study "A Study of Low-Volatility Portfolio Construction Methods," found a 0.2 correlation between the BAB (betting against beta) factor and the duration factor. Using U.S. data going back to 1929 and global data starting from 1988, David Blitz, Bart van der Grient, and Pim van Vliet found similar results in their 2014 paper "Interest Rate Risk in Low-Volatility Strategies." They did add, however, that the bond exposure of low-volatility strategies does not fully explain their long-term added value.

Given their positive exposure to term risk, low-volatility stocks have benefited from the cyclical bull market in bonds that we have experienced since 1982. That rally cannot be repeated now, with interest rates at historic lows.

SUPPORT FOR LOW BETA

The aforementioned 2014 study by Andrea Frazzini and Lasse Heje Pedersen, "Betting Against Beta," found strong support for low-beta strategies. They found that for U.S. stocks, the Betting Against Beta (BAB) factor (a portfolio that holds low-beta assets, leveraged to a beta of 1, and that shorts high-beta assets, de-leveraged to a beta of 1) realized a Sharpe ratio of 0.78 between 1926 and March 2012. That is about twice the Sharpe ratio of the value effect and 40 percent higher than that of momentum over the same time period. And they found that the BAB factor has highly significant risk-adjusted returns after accounting for its realized exposure to the market beta, value, size, momentum, and liquidity factors. In fact, BAB realized a significant positive return in each of the four 20-year subperiods between 1926 and 2012. Additionally, their analysis of 19 international equity markets revealed similar results. The authors further found that BAB returns have been consistent across countries, across time, within deciles sorted by size, and within deciles sorted by idiosyncratic risk, as well as consistently robust to a number of specifications. These consistent results suggest that coincidence or data mining are unlikely explanations.

254 | APPENDIX D

As further supporting evidence, Frazzini and Pedersen found that in each asset class they examined (stocks, U.S. Treasury bonds, credit markets, and futures markets for currencies and commodities), alphas and Sharpe ratios declined almost monotonically as beta increased. They concluded: "This finding provides broad evidence that the relative flatness of the security market line is not isolated to the U.S. stock market but that it is a pervasive global phenomenon. Hence, this pattern of required returns is likely driven by a common economic cause."

Evidence for low-volatility strategies extends to international equities as well. In their 2007 article "The Volatility Effect: Lower Risk without Lower Return," David Blitz and Pim van Vliet find that low volatility works globally for developed market large-cap stocks, with an annual spread between the lowest- and highest-volatility stocks of 5.9 percent from 1986 through 2006. The lowest risk decile had a Sharpe ratio of 0.72, compared to 0.40 for the market and 0.05 for the highest-volatility decile. Results also held for the U.S., European, and Japanese markets. And in their 2013 study "The Volatility Effect in Emerging Markets," David Blitz, Juan Pang, and Pim Van Vliet extended these results to emerging markets. Using data from 30 emerging market countries covering the period from 1988 through 2010, they found an annual spread of 2.1 percent. Interestingly, returns increased with volatility until the highest-volatility quintile, whose returns lagged the rest.

The preceding evidence presents a strong case for the pervasiveness of the low-beta factor, as well as for its persistence and robustness. And, as we have discussed, there are limits to arbitrage and other constraints that provide intuitive explanations for why the premium should persist. Thus, perhaps low beta does meet all of our criteria. With that said, we do offer caution before investing in this strategy, at least as it applies to equities.

HAVE LOW-VOLATILITY STRATEGIES BECOME OVERGRAZED?

As is the case with so many well-known anomalies and factors, the problem of potential overgrazing does exist. Published research on the premium, combined with the bear market caused by the Great Recession of 2008, led to a dramatic increase in the popularity of low-volatility strategies. For example, as of April 2016, there were five ETFs with at least $2 billion in assets under management (AUM):

- PowerShares S&P 500 Low Volatility Portfolio (SPLV): $6.8 billion
- iShares Edge MSCI Minimum Volatility USA ETF (USMV): $12.4 billion
- iShares Edge MSCI Minimum Volatility Emerging Markets ETF (EEMV): $3.4 billion
- iShares Edge MSCI Minimum Volatility Global ETF (ACWV): $2.8 billion
- iShares Edge MSCI Minimum Volatility EAFE ETF (EFAV): $6.7 billion

Cash inflows have raised the valuations of defensive (low-volatility/low-beta) stocks, dramatically reducing their exposure to the value premium from quite high to near zero or negative, and thus lowering expected returns. Specifically, as low-volatility stocks are bid up in price, low-volatility portfolios can lose their value characteristics, which would reduce their forward-looking returns.

Specifically, we will take a look at the valuation metrics of the two largest low-volatility ETFs: the iShares Edge MSCI Minimum Volatility USA ETF (USMV) and the PowerShares S&P 500 Low Volatility Portfolio (SPLV). We will then compare their value metrics to those of the iShares Russell 1000 EFT (IWB), which is a market-oriented fund, and the iShares Russell 1000 Value ETF (IWD). Table D.1 below is based on Morningstar data as of the end of April 2016.

TABLE D.1: VALUE METRICS

	USMV	SPLV	IWB	IWD
PRICE-TO-EARNINGS	21.2	19.9	18.3	16.5
PRICE-TO-BOOK	3.1	3.1	2.4	1.6
PRICE-TO-CASH FLOW	11.9	11.6	9.3	7.9

What is clear from the data is that the demand for these strategies has altered their very nature. In the past, the valuation metrics of USMV and SPLV were more value-oriented than the Russell 1000. However, now these metrics certainly do not look like what a value-oriented fund would have. Their price-to-earnings, book-to-market, price-to-sales, and price-to-cash flow ratios are all quite a bit higher than those of IWD. In fact, their metrics indicate that both funds are now more "growthy" than the market-like IWB. In other words, because there is an ex-ante value premium, what low volatility is predicting at this point in time is not higher returns, just low future volatility.

While investors should always prefer buying stocks at lower valuations, what we do not know is how big of an impact valuations will have on low-volatility strategies. Research from a 2012 paper by Pim van Vliet, "Enhancing a Low Volatility Strategy is Particularly Helpful When Generic Low Volatility is Expensive," sheds some light on this question. Using data from 1929 through 2010, he found that while on average low-volatility strategies tend to have exposure to the value factor, that exposure is time-varying. The low-volatility factor spends about 62 percent of the time in a value regime and 38 percent of the time in a growth regime.

This regime-shifting behavior impacts the performance of low-volatility strategies. When low-volatility stocks have value exposure, they have outperformed the market, returning an average of 9.5 percent annually versus the market's 7.5 percent. The low-volatility factor has also exhibited lower volatility, with an annual standard deviation of 13.5 percent versus the market's 16.5 percent. However, when low-volatility stocks have growth exposure, they have underperformed, returning an average of 10.8 percent annually versus the market's 12.2 percent. The low-volatility factor did continue to have lower annual volatility, at

15.3 percent versus 20.3 percent for the market. The result has been a higher *risk-adjusted* return in either regime. The bottom line is that in either regime, low volatility predicts future low volatility. However, when low volatility has negative exposure to the value factor (as it did in mid-2016), it also forecasts below-market returns.

The evidence suggests that you might be better served by investing in vehicles that screen out high-volatility (or high-beta), high-risk stocks. In other words, invest directly in size, value, and profitability, rather than doing so indirectly (like defensive strategies do).

Finally, it is important to remember that the anomaly is much more about the underperformance of high-volatility (or high-beta) stocks and not so much about the outperformance of low-volatility (or low-beta) stocks. Thus, to take advantage of the anomaly, you can either avoid high-volatility/high-beta stocks or invest in funds that screen them out.

Our conclusion is that there does seem to be evidence that low volatility is a unique factor, partly driven by limits to arbitrage and some investors' preference for lottery stocks. Low volatility historically has characteristics related to the term, value, and profitability factors, and the premiums associated with them. However, you should be wary. With interest rates at historic lows, the term premium aspect is unlikely to pay off as it has in the past. Furthermore, recent strong demand for low volatility has caused it to lose the value exposure typical of it over the last several decades.

The extent of the interaction between low volatility and these other factors continues to be the subject of active research. We do not yet know how it will all play out, but the combination of high valuations and low interest rates does give us concern.

APPENDIX E
THE DEFAULT FACTOR

The default premium (referred to as DEF) is defined as the return on long-term investment-grade bonds (20-year) minus the return on long-term government bonds (also 20-year). From 1927 through 2015, the annual average premium of DEF was just 0.3 percent. Clearly, corporate bonds have more default risk than bonds that carry the full faith and credit of the of the U.S. government, which is why there has been no debate (unlike with several of the other factors we examined) about the source of the premium.

While there is no debate about its source, taking credit risk has not been well-rewarded historically, with a premium of just 0.3 percent. In addition, the premium's t-statistic over the period was just 0.61, indicating that it was not statistically different from zero. And for bond mutual funds, the premium for taking the risks of investment-grade corporate debt instruments (versus U.S. government, U.S. government agency, or government-sponsored entities) historically has been very close to zero, or even negative. Examples of U.S. government agencies include the Federal Home Loan Bank and Tennessee Valley Authority; examples of government-sponsored entities (GSEs) include Fannie Mae or Freddie Mac. This is one reason why the only exhibit in the bond section of the factor zoo we recommend visiting is the term factor.

It is important to note that the slim 0.3 percent default premium does not take into consideration the higher costs involved with trading corporate bonds, nor the typically higher expense ratios of corporate bond funds. The market for U.S. government bonds is the most liquid in the world and, therefore, has the lowest trading costs. Because U.S. government obligations do not carry any credit risk for domestic investors, there is no need to diversify the risk of default. However, if you invest in corporate bonds, you should diversify default risk. Diversification is the main benefit of owning mutual funds, so you will incur the expense ratio of the fund as well as its trading costs. The result is a lower premium than the one seen on paper. On the other hand, investors can avoid mutual fund expenses by purchasing U.S. Treasury bonds directly from the government.

There is another issue that favors avoiding the default factor. Unless investors' funds are held in 401(k) plans, other similar retirement plans, or 529 plans, individuals can purchase FDIC-insured CDs, which typically carry higher yields than U.S. Treasuries and government agencies (although CD maturities are generally limited to 10 years), while also avoiding credit risk. For example, as of this writing, the yields on five- and 10-year CDs are approximately 0.75 percent above the yields of comparable U.S. Treasuries. That is an amount far greater than the default premium, and you have none of the fund expenses or trading costs incurred through corporate bond funds. The only remaining benefit, then, of mutual funds would be their convenience.

While corporate bonds do come with higher yields than government issues of the same maturity, the incremental yield historically has been offset by credit losses, the typically higher expense ratios of corporate bond funds relative to government bond funds (resulting from the need to analyze the credit risk of corporate issuers), and other features incorporated into corporate bonds (such as a call option). A call option gives the issuer the right to call in (prepay) the bonds. The issuer will do so if interest rates drop sufficiently to warrant the expense of the recall and reissuance of new bonds at the then-prevailing lower rate. The investor holding the high-yielding bond and then having it paid off early will have to purchase a new bond at the new lower rates. There are very few U.S. Treasury issues with call features.

Another problem for the default factor is that is has exhibited less persistence than any of the factors we have recommended. Table E.1 shows the persistence of the default premium over the period from 1927 through 2015. Note how much lower it is than the term premium (which can be found in Table 6.1) or, indeed, any of the other premiums discussed.

TABLE E.1: ODDS OF OUTPERFORMANCE (%)

	1-YEAR	3-YEAR	5-YEAR	10-YEAR	20-YEAR
DEFAULT	53	54	56	58	61

Over the same period, the Sharpe ratio for the default premium was just 0.06, much lower than the lowest of the Sharpe ratios for the factors we have recommended (the lowest of which was 0.24).

While the data are for a relatively short period, we do have evidence of a global credit premium as measured by the difference in the annual average returns of the Barclays Global Aggregate Corporate Index and the Barclays Global Treasury Index. For the period from 2001 through 2015, the annual premium was 0.9 percent, quite a bit smaller than any of the premiums on the factors we have recommended. And again, the premium ignores implementation costs, as well as the higher returns available (relative to government bonds) on riskless, FDIC-insured CDs. Factoring in both of these issues would likely offset much of the premium.

In addition to the miniscule realized premium, another problem for corporate debt is that default risk does not mix well with equity risk. The risk of default has a nasty tendency to show up at the same time equity risk rears its head.

In their 2001 paper "Explaining the Rate Spread on Corporate Bonds," Edwin J. Elton, Martin J. Gruber, Deepak Agrawal, and Christopher Mann demonstrated that a substantial portion of the credit spread is attributable to factors related to the equity risk premium. This makes intuitive sense: Both bonds and equities are investments in companies, so both carry the risk of the business doing poorly. They found that expected losses account for no more than 25 percent of the corporate spread. In the case of a 10-year, A-rated corporate bond, just 18 percent of the spread was explained by default risk. They also found that the Fama–French three-factor model explains as much as 85 percent of the spread not already explained by taxes and expected default loss. Furthermore, they found that the lower the credit rating (and the longer the maturity), the greater the explanatory power of the model. Thus, much of the expected return to high-yield debt is explained by risk premiums associated with equities, not debt. These risks are systematic and cannot be diversified away.

EVIDENCE SUPPORTED BY THEORY

The case for an equity component in higher-yield bonds — effectively making them hybrid securities — is supported by theory. Martin Fridson explained in his 1994 paper "Do High-Yield Bonds Have an Equity Component?": "In effect, a corporate bond is a combination of a pure interest rate instrument and a short position in a put on the issuer's equity. The put is triggered by a decline in the value of the issuer's assets to less than the value of its liabilities. A default, in other words, results in the stockholders putting the equity to the bondholders, who then become the company's owners. For a highly-rated company, the put is well out of the money and is not likely to be exercised. The option consequently has a negligible impact on the price movement of the bonds, which is more sensitive to interest rate fluctuations. In the case of a noninvestment-grade bond, however, default is a realistic enough prospect to enable the equity put to affect the bond's price materially. With the equity-related option exerting a greater influence on its price movement, the noninvestment-grade bond is bound to track government bonds (pure interest rate instruments) less closely than the investment-grade bond does."

ISOLATING INTEREST RATE RISK

Attakrit Asvanunt and Scott Richardson, authors of the 2016 paper "The Credit Risk Premium," took a new and interesting look at the credit premium. Their innovation was to first remove the influence of term risk. Past research, for the most part, computed the credit premium as the difference between long-term corporate bond returns and long-term government bond returns. However, that creates a problem because these two types of bonds have different exposures to interest rate sensitivities. The higher yields on long-term corporate debt result in their having shorter durations than long-term government bonds. And given the historical term premium, a matching of maturities (instead of duration) will result in an understating of the credit premium. The authors also raise the issue that if you only look at the safest issuers (investment-grade debt), you could underestimate the credit premium.

We would add two issues not fully considered by the authors. The first is that most long-term corporate debt has a call feature, which impacts interest rate sensitivities. Part of the premium on corporate debt is compensation for that asymmetric call risk (and thus not related to default risk). With that said, in the latter part of the sample data (1988 onward), the authors do use an option-adjusted duration measure, therefore accounting for callability. The second issue is that while interest on U.S. government securities is not taxed at the state or local levels, interest on corporate debt is. Investors must be compensated for that tax differential, which results in a tax premium on corporate debt not related to default risk.

The following is a summary of Asvanunt and Richardson's findings:

- By isolating interest rate sensitivity, they "confirm the existence of a positive premium for bearing exposure to default risk." They refer to this premium as the credit excess return.
- The average annual credit excess return on investment-grade corporate bonds over the period from 1936 through 2014 was about 1.4 percent with a Sharpe ratio of 0.37.

Asvanunt and Richardson also found that there is a consistently positive exposure of credit excess returns to equity excess returns (the correlation is about 0.3). In other words, they confirmed the results of prior research that found the equity premium (market beta) captures a considerable portion of the default premium. They also found that the credit risk premium varies over time with economic growth, and is subject to tail risk. Also keep in mind that this premium does not take into account the higher yields available on CDs, or the expenses or trading costs of a mutual fund. If we assume an additional yield (say, 0.75 percent) available on CDs, and trading costs and the expense ratio of a corporate bond fund, even a 1.4 percent default premium might disappear.

Evidence that the default premium contains equity-like risk is also provided by Jennie Bai, Pierre Collin-Dufresne, Robert Goldstein, and Jean Helwege, authors of the 2015 study "On Bounding Credit-Event Risk Premia." They examined the historical evidence to determine how much of the spread in corporate bonds was related to credit-event risk, and how much was related to contagion-event risk.

Their study, which covered the period from 2001 through 2010, defined a credit event as having occurred if the credit default swap (CDS) spread (or the firm-level bond yield spread) jumped by 100 basis points or more within a three-day window. They also required that firms start the pre-event period with a CDS spread of no higher than 400 basis points or with a bond price no lower than $80. The authors chose these criteria because, even though all the bonds in their sample were investment grade prior to the event, ratings sometimes lag the market. In other words, investment-grade bonds with high spreads may no longer actually be perceived as investment grade by market participants. The study covered 128 events using the CDS sample and 330 events using the corporate bond data.

Consistent with prior research, Bai and colleagues found that credit-event risk explains only a small percentage of the premium. A large majority of the premium is explained by contagion risk, meaning that credit markets tend to perform poorly when the equity market portfolio also performs poorly. They wrote: "The implication is that contagion risk is economically significant, even for medium-sized firms." Finally, they concluded: "Since only credit-event risk, and not contagion risk, can explain large short-maturity spreads, our findings suggest that short-maturity spreads are not due to credit-event risk, but rather to noncredit factors, such as liquidity and tax effects."

The bottom line is that the failure to account for contagion risk leads to an upward bias in the estimated credit-event premium, and that bias is likely to be very large. For investors, the implication of this study is that all but short-maturity corporate bonds contain equity-like risks. And the lower the credit rating, the greater the contagion risk. Thus, investors who choose to include an allocation to either high-yield bonds or longer-term investment-grade bonds should consider them as hybrid instruments, combining the characteristics of both U.S. Treasuries and equities.

DIVERSIFICATION BENEFITS?

One of the arguments made in favor of including an allocation to higher-yield debt in portfolios is that it provides a diversification benefit that can be seen in the relatively low correlations of high-yield debt to both stocks and U.S. Treasury bonds. However, there is a very logical explanation for these low correlations, and it is not one that is ultimately favorable to including credit risk in your portfolio.

HIGH-YIELD BONDS: EXPLAINING THE LOW CORRELATIONS

It is easy to understand why high-yield bonds have relatively low correlation with investment-grade bonds (and, as we explained earlier, with equities). As we discussed, the higher yield of low-grade bonds makes their duration shorter, making them less sensitive to movements in interest rates than investment-grade bonds. And their *effective* duration is lower because low-grade bonds are often called by the issuer earlier (they have weaker call protection than investment-grade bonds). In addition, their credit ratings are more likely to rise, and this difference in potential behavior could lower the return correlation. Low-grade bonds are also more sensitive to changes in stock prices than investment-grade bonds (which, with rare exception, respond only to changes in rates). U.S. Treasury bonds, of course, only respond to changes in interest rates.

OTHER CONSIDERATIONS

One of the beneficial characteristics of Treasury securities is that, for U.S. investors, there is no need to diversify credit risk because there is virtually none. All of the risk is interest rate (or term) risk. As you move down the spectrum from U.S. Treasuries to investment-grade bonds and then to junk bonds (which are lower-rated but higher-yielding), you begin to take on risk that can be diversified away (the idiosyncratic risks of the individual companies). Investors are not compensated with higher expected returns for taking diversifiable risks. The need for diversification increases as you move down the credit spectrum because the lower the credit rating, the more equity-like the investment. The implication in terms of portfolio construction is that once you move beyond U.S. Treasury securities, prudence dictates the need to diversify credit risk. And that means incurring the expenses of a mutual fund, which can be avoided if you limit investments to U.S. Treasuries or FDIC-insured CDs. Thus, some of the risk premium built into the prices of higher-yielding debt will be eroded by the incremental costs incurred.

While Asvanunt and Richardson make the case that the default premium has been understated, we cannot find a compelling reason for individual investors to include higher-yielding corporate debt in portfolios. However, we do point out that institutional constraints can lead some investors to a preference for corporate debt. Consider a pension plan that has a provision in its charter that the equity allocation of its portfolio cannot exceed 60 percent. And assume that the plan is already at that limit. In an effort to boost returns, however, it wishes to increases its exposure to equity risk. It can do so by lowering its exposure to government bonds and increasing it to corporate bonds. This "preference," caused by institutional constraints, could help explain the small realized default premium.

TIME-VARYING CORRELATIONS OF STOCKS AND BONDS

Over the long term, the correlation of U.S. Treasury bonds (whether short-, intermediate-, or long-term) to stocks has been virtually zero. However, there is substantial variation in the correlations over time. Naresh Bansal, Robert Connolly, and Chris Stivers, authors of the 2015 paper "Equity Volatility as a Determinant of Future Term-Structure Volatility," contribute to our understanding of how the equity and bond markets interact. They found that equity risk helps us understand movements in the term structure (beyond an approach that looks only at the bond market in isolation), and that stock–bond return correlations are appreciably more negative for observations following high realized stock volatility.

The authors' finding that a stronger relationship occurs during periods of higher stress/volatility in the stock market is evidence that should be expected through the flight-to-quality avenue. When the stock market is perceived as being riskier, some investors flee to the safety of lower-risk government bonds. Thus, there is an episodic nature to the time-varying relationship between stock and bond market volatility.

Bansal and colleagues also found that U.S. Treasury bonds have served as a good diversification instrument against bad stock market outcomes, and that such diversification benefits have been relatively stronger following periods with higher realized stock volatility. When the stock return was extreme, they found a sizeable, opposite average U.S. Treasury bond return.

The authors concluded: "The intertemporal aspect of our findings supports the notion that equity risk can help us to understand movements in the term structure, beyond an approach that only looks at the bond market in isolation."

An important point is that the diversification benefit the authors found only applies to the highest-quality bonds. The best example of this is what happened in 2008, when the S&P 500 Index fell 37.0 percent. Vanguard's Intermediate-Term Treasury Fund Investor Shares (VFITX) provided shelter from the storm, returning 13.3 percent. On the other hand, Vanguard's Intermediate-Term Investment-Grade Fund Investor Shares (VFICX) lost 6.2 percent, and the firm's High-Yield Corporate Fund Investor Shares (VWEHX) lost 21.3 percent. Just when the safety that bonds are supposed to provide in a portfolio was needed most, credit risk showed up, exacerbating equity portfolio losses instead of mitigating them.

We are not done with pointing out the negative characteristics of higher-yielding debt. Like many risky assets, high-yield debt does not have a normal return distribution.

NON-NORMAL DISTRIBUTION
OF RETURNS

As we have discussed, behavioral finance studies have found that, in general, people like assets with positive skewness. This is evidenced by their willingness to accept low, or even negative, expected returns for assets that exhibit this property. The classic example is a lottery ticket, which has negative expected returns but also has positive skewness. As we all know, there are precious few who win the lottery (a positive outcome) and an enormous number who lose (a negative outcome). However, the benefit of a positive outcome is much greater than the cost of a negative one.

On the other hand, most people do not like assets with negative skewness. This explains why people generally purchase insurance against low-frequency events, such as disability or fires. While these events are unlikely to occur, they carry the potential for large losses. The problem for investors is that high-yield debt exhibits negative skewness. It also has excess kurtosis (exceptional values called "fat tails," indicating a higher percentage of very low and very high returns than would be expected with a normal distribution).

For the period from 1984 through 2015, the Barclays Intermediate U.S. Treasury Bond Index had a monthly skewness of 0.1 and a monthly kurtosis of 3.4. In contrast, the Barclays U.S. Intermediate Credit Index had a monthly skewness of –0.8 and a monthly kurtosis of 7.6, and the Barclays U.S. Corporate

High Yield Index had a monthly skewness of –0.9 and a monthly kurtosis of 11.3. As you can see, the greater the increase to credit risk exposure, the more negative the skewness and the larger the excess kurtosis. The very high kurtosis exhibited by high-yield debt reflects the risk of downgrades, defaults, and bankruptcies. And when you combine the data on skewness and kurtosis, it is easy to see that high-yield bonds have a lot in common with equities, which is, of course, why they have exposure to equity risk. However, as you will see, they have not provided investors a "bang" for their buck.

The only right way to consider an investment is to determine how adding an allocation to it impacts the risk and return of the overall portfolio. Thus, we will now examine the impact of adding credit risk in that light.

IMPACT OF CREDIT RISK ON PORTFOLIOS

We will compare four portfolios, each with an allocation of 60 percent to the S&P 500 Index. The data cover the 32-year period from 1984 through 2015. Portfolio A will invest its fixed income in the Barclays Intermediate U.S. Treasury Index. Portfolio B will be allocated 30 percent to the Barclays Intermediate U.S. Treasury Index and 10 percent to the Barclays U.S. Corporate High Yield Index. Portfolio C will be allocated 20 percent to the Barclays Intermediate U.S. Treasury Index and 20 percent to the Barclays U.S. Corporate High Yield Index. Portfolio D will put all of its 40 percent fixed income allocation in the Barclays U.S. Corporate High Yield Index.

Before reviewing the results, we will first examine the performance of the three indices.

TABLE E.2: ANNUALIZED RETURNS, STANDARD DEVIATIONS, AND SHARPE RATIOS (1984–2015)

	ANNUALIZED RETURN (%)	ANNUAL STANDARD DEVIATION (%)	SHARPE RATIO
S&P 500 INDEX	10.85	17.08	0.50
BARCLAYS INTERMEDIATE U.S. TREASURY INDEX	6.53	5.14	0.73
BARCLAYS U.S. CORPORATE HIGH YIELD INDEX	8.84	15.46	0.38

Despite providing a 2.31 percent higher annualized return than the government intermediate index, the high-yield index produced a Sharpe ratio about one-half that of the government intermediate index. And because its standard deviation was close to that of the S&P 500, its 2.01 percent lower annualized return resulted in a Sharpe ratio 24 percent below the S&P 500's.

We now turn to the analysis of the four portfolios.

TABLE E.3: PORTFOLIO RETURNS (1984–2015)

	ANNUALIZED RETURN (%)	ANNUAL STANDARD DEVIATION (%)	SHARPE RATIO
PORTFOLIO A	9.52	10.46	0.62
PORTFOLIO B	9.74	11.42	0.59
PORTFOLIO C	9.93	12.52	0.56
PORTFOLIO D	10.24	15.00	0.50

As we might expect, given the higher return of the high-yield index, Portfolio D produced the highest annualized return. However, as we increased the allocation to the high-yield index, the combination of its higher volatility and much higher correlation with the S&P 500 Index resulted in ever lower Sharpe ratios. Over the period, the annual correlation of the government index with the S&P 500 Index was virtually zero (0.01). In contrast, the annual correlation of the high-yield index with the S&P 500 Index was a high 0.58.

Also of interest is that a portfolio allocated 80 percent to the S&P 500 Index and 20 percent to the Barclays Intermediate U.S. Treasury Index would have provided virtually the same return (10.27 percent) as Portfolio D, but with an annual standard deviation of just 13.71 percent (about 9 percent less volatility) and a Sharpe ratio of 0.54 (about 8 percent higher).

And finally, remember that for individual investors with access to FDIC-insured CDs, using them in place of government bonds of the same maturity would make the results look even more unfavorable for taking on default risk.

The bottom line is that, historically, adding default risk has been an inefficient way to improve the risk-adjusted returns of a portfolio. It is why a detour from that exhibit is recommended.

APPENDIX F
TIME-SERIES MOMENTUM

Time-series momentum examines the trend of an asset with respect to its own past performance. This is different from cross-sectional momentum, which compares the performance of an asset with respect to the performance of another asset. Indeed, time-series momentum is the one factor in this book that is not applied cross-sectionally, which is the main reason why we have placed it in an appendix. Ian D'Souza, Voraphat Srichanachaichok, George Jiaguo Wang, and Chelsea Yaqiong Yao, the authors of the 2016 study "The Enduring Effect of Time-Series Momentum on Stock Returns over Nearly 100-Years," provide evidence supportive of the view that time-series momentum (also referred to as trend-following) is one of the few factors that meet all of our criteria for inclusion in a portfolio. Their study covered the 88-year period from 1927 to 2014. The following is a summary of their findings:

- A value-weighted strategy of going long stocks with positive returns in the prior 12 months (skipping the most recent month) and going short stocks with negative returns during the same period of time produced an average monthly return of 0.55 percent, and was highly significant (t-stat = 5.28). It has also been present following both up and down markets, producing an average monthly return of 0.57 percent (t-stat = 2.09) following down markets and 0.54 percent (t-stat = 5.30) following up markets. What is more, it was persistent across all four sub-periods the authors studied, with average monthly returns of 0.69 percent (t-stat = 2.41) in the period from 1927 through 1948, 0.47 percent (t-stat = 3.60) in the period from 1949 through 1970, 0.62 percent (t-stat = 3.84) in the period from 1971 through 1992, and 0.42 percent (t-stat = 1.91) in the period from 1993 through 2014. Thus, it meets the persistence criteria.

- Time-series momentum produced positive risk-adjusted returns in all 13 international stock markets the authors examined for the period from 1975 through 2014. And it was statistically significant at the 95 percent confidence level in 10 of the 13 countries. The highest return for a value-weighted strategy was in Denmark, where it had a monthly return of 1.15 percent (with a t-statistic of 5.06). Thus, it meets the pervasive criteria.

- Time-series stock momentum was profitable regardless of formation and holding periods for 16 different combinations. Thus, it meets the robust criteria.

- Time-series stock momentum fully subsumes cross-sectional stock momentum, while cross-sectional stock momentum cannot capture time-series stock momentum. In addition, the other common factors of market beta, size, and value have little power to explain time-series momentum. Thus, it is also not subsumed by other factors.

- Unlike with cross-sectional momentum, time-series momentum does not experience losses in January (a seasonal effect) or crashes (which occur with cross-sectional momentum during market reversals).

- The time-series premium can be at least partially explained by two prominent theories that describe investor underreaction (both the gradual information diffusion model and what is called the frog-in-the-pan model). For example, if time-series momentum came from gradual information flow, there should be greater time-series momentum in small-cap stocks (for which information diffuses more slowly). In fact, they found that the small size group produces the highest momentum profits (0.78 percent per month with an associated t-statistic of 5.52), while the large size group generates the lowest momentum profits (0.47 percent per month with an associated t-statistic of 4.33). As we discussed in Chapter 4, the frog-in-the-pan hypothesis suggests that investors are less aware of information that arrives continuously and in small amounts than they are of information that arrives in large amounts at discrete points in time. The analogy is that frogs will jump out of a pan of water following a sudden increase in temperature, but will underreact to increasing water temperature in the pan if it is brought to a boil slowly, and so are cooked. According to the frog-in-the-pan hypothesis, if investors underreact to small amounts of information that arrive continuously, it induces strong persistent return continuation. The authors found a monotonic increase in momentum profits for stocks with discrete information compared to stocks with continuous information. Thus, we have evidence that time-series momentum meets the explanation criteria.

D'Souza, Srichanachaichok, Wang, and Yao also examined a strategy that combined the two (time-series and cross-sectional) momentum strategies. Their dual-momentum strategy buys the strongest winner portfolio and sells short the weakest loser portfolio, basically making it a market-neutral strategy. They found that the average annualized return of the dual-momentum strategy was 22.4 percent. The strategy, however, was associated with high volatility (37.5 percent per year). The data were statistically significant and also held up to tests that employed different combinations of formation and holding periods.

FURTHER EVIDENCE

Using historical data from a number of sources, the 2014 study "A Century of Evidence on Trend-Following Investing" by Brian Hurst, Yao Hua Ooi, and Lasse H. Pedersen constructed an equal-weighted combination of one-month, three-month, and 12-month time-series momentum strategies for 67 markets across four major asset classes (29 commodities, 11 equity indices, 15 bond markets, and 12 currency pairs) from January 1880 to December 2013.

Their results include implementation costs based on estimates of trading costs in the four asset classes. They further assumed management fees of 2 percent of asset value and 20 percent of profits, the traditional fee for hedge funds. The following is a summary of these AQR researchers' findings:

- The performance was remarkably consistent over an extensive time horizon that included the Great Depression, multiple recessions and expansions, multiple wars, stagflation, the global financial crisis of 2008, and periods of rising and falling interest rates.

- Annualized gross returns were 14.9 percent over the full period, with net returns (after fees) of 11.2 percent, higher than the return for equities but with about half the volatility (an annual standard deviation of 9.7 percent).
- Net returns were positive in every decade, with the lowest net return being the 5.7 percent return for the period beginning in 1910. There were also only five periods in which net returns were in the single digits.
- There was virtually no correlation to either stocks or bonds. Thus, the strategy provides strong diversification benefits while producing a high Sharpe ratio of 0.77. Even if future returns are not as strong, the diversification benefits would justify an allocation to the strategy.

The researchers at AQR observed that "a large body of research has shown that price trends exist in part due to long-standing behavioral biases exhibited by investors, such as anchoring and herding [and we would add to that list the disposition effect and confirmation bias], as well as the trading activity of non-profit-seeking participants, such as central banks and corporate hedging programs. For instance, when central banks intervene to reduce currency and interest-rate volatility, they slow down the rate at which information is incorporated into prices, thus creating trends."

AQR's researchers continued: "The fact that trend-following

strategies have performed well historically indicates that these behavioral biases and non-profit-seeking market participants have likely existed for a long time."

They noted that trend-following has done particularly well in extreme up or down years for the stock market, including the most recent global financial crisis of 2008. In fact, they found that during the 10 largest drawdowns experienced by the traditional 60/40 portfolio over the past 135 years, the time-series momentum strategy experienced positive returns in eight of these stress periods and delivered significant positive returns during a number of these events.

AQR also noted that these results were achieved even with a "2-and-20" fee structure. Today, there are funds that can be accessed with much lower, although still not exactly cheap, expenses (including AQR's own Managed Futures Strategy I Fund, AQMIX, which has an expense ratio of 1.21 percent, as well as the R6 version of the fund, AQMRX, which has a lower expense ratio of 1.13 percent). Additionally, AQR has found that its actual trading costs have been only about one-sixth of the estimates used for much of the sample period (1880 through 1992) and approximately one-half of the estimates used for the more recent period (1993 through 2002). These results demonstrate that time-series momentum also meets our criteria of investability and implementability.

Further evidence on time-series momentum comes from Akindynos-Nikolaos Baltas and Robert Kosowski, authors of the 2013 study "Momentum Strategies in Futures Markets and Trend-Following Funds." They studied "the relationship between time-series momentum strategies in futures markets and commodity trading advisors (CTAs), a subgroup of the hedge fund universe that was one of the few profitable hedge fund styles during the financial crisis of 2008, hence attracting much attention and inflows in its aftermath." The authors noted that following inflows over the subsequent years, the size of the industry had grown substantially, and CTA funds exceeded $300 billion of the total $2 trillion assets under management (AUM) invested in hedge funds by the end of 2011. Their study covered the period from December 1974 through January 2012 and included 71 futures contracts across several assets classes, specifically 26 commodities, 23 equity indices, 7 currencies, and 15 intermediate-term and long-term bonds. The following is a summary of their findings:

- Time-series momentum exhibits strong effects across monthly, weekly, and daily frequencies.
- Strategies with different rebalancing frequencies have low cross-correlations and therefore capture distinct return patterns.
- Momentum patterns are pervasive and fairly robust over the entire evaluation period and within sub-periods.
- Different strategies achieve annualized Sharpe ratios of above 1.20 and perform well in up and down markets, which renders them good diversifiers in equity bear markets.

- Commodity futures-based momentum strategies have low correlation with other futures strategies. Thus, despite the fact that they have a relatively low return, they do provide additional diversification benefits.

Importantly, the authors found that momentum profitability is not limited to illiquid contracts. Rather, momentum strategies are typically implemented by means of exchange-traded futures contracts and forward contracts, which are considered relatively liquid and have relatively low transaction costs compared to cash equity or bond markets. In fact, they found that "for most of the assets, the demanded number of contracts for the construction of the strategy does not exceed the contemporaneous open interest reported by the Commodity Futures Trading Commission (CFTC) over the period 1986 to 2011." They also found that the "notional amount invested in futures contracts in this hypothetical scenario is a small fraction of the global OTC derivatives markets (2.3% for commodities, 0.2% for currencies, 2.9% for equities and 0.9% for interest rates at end of 2011)." Thus, they concluded: "Our analyses based on the performance-flow regressions and the hypothetical open interest exceedance scenario do not find statistically or economically significant evidence of capacity constraints in time-series momentum strategies."

However, following strong performance in 2008, the aggregate performance of trend-following CTA funds has been relatively weak. For example, from January 2009 to June 2013, the annualized return of the SG CTA Trend Sub-Index (formally the Newedge Trend Index) was –0.8 percent, versus 8.0 percent over the prior five-year period. This occurred during a period of slow recovery in the United States and prolonged crisis in the Eurozone. Relatively poor performance, combined with large inflows following the strong performance, leads investors to question both whether the trend-following strategy has already become too crowded and if it will work in the future.

Mark C. Hutchinson and John O'Brien contribute to the literature on time-series momentum with their 2014 paper, "Is This Time Different? Trend Following and Financial Crises." Using almost a century of data on trend-following, they investigated what happened to the performance of the strategy subsequent to the U.S. subprime and Eurozone crises, and whether it was typical of what happens after a financial crisis.

The authors note: "Identifying a list of global and regional financial crises is problematic." Thus, they chose to use the list of crises from two of the most highly cited studies on financial crises, "Manias, Panics, and Crashes: A History of Financial Crises" (originally published in 1978) and "This Time Is Different: Eight Centuries of Financial Folly" (originally published in 2009). The six global crises studied were: the Great Depression in 1929, the 1973 Oil Crisis, the Third World Debt crisis of 1981, the Crash of October 1987, the bursting of the dot-com bubble in 2000, and the Sub-Prime/Euro crisis beginning in 2007. The regional crises studied (with year of inception in parentheses) were: Spain (1977), Norway (1987), Nordic (1989), Japan (1990),

Mexico (1994), Asia (1997), Colombia (1997), and Argentina (2000). The start date for each crisis was the month following the equity market high preceding the crisis. Because neither of the two aforementioned studies provided guidance on the length or end date of each crisis, rather than attempting to define when each individual crisis finished, the authors instead focused on two fixed time periods: 24 months and 48 months after the prior equity market high.

Hutchinson and O'Brien's dataset for the global analysis consisted of 21 commodities, 13 government bonds, 21 equity indices, and currency crosses derived from nine underlying exchange rates covering a sample period from January 1921 to June 2013. Their results include estimates of trading costs as well as the typical hedge fund fee of 2 percent of assets and 20 percent of profits. The following is a summary of their findings:

- Time-series momentum has been highly successful over the long term. The average net return for the global portfolio from 1925 to 2013 was 12.1 percent, with volatility of 11 percent. The Sharpe ratio was an impressive 1.1 (a finding consistent with that of other research).
- There is a breakdown in futures market return predictability during crisis periods.
- In no-crisis periods, market returns exhibit strong serial correlation at lags of up to 12 months.
- Subsequent to a global financial crisis, trend-following performance tends to be weak for four

years on average. This lack of time-series return predictability reduces the opportunity for trend-following to generate returns.

- Comparing the performance of crisis and no-crisis periods, the average return (4.0 percent) in the first 24 months following the start of a crisis is less than one-third of the return (13.6 percent) earned in no-crisis periods. Performance in the 48 months after a crisis starts was well under half (6.0 percent) the return (14.9 percent) in that of no-crisis periods.

- Across stocks, bonds, and currencies, the results were consistent. The exception was commodities, where returns were of similar magnitude in pre- and post-crisis periods.

- They found a similar effect when examining portfolios formed of local assets during regional financial crises.

The authors noted that behavioral models link momentum to investor overconfidence and decreasing risk aversion, with both leading to return predictability in asset prices. Under these models, overconfidence should fall and risk aversion should increase following market declines, so it seems logical that return predictability would fall following a financial crisis. It is also important to note, as the authors did, that "governments have an increased tendency to intervene in financial markets during crises, resulting in discontinuities in price patterns."

Such interventions can lead to sharp reversals, with negative consequences for trend-following.

Hutchinson and O'Brien concluded: "The performance of these types of strategies [trend-following] is much weaker in crisis periods, where performance can be as little as one-third of that in normal market conditions. This result is supported by our evidence for regional crises, though the effect seems to be more short lived. In our analysis of the underlying markets, our empirical evidence indicates a breakdown in the time series predictability, pervasive in normal market conditions, on which trend following relies."

SUMMARY

As an investment style, trend-following has existed for a long time. The data from the aforementioned studies provide strong out-of-sample evidence beyond the substantial evidence that already existed in the literature. It also provides consistent, long-term evidence that trends have been pervasive features of global markets.

Addressing the issue of whether we should expect trends to continue, Hurst and his colleagues concluded: "The most likely candidates to explain why markets have tended to trend more often than not include investors' behavioral biases, market frictions, hedging demands, and market interventions by central banks and governments. Such market interventions and hedging programs are still prevalent, and investors are likely to continue to suffer from the same behavioral biases that have influenced price behavior over the past century, setting the stage for trend-following investing going forward."

The bottom line is that, given the diversification benefits and the downside (tail-risk) hedging properties, we believe that a moderate portfolio allocation to trend-following strategies merits consideration. We do note that the generally high turnover of trend-following strategies renders them tax inefficient. Thus, there should be a strong preference to hold them in tax-advantaged accounts.

APPENDIX G
MARGINAL UTILITY OF INCREMENTAL FACTORS ON FUND RETURNS

Professors Eugene F. Fama and Kenneth R. French, in their 2015 paper "Incremental Variables and the Investment Opportunity Set," provide some important insights for investors who are considering funds designed to supply exposure to multiple factors, or styles, of investing.

In their study, Fama and French note: "Much asset pricing research is a search for variables that improve understanding of the cross section of expected returns. Researchers often claim success if a sort on their candidate produces a large spread in average returns. A better measure, however, is the variable's incremental contribution to the return spread produced by a model that includes the variables already known to predict returns."

The paper's important message is that factors (the systematic variables we have discussed, such as momentum and profitability) that possess strong marginal explanatory power in cross-sectional asset-pricing regressions and exhibit large premiums typically show less power to produce incremental improvements to the returns of portfolios that already have exposure to other factors (such as size and value) shown to have explanatory power.

Once you have decided on which factors you want exposure to, the next decision should involve whether to target the factors separately or through a multi-style fund. For instance, an investor could decide to own three funds, each of which targets the size, value, and momentum factors individually. Alternatively, the investor could choose to invest in one multi-style fund that targets all three.

As Roger Clarke, Harindra de Silva, and Steven Thorley explain in their 2016 paper "Factor Portfolios and Efficient Factor Investing," it is far better to combine individual securities to achieve optimal portfolios than to combine independent factor portfolios. This is intuitive. For example, suppose one chooses to invest in both the size and value factors. Constructing a portfolio at the security level would mean purchasing stocks that combine both small and value characteristics. But building it at the factor level would mean independently buying a bunch of small-cap stocks and then also a bunch of value stocks. The small-cap stocks would include some with a lot of growth exposure (little value), while the value stocks would include some that are large (not small). This would be less optimal.

It would be even less optimal if the strategy involved both long and short positions in the factors. One factor could be long a security and the other factor could be short. Thus, if the factors were targeted separately, the investor would not only be paying two fees for no net position, but also would be incurring unnecessary trading costs. Using multi-style funds is clearly optimal.

There are trade-offs involved in how one combines factors. Consider value and momentum, for example, which are negatively correlated. Ideally, you want a portfolio with stocks that have high exposure to both these factors and to avoid those with negative exposure. In doing so, you can certainly combine them in such a way that high-value (but low-momentum) stocks are excluded, as are high-momentum (but low-value) stocks. However, the more stocks you exclude, the less diversification you will have across securities. In addition, the portfolio will move away from holding the deepest-exposure equities because many of the high-value (momentum) stocks have low momentum (value). The portfolio will move more to the middle of the factors. Therefore, thoughtful consideration of combining factors is warranted, including issues such as exposures to factors, number of holdings, turnover, and liquidity.

And that brings us back to the issue addressed by Fama and French: What is the incremental impact of adding exposures to additional factors? Here again, intuition can help us. Even the simple three-factor model explains more than 90 percent of the differences in returns between diversified portfolios. Adding momentum brings that figure up to a percentage in the mid-90s. As Fama and French explain in their paper, adding a variable with marginal explanatory power always shrinks the values of other explanatory variables. In other words, if a portfolio already has exposure to market beta, size, and value, adding exposure to momentum cannot contribute that much more in the way of incremental returns (certainly nothing anywhere close to the 9.6 percent annual premium momentum has provided, or even half that for a long-only portfolio). The reasons again are intuitive.

If you add exposure to a factor with a positive correlation to the other factors already in the portfolio, part of the explanatory power of the new factor is already accounted for by the exposure to the original factors. Fama and French explain: "Attenuation of variables already in the model almost always limits an incremental variable's contribution to the expected return spread produced by a multivariate model."

Thus, exposure to a new factor cannot add that factor's full premium to the portfolio's return. And if the factor being added is negatively correlated (as is the case with momentum and value) with existing factors, adding exposure to one factor (enhancing the expected return) will reduce the exposure to the other (subtracting some expected return).

This does not mean, however, that there may not be an improvement in the efficiency of the portfolio. Adding factors that are not perfectly correlated can provide a diversification benefit. Another benefit is that adding negatively correlated factors can reduce the risk of catching the dreaded disease known as "tracking error regret," which we discussed in Appendix A. Investors regret it when their differentiated portfolio underperforms "the market" as represented by such indices as the S&P 500. In fact, for many investors, once you get beyond the three factors of market beta, size, and value, minimizing the risk of tracking error regret may be the biggest incremental benefit of adding exposure to more factors.

Finally, another issue to consider is that, when adding exposure to additional factors, you may also *increase* the turnover of the portfolio, raising trading costs and reducing tax efficiency.

APPENDIX H
SPORTS BETTING
AND ASSET PRICING

Academic research has uncovered the fact that combining value and momentum strategies results in more efficient portfolios (because their correlation is highly negative). Importantly, this holds true across the globe and across asset classes (meaning that it is the case not only for stocks, but also for bonds, commodities, and currencies). While the existence and explanatory power of the value and momentum factors is not debated (as we have discussed), two competing theories attempt to explain the sources of their premiums: risk-based explanations (what we might refer to as the Eugene Fama — father of the efficient-market hypothesis — camp) and behavioral-based explanations (the Robert Shiller camp). Interestingly enough, Fama and Shiller shared the 2013 Nobel Prize in economics.

Behavioral research has found that prices can deviate from their fundamental values due to cognitive biases (leading some investors to underreact and overreact to news) or to erroneous beliefs. And because arbitrageurs cannot keep the market efficient by their actions, thanks to costs and limits to arbitrage, mispricings can persist.

Yale University professor Toby Moskowitz sought to shed some light on the risk versus behavioral explanations for these premiums by testing the momentum and value effects in the world of sports betting. The hypothesis is that if behavioral pricing models work, they should explain returns across all markets, from investing to gambling. Alternatively, if they do not work, it becomes clear we need different models for different markets and/or asset types.

WHY SPORTS BETTING?

Sports betting provides a great laboratory, primarily because there are no macroeconomic risk explanations to account for the existence of a factor. In short, the only explanation possible is behavior-related.

If the value and momentum factors that appear in investing are indeed based on behavioral mistakes, then the same behavioral errors that materialize in investing should show up in sports betting. What is more, sports betting (where terminal values are found very quickly) provides an excellent out-of-sample testing ground for behavioral theory because any pricing errors are discovered quickly when bets pay off. So the question becomes: Do we find the same patterns in sports betting and investing?

To supply an answer, Moskowitz looked at different sports

betting markets to see if similar relationships and patterns appeared. He examined four sports — baseball (MLB), football (NFL), basketball (NBA), and hockey (NHL) — and three different contracts. That makes a total of 12 tests, greatly reducing the odds that any finding showing a consistent relationship was just a lucky coincidence. The three contracts were:

A. Point spread: For example, a team is favored by 3½ points. If you bet on the favorite and it either loses or it wins by less than 3½ points, you lose the bet.

B. The over/under: This contract pertains to the total amount of points scored. For example, in an NBA basketball game, the over/under is 200 points. If you bet over and the total points scored add up to less than 200, you lose the bet.

C. Money line: If you put money on the favorite, you might have to bet $180 to win $100, for example. And if you put money on the underdog, you may only have to bet $100 to win $170.

In contracts A and B, it is typical to have to bet $110 in order to win $100. This is the bookie's cut, otherwise known as the vigorish (or "the vig"). Thus, transaction costs are high.

The data that Moskowitz examined covered the period from 1999 through 2013 and about 120,000 different contracts and came from the largest Las Vegas and online sports gambling books. Moskowitz analyzed the returns to the three types of bets across time: from the opening price, which is set by the bookies; afterward, during which time individual betters are setting prices by their actions, until the game begins and betting ends; and the terminal value.

The theory he was testing was: Do the behavioral models explain returns or are the markets efficient? In other words, if markets were efficient, "sentiment" (what might be called "animal spirits" or irrational exuberance) should not predict outcomes; only new information (such as disclosure of an injury to a key player) should.

Alternatively, if new information is incorporated only slowly (the market underreacts) or there is an overreaction (prices move up or down by too great an amount), we have a behavioral explanation that would be consistent with what we can observe in financial markets.

To reduce the risks of data mining, Moskowitz examined different momentum and value metrics, and different horizons, and averaged the results. He even tested for outcomes using only even and odd years as different metrics.

MEASURING MOMENTUM AND VALUE

In finance, there are conventional measures of momentum and value — not so in the world of sports betting. With momentum, it is relatively easy to come up with some appropriate and usable metrics. For example, Moskowitz examined lagged measures of performance based on metrics such as wins, point differentials, and dollar returns on the same team and contract type over the past one, two, and even eight games (eight games is roughly 10 percent of the NBA season, for instance).

Value is more difficult to measure. Moskowitz chose to use long-term reversals as one value metric. With equities, stocks that have done poorly over the past five years are considered value stocks. Thus, as a measure of value, he used past performance during the previous one, two, and three seasons.

As for other measures of value, Moskowitz took various book values of the team franchise — including book value of the team, ticket revenue, total revenue (gate sales plus souvenir sales, TV rights, and concessions), and player payroll — and then divided each by the current spread on the spread-betting contract. Moskowitz also used the sabermetric (the statistical analysis of sports) score known as the Pythagorean expectation formula. The formula provides an expected win percentage for each team based on past wins, point differentials, and strength of schedule, much like a power ranking. He used the score as a relative strength measure by taking the difference between the measures for each team and then dividing that difference by the current betting line or contract price (similar to an earnings-to-price, or E/P, ratio).

FAMA AND THALER ON MOMENTUM AND VALUE MEASURES IN SPORTS BETTING

Of particular interest is that, before running the data, Moskowitz asked his colleagues Eugene Fama (a leading "cheerleader" of the efficient markets perspective and risk-based explanations for premiums) and Richard Thaler (a leading "cheerleader" of the inefficient markets perspective and behavioral explanations for premiums) if they agreed with the choice of metrics.

Fama and Thaler had to base their evaluation ex-ante, not ex-post (after seeing the results). And they both generally agreed that the choice of value and momentum metrics were good and consistent with the way those terms are defined in financial markets. The following is a summary of Moskowitz's findings:

- Aggregate returns in sports betting are flat before expenses and slightly negative after expenses (because of the vig), indicating that systematically betting on the home team, the favored team, or the over is not profitable. Markets are efficient with respect to these attributes.

- As you would expect, Moskowitz discovered no correlation between the outcomes of sports bets and stock market returns. This demonstrates that sports bets are, in fact, independent.

- When betting lines move between the open of "trading" and the close of "trading," the return from open-to-close is slightly positively correlated with the open-to-end return, and is negatively correlated with the close-to-end return.

- Sports betting markets do exhibit a tendency toward overreaction in prices. The overreaction is revealed (reversed) at the terminal value (when the game ends).

- There is a strong pattern that indicates momentum exists and it predicts returns. Just as in financial markets, bettors push up prices. And again, just as in financial markets, there is predictive value (reversal at terminal value occurs, meaning there is a delayed overreaction). In other words, the opening price (set by the bookies) was more correct than the price that existed when betting was closed at the start of the game. This was true across the different sports and different (and uncorrelated) betting contracts. And with the exception of hockey, the t-statistics were significant.

- There is also a strong, though opposite, pattern with value. Cheap bets tend to get cheaper as time passes, and then a reversal occurs as the true value is revealed at the terminal date when the results become known. This negative relationship between momentum and value is the same as we see in financial markets. However, while a strong pattern for value bets did exist, the results didn't come with the same strong statistical significance as they did with momentum. And, while it is easy to come up with the momentum definitions, it is not so clear-cut with value.

- Moskowitz also examined the size effect. To measure size, he used annual franchise value, ticket revenue, total revenue, and player payroll. These measures are highly correlated with the size of the local market in which the team resides. He found no explanatory or predictive value in the data.

- The returns generated from momentum and value per unit of risk (volatility) are about one-fifth as large as those found in financial markets, suggesting that the majority of the return premiums in financial markets could be coming from other (risk-based) sources. Or it could be that the measures being used in sports betting markets are noisy and hence do not give predictive content as clearly.

Moskowitz went on to examine the data from a different perspective. He wrote: "An additional implication of the overreaction is that the effects are greater when there is more uncertainty or ambiguity about valuations." Because the quality of any team is more uncertain near the beginning of a season, Moskowitz separately examined games early in each season and also instances where the volatility of betting prices was higher. He found results consistent with overreaction: Momentum and subsequent reversals were stronger, while value effects were weaker.

Moskowitz applied the same idea to the returns of financial securities by using the passage of time from the most recent earnings announcement. He found: "Immediately following an earnings announcement, firm valuation should be more certain, since earnings provide an important piece of relevant information." Splitting firms into two groups — companies that recently announced earnings versus companies whose last earnings announcement was several months prior (greater uncertainty) — Moskowitz found stronger momentum profits and subsequent reversals for the firms with stale earnings and negligible profits for firms that recently posted earnings.

The opposite held for value. Value profits are strongest among firms with recent earnings and nonexistent among firms with stale earnings. Moskowitz explains: "These results match those found in sports betting markets and are consistent with a delayed overreaction story, where sports betting provides a novel test and new set of results for momentum and value in financial markets."

He concluded: "The remarkably consistent patterns found across different sports and different contracts within a sport make the results very unlikely to be driven by chance. The evidence is consistent with momentum and value return premia being generated by investor overreaction, providing an out of sample test of behavioral theories. In addition, the returns are wiped out by trading costs in sports betting markets, preventing arbitrageurs from eliminating these patterns in prices and allowing them to persist."

WHAT, IF ANY, CONCLUSIONS CAN BE DRAWN?

Given the nature of Moskowitz's findings, what conclusions can we draw? First, the momentum and value effects move betting prices from the open to the close of betting. These patterns are completely reversed by the game's outcome, and in a manner that is consistent with how these premiums work in financial markets.

Second, the fact that both momentum and value have predictive value in sports betting markets, and that these factors have the same negative relationship (momentum pushes prices up and value pushes prices down) that they demonstrate in the financial markets, provides support for the idea that these factors do incorporate at least some behavioral components in financial markets.

In other words, the risk-based versus behavioral-based explanations are not really competing, but complementary. The answer is not black or white; rather, some combination of the two competing theories is likely the correct explanation. We think about it this way: The value and momentum premiums are not free lunches (which would be the case if we were simply taking advantage of others' behavioral flaws), but they might be a free stop at the dessert tray.

Third, given the independent nature of the tests (which were across four different sports and three different contracts, for a total of 12 betting markets), as Moskowitz noted, it would be a remarkable coincidence, and difficult to believe, that the findings were just a random outcome.

Also of interest is that Moskowitz found, just as in the world of investing where frictions prevent the "smart money" (arbitrageurs) from correcting mispricings, there are frictions

SPORTS BETTING AND ASSET PRICING

(the cost of betting in the form of the bookie's spread) that prevent the smart money from correcting the pricing errors of individual bettors. In other words, frictions allow the mispricings to persist even when the smart money knows they exist. In addition, the finding provides evidence that, after the cost of implementing a strategy is considered, the sports betting markets — like the financial markets — can be considered highly efficient.

With that said, if you can make "friendly" bets (without a bookie in the middle taking the vig), the evidence suggests you should be able to exploit mispricings that occur after the opening line is established by the bookies, especially if you combine the two strategies of value and momentum.

Finally, Moskowitz noted that, predictably, competition from online betting sites has led to spreads smaller than the traditional 10 percent set by bookies. However, even lower spreads (as low as about 7 percent) are not low enough to exploit mispricings. We will leave you with one last item of interest. Moskowitz is also the co-author of an outstanding book on sports and statistics. In our opinion, "Scorecasting: The Hidden Influences Behind How Sports Are Played and Games Are Won" is a must-read for sports fans.

APPENDIX I
REEVALUATING
THE SIZE PREMIUM

Many investors and advisors who implement multifactor portfolios tend to focus on capturing the value premium over the size premium, often for the simple reason that, historically, the value premium has been larger. Others have even challenged the size premium's very existence, citing a weak and varying historical record. In both situations, it may be that the size premium, and specifically the construction of the size factor, is not fully understood. To clarify this issue, we begin with basic definitions.

The size factor, as defined by Eugene Fama and Kenneth French, is constructed by sorting all stocks by market capitalization (as determined by market capitalizations of NYSE stocks) into deciles and then taking the weighted average annual return of deciles 6–10 (small-cap stocks) minus the weighted average annual return of deciles 1–5 (large-cap stocks). In other words, it is the bottom 50 percent of stocks ranked by size minus the top 50 percent. Contrast this with the value factor, which is constructed by sorting stocks on book-to-market ratios and then taking the weighted average annual return from deciles 1–3 (value stocks) minus the weighted average annual return from deciles 8–10 (growth stocks). In other words, it is the top 30 percent of stocks ranked by the valuation metric minus the bottom 30 percent. In this construct, deciles four through seven are considered core stocks. The 30/40/30 construction is also used for other established risk factors, such as momentum, profitability, quality, and low beta/low volatility. The size factor is the only exception.

Using data from the University of Chicago's Center for Research in Security Prices (CRSP), Table I.1 presents historical returns for grouped market capitalization deciles.

TABLE I.1: CRSP DECILES: ANNUALIZED RETURNS (1926–2015)

	1–2	3–5	6–8	9–10
ANNUALIZED RETURN (%)	9.47	10.99	11.39	11.98

As illustrated with these market capitalization deciles, if there is a premium in some category of stocks over another, then that premium will be larger the more strictly that category is defined. As we can see with the narrower size grouping, as stocks get smaller, their returns get higher. In addition, the more strictly the category is defined, the more difficult it should be to capture because there will be fewer stocks from which to choose. So in trying to understand the size premium, we ask: How does the construction of the size factor affect the amount of the premium that a portfolio can capture?

Kenneth French's data library provides returns for a variety of percentile sorts on market capitalization. Using these, we are able to build several different versions of the size factor in an attempt to answer our question. The standard size factor, defined before as the weighted average return of the smallest 50 percent of stocks less that of the largest 50 percent, will be designated 50/50. We then construct size factors using the smallest (largest) 30 percent, 20 percent, and 10 percent of stocks, which we will call 30/30, 20/20, and 10/10, respectively. Table I.2 shows the historical annual premium for these various definitions of the size factor.

TABLE I.2: HISTORICAL PREMIUM (1927–2015)

	SIZE FACTOR CONSTRUCTION			
	50/50	30/30	20/20	10/10
ANNUAL PREMIUM (%)	3.28	5.22	6.15	7.65
t-STATISTIC	2.22	2.34	2.27	2.44

As expected, the more narrowly we define "small-cap" versus "large-cap," the larger the annual premium. The standard 50/50 size factor has the smallest annual premium and, notably, the premium resulting from the 30/30 construction is actually larger than the value premium (which is 4.83 percent). Furthermore, all the annual premiums are statistically significant (they have a t-statistic greater than 2.0).

To measure how much of a given premium a portfolio is able to capture, multifactor investors turn to estimated factor loadings from a factor model regression. For three small-cap indices, Table I.3 shows the estimated size factor loadings from a four-factor model for our various size factor constructions.

TABLE I.3: MONTHLY SIZE FACTOR LOADINGS,
FOUR-FACTOR MODEL (1998–2015)

INDEX	SIZE FACTOR CONSTRUCTION			
	50/50	30/30	20/20	10/10
RUSSELL 2000 INDEX	0.77	0.59	0.50	0.42
S&P 600 SMALL CAP INDEX	0.68	0.50	0.41	0.34
DOW JONES U.S. SMALL CAP INDEX	0.58	0.44	0.37	0.32

Again, we find that the more narrowly we define the construction of the size factor, the more difficult it is to capture the premium. For each index, the more narrowly the size factor is defined, the smaller the estimated loading is. Note that all the estimates shown in Table I.3 are statistically significant. We can perform the same exercise for live funds as well. Consider Table I.4, which shows the results for the same exercise as Table I.3 but using three small-cap funds.

TABLE I.4: MONTHLY SIZE FACTOR LOADINGS,
FOUR-FACTOR MODEL (1998–2015)

FUND	SIZE FACTOR CONSTRUCTION			
	50/50	30/30	20/20	10/10
DFA U.S. MICRO CAP	1.01	0.82	0.73	0.64
DFA U.S. SMALL CAP	0.83	0.65	0.56	0.48
VANGUARD SMALL CAP INDEX	0.73	0.56	0.47	0.40

Again, we find that the more narrowly the size factor is defined, the smaller the estimated loading. In this case, consider that even though there is significant variation between funds for a given size factor construction method, each fund still shows a decrease in estimated loadings with stricter size factor definitions.

We have now fleshed out our hypotheses concerning the effect of size factor construction on the magnitude of the size premium and on a portfolio's ability to capture it. Using two funds, the DFA U.S. Micro Cap Fund from Table I.4 and the DFA Large Cap Value Fund, we can take a look at how the differences in construction between the size factor and the value factor affect the amount of the premium a portfolio is able to capture. This is measured simply by multiplying a portfolio's estimated factor loading by the respective annual premium. Table I.5 shows this calculation for the two funds.

TABLE I.5: ANNUAL SIZE VERSUS VALUE PREMIUM CAPTURE
(1998–2015)

	PREMIUM TARGET	LOADING	PREMIUM	CAPTURED PREMIUM
DFA U.S. MICRO CAP	SIZE	1.01	3.28	3.31
DFA LARGE CAP VALUE	VALUE	0.60	4.83	2.89

Despite the value premium being larger than the size premium, the portfolio targeting the size factor — the DFA U.S. Micro Cap Fund — actually captures more factor premium. This reflects the higher factor loading, which, we have shown, results directly from the less strict construction of the size factor.

Although brief, this example clearly shows that the magnitude of factor premiums should not be the sole consideration for multifactor investors when choosing their allocation to factors. The important takeaway is that size factor construction — and thus a portfolio's increased ability to capture the size premium — needs to be considered when evaluating the size premium. The investor who ignores the size premium may very well be missing out on a very sizable factor premium indeed.

APPENDIX J
IMPLEMENTATION:
MUTUAL FUNDS AND ETFs

The following is a list of funds you should consider when constructing your portfolio.[12] Where there is more than one share class available for a mutual fund, the lowest-cost version is shown. That fund version may not be available to all investors because minimums may be required. AQR, Bridgeway, and DFA funds are available through approved financial advisors and in retirement and 529 plans. (Note that for some AQR funds, lower-cost R Share versions may be available to some investors.) Considerations should include how much exposure to each of the factors a fund provides, its expense ratio, and the amount of diversification it provides (that is, the number of securities held). For ETFs, an added consideration is the liquidity of the fund. Thus, the recommendation is that the ETFs you are considering should have in excess of $100 million in assets and an average trading volume in excess of $5 million.

---

12 Because of Andrew Berkin's position at a mutual fund company, to avoid potential conflicts of interest, he did not participate in the selections in this appendix. The recommendations here reflect those of Buckingham Strategic Wealth's Investment Policy Committee.

SINGLE-STYLE FUNDS

MARKET BETA

DOMESTIC	
FUND	**EXPENSE RATIO**
FIDELITY SPARTAN TOTAL MARKET INDEX (FSTVX)	0.05
SCHWAB U.S. BROAD MARKET (SCHB)	0.03
VANGUARD TOTAL STOCK MARKET INDEX (VTI/ VTSAX)	0.05/0.05
ISHARES CORE S&P TOTAL US MARKET (ITOT)	0.03

INTERNATIONAL DEVELOPED MARKETS	
FUND	**EXPENSE RATIO**
FIDELITY SPARTAN INTERNATIONAL INDEX (FSIIX)	0.20
VANGUARD FTSE ALL-WORLD EX-US (VEU/VFWAX)	0.13/0.13
VANGUARD TOTAL INTERNATIONAL STOCK (VXUS/VTIAX)	0.13/0.12
SCHWAB INTERNATIONAL EQUITY (SCHF)	0.08
ISHARES CORE MSCI EAFE (IEFA)	0.12

EMERGING MARKETS	
FUND	**EXPENSE RATIO**
DFA EMERGING MARKETS (DFEMX)	0.57
SCHWAB EMERGING MARKETS (SCHE)	0.14
VANGUARD FTSE EMERGING MARKETS (VWO/VEMAX)	0.15/0.15

SIZE

DOMESTIC	
FUND	**EXPENSE RATIO**
BRIDGEWAY ULTRA-SMALL COMPANY MARKET (BRSIX)	0.73
DFA US MICRO CAP (DFSCX)	0.52
DFA US SMALL CAP (DFSTX)	0.37
DFA TAX-MANAGED US SMALL CAP (DFTSX)	0.52
ISHARES RUSSELL MICROCAP (IWC)	0.60
VANGUARD SMALL CAP INDEX FUND (VB/VSMAX)	0.08/0.08
SCHWAB U.S. SMALL CAP (SCHA)	0.08
ISHARES CORE S&P SMALL-CAP (IJR)	0.12

INTERNATIONAL DEVELOPED MARKETS	
FUND	**EXPENSE RATIO**
DFA INTERNATIONAL SMALL COMPANY (DFISX)	0.54
SPDR S&P INTERNATIONAL SMALL CAP ETF (GWX)	0.40
VANGUARD FTSE ALL-WORLD EX-US SMALLCAP (VSS/VFSVX)	0.17/0.31
SCHWAB INTERNATIONAL SMALL-CAP EQUITY (SCHC)	0.16

EMERGING MARKETS	
FUND	**EXPENSE RATIO**
DFA EMERGING MARKETS SMALL (DEMSX)	0.72
SPDR S&P EMERGING MARKETS SMALL CAP (EWX)	0.65

LARGE AND VALUE

DOMESTIC	
FUND	**EXPENSE RATIO**
DFA US LARGE CAP VALUE III (DFUVX)	0.13
DFA TAX-MANAGED US MARKETWIDE VALUE II (DFMVX)	0.22
DFA US VECTOR EQUITY (DFVEX)	0.32
SCHWAB US LARGE-CAP VALUE (SCHV)	0.06
VANGUARD VALUE INDEX (VTV/VVIAX)	0.08/0.08

INTERNATIONAL DEVELOPED MARKETS	
FUND	**EXPENSE RATIO**
DFA INTERNATIONAL VALUE III (DFVIX)	0.25
DFA TAX-MANAGED INTERNATIONAL VALUE (DTMIX)	0.53
DFA INTERNATIONAL VECTOR EQUITY (DFVQX)	0.50
ISHARES MSCI EAFE VALUE (EFV)	0.40
SCHWAB FUNDAMENTAL INTERNATIONAL LARGE COMPANY (FNDF)	0.32

EMERGING MARKETS	
FUND	**EXPENSE RATIO**
DFA EMERGING MARKETS VALUE (DFEVX)	0.56
SCHWAB FUNDAMENTAL EMERGING MARKETS LARGE CO. (FNDE)	0.48

SIZE AND VALUE

DOMESTIC	
FUND	**EXPENSE RATIO**
BRIDGEWAY OMNI SMALL CAP VALUE (BOSVX)	0.60
BRIDGEWAY OMNI TAX-MANAGED SMALL-CAP VALUE (BOTSX)	0.60
DFA US SMALL CAP VALUE (DFSVX)	0.52
DFA US TARGETED VALUE (DFFVX)	0.37
DFA TAX-MANAGED US TARGETED VALUE (DTMVX)	0.44
ISHARES S&P SMALL-CAP 600 VALUE (IJS)	0.25
VANGUARD SMALL CAP VALUE (VBR/VSIAX)	0.08/0.08
SCHWAB FUNDAMENTAL US SMALL COMPANY (FNDA)	0.32
INTERNATIONAL DEVELOPED MARKETS	
FUND	**EXPENSE RATIO**
DFA INT'L SMALL CAP VALUE (DISVX)	0.69
DFA WORLD EX US TARGETED VALUE (DWUSX)	0.65

MOMENTUM

DOMESTIC	
FUND	**EXPENSE RATIO**
AQR MOMENTUM STYLE (AMOMX)	0.40
ISHARES MSCI USA MOMENTUM FACTOR (MTUM)	0.15
INTERNATIONAL DEVELOPED MARKETS	
FUND	**EXPENSE RATIO**
AQR INTERNATIONAL MOMENTUM STYLE (AIMOX)	0.55

PROFITABILITY/QUALITY

DOMESTIC	
FUND	**EXPENSE RATIO**
ISHARES MSCI USA QUALITY FACTOR ETF (QUAL)	0.15

INTERNATIONAL DEVELOPED MARKETS	
FUND	**EXPENSE RATIO**
ISHARES MSCI INTERNATIONAL DEVELOPED QUALITY FACTOR ETF (IQLT)	0.30

TERM

FUND	**EXPENSE RATIO**
DFA FIVE-YEAR GLOBAL FIXED INCOME (DFGBX)	0.27
DFA DIVERSIFIED FIXED INCOME (DFXIX)	0.15
DFA INTERMEDIATE GOVT. FIXED-INCOME (DFIGX)	0.12
DFA WORLD EX US GOVERNMENT FXD INC (DWFIX)	0.20
DFA INTERMEDIATE-TERM MUNICIPAL BD (DFTIX)	0.23
ISHARES BARCLAYS 7-10 YEAR TREASURY (IEF)	0.15
VANGUARD INTERMEDIATE-TERM TREASURY (VGIT/VFIUX)	0.10/0.10

CARRY

FUND	**EXPENSE RATIO**
POWERSHARES DB G10 CURRENCY HARVEST ETF (DBV)	0.76

MULTI-STYLE FUNDS

SIZE + VALUE + PROFITABILITY/QUALITY

DOMESTIC	
FUND	**EXPENSE RATIO**
DFA US CORE EQUITY 1 (DFEOX)	0.19
DFA US CORE EQUITY 2 (DFQTX)	0.22
DFA TA US CORE EQUITY 2 (DFTCX)	0.24

INTERNATIONAL	
FUND	**EXPENSE RATIO**
DFA INT'L CORE EQUITY (DFIEX)	0.38
DFA WORLD EX US CORE EQUITY (DFWIX)	0.47
DFA TA WORLD EX US CORE EQUITY (DFTWX)	0.45

SIZE + MOMENTUM

DOMESTIC	
FUND	**EXPENSE RATIO**
AQR SMALL CAP MOMENTUM STYLE (ASMOX)	0.60

VALUE + MOMENTUM + PROFITABILITY/QUALITY

DOMESTIC	
FUND	**EXPENSE RATIO**
AQR LARGE CAP MULTI-STYLE (QCELX)	0.45
AQR TM LARGE CAP MULTI-STYLE (QTLLX)	0.45
GOLDMAN SACHS ACTIVEBETA US LARGE CAP EQUITY ETF (GSLC)	0.09

INTERNATIONAL	
FUND	**EXPENSE RATIO**
AQR INTERNATIONAL MULTI-STYLE (QICLX)	0.60
AQR TM INTERNATIONAL MULTI-STYLE (QIMLX)	0.60

EMERGING MARKETS	
FUND	**EXPENSE RATIO**
AQR EMERGING MULTI-STYLE (QEELX)	0.75
AQR TM EMERGING MULTI-STYLE (QTELX)	0.75

SIZE + VALUE + MOMENTUM + PROFITABILITY/QUALITY

DOMESTIC	
FUND	**EXPENSE RATIO**
AQR SMALL CAP MULTI-STYLE (QSMLX)	0.65
AQR TM SMALL CAP MULTI-STYLE (QSSLX))	0.65

VALUE + MOMENTUM + QUALITY + DEFENSIVE
(STOCKS, BONDS, CURRENCIES, AND COMMODITIES)

FUND	EXPENSE RATIO
AQR STYLE PREMIA (QSPIX)	1.50
AQR STYLE PREMIA ALTERNATIVE LV (QSLIX)	0.85

TREND-FOLLOWING
(STOCKS, BONDS, CURRENCIES, AND COMMODITIES)

FUND	EXPENSE RATIO
AQR MANAGED FUTURES (AQMIX)	1.25
AQR MANAGED FUTURES STRATEGY HV (QMHIX)	1.55

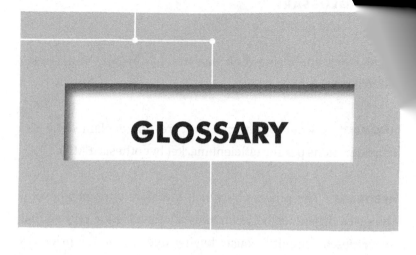

GLOSSARY

ACTIVE MANAGEMENT The attempt to uncover securities the market has either undervalued or overvalued and/or the attempt to time investment decisions to be more heavily invested when the market is rising and less so when the market is falling.

ALPHA A measure of risk-adjusted performance relative to a benchmark. Positive alpha represents outperformance; negative alpha represents underperformance. Positive or negative alpha may be caused by luck, manager skill, costs, and/or wrong choice of benchmark.

ANCHORING A form of cognitive bias in which people place an inordinate amount of importance on certain values or attributes, which then act as a reference point, and inappropriately weight the influence of subsequent data to support their initial assessment. For example, some investors will tend to hang on to a losing investment because they are waiting for it to at least

ak even, anchoring their investment's present value to the
alue it once had.

ANOMALY   Security returns that are not explained by risk considerations per the efficient market hypothesis (EMH).

ARBITRAGE   The process by which investors attempt to exploit the price difference between two exactly alike (or very similar) securities by simultaneously buying one at a lower price and selling the other at a higher price (thereby avoiding or minimizing risk). The trading activity of arbitrageurs eventually eliminates these price differences.

ASSET ALLOCATION   The process of determining what percentage of assets should be dedicated to specific asset classes. Also, the end result of this process.

ASSET CLASS   A group of assets with similar risk and expected return characteristics. Cash, debt instruments, real estate, and equities are examples of asset classes. Within a major asset class, such as equities, there are more specific classes, such as large- and small-cap company stocks and domestic and international stocks.

BASIS POINT One one-hundredth of 1 percent, or 0.0001.

BENCHMARK   An appropriate standard against which mutu̶ funds and other investment vehicles can be judged. Domestic large-cap growth funds should be judged against a domestic large-cap growth index, such as the S&P 500 Growth Index, while small-cap managers should be judged against a small-cap index, such as the Russell 2000 Index.

BETA   The exposure of a stock, mutual fund, or portfolio to a factor.

BID-OFFER SPREAD   The bid is the price at which you can sell a security, and the offer is the price you must pay to buy a security. The spread is the difference between the two prices and represents the cost of a round-trip trade (purchase and sale) excluding commissions.

BOOK-TO-MARKET VALUE (BTM)   The ratio of the book value per share to the market price per share, or book value divided by market capitalization.

BOOK VALUE   An accounting concept that reflects the value of a company based on accounting principles. It is often expressed in per-share terms. Book value per share is equal to book equity divided by the number of shares.

CALL   An option contract that gives the holder the right, but not the obligation, to buy a security at a predetermined price on a specific date (European call) or during a specific period (American call).

CAPITAL ASSET PRICING MODEL (CAPM)   The first formal asset pricing model. It uses a single factor (market beta) that describes the relationship between risk and expected return, and is used in the pricing of risky securities.

COMMODITY   A physical good (such as corn, oil, or gold) that is supplied without significant qualitative differentiation.

CONFIRMATION BIAS   The tendency to search for, interpret, favor, and recall information in a way that confirms one's preexisting beliefs or hypotheses, while giving disproportionately less consideration to alternative possibilities.

CREDIT DEFAULT SWAP (CDS)   A financial swap agreement in which the seller of the CDS will compensate the buyer (usually the creditor of the reference loan) in the event of a loan default (by the debtor) or other credit event. In effect, the seller of the CDS insures the buyer against some reference loan defaulting. The buyer of the CDS makes a series of payments (the CDS "fee" or "spread") to the seller and, in exchange, receives a payoff if the loan defaults.

CRSP   The Center for Research in Security Prices is a financial research group at the University of Chicago Business School. The CRSP deciles refer to groups of U.S. stocks ranked by their market capitalization, with CRSP 1 being the largest and CRSP 10 the smallest.

CURRENCY RISK The risk that an investment's value will be affected by changes in exchange rates.

DATA MINING A technique for attempting to build predictive real-world models by discerning patterns in masses of historical data.

DEFAULT Failure to pay principal or interest in a timely manner.

DISPOSITION EFFECT The tendency for investors to sell winning investments prematurely to lock in gains and hold losing investments too long in the hope of breaking even.

DISTRESSED STOCKS Stocks with high book-to-market values and/or low price-to-earnings ratios; another name for value stocks.

DIVERSIFICATION Dividing investment funds among a variety of investments with different risk–return characteristics to minimize portfolio risk.

DURATION The expected percentage change in the price of a bond given a percentage change in the yield on that bond. A higher duration number indicates a greater sensitivity of that bond's price to changes in interest rates.

EAFE INDEX The Europe, Australasia, and Far East Index, which consists of the stocks of companies from the developed EAFE countries. Very much like the S&P 500 Index, the stocks within the EAFE index are weighted by market capitalization.

EFFICIENT MARKET HYPOTHESIS (EMH) A theory that, at any given time and in a liquid market, security prices fully reflect all available information. The EMH contends that because markets are efficient and current prices reflect all information, attempts to outperform the market are essentially a game of chance rather than one of skill.

EMERGING MARKETS The capital markets of less-developed countries that are beginning to acquire characteristics of developed countries, such as higher per-capita income. Countries typically included in this category would be Brazil, Mexico, Romania, Turkey, and Thailand.

EMH *See efficient market hypothesis.*

EVENT RISK The risk that something unexpected will occur (war, political crisis, flood, or hurricane), negatively impacting the value of a security.

EXCHANGE TRADED FUNDS (ETFs) For practical purposes, these funds act like open-ended, no-load mutual funds. Like mutual funds, they can be created to represent virtually any index or asset class. They are not actually mutual funds. Instea these new investment vehicles represent a cross between a exchange-listed stock and an open-ended, no-load mutual fund. Like stocks (but unlike mutual funds), they trade on a stock exchange throughout the day.

EX-ANTE Before the fact.

EXPENSE RATIO The operating expenses of a mutual fund expressed as a percentage of total assets. These expenses are subtracted from the investment performance of a fund to determine the net return to shareholders. They cover manager fees, administrative costs, and, in some cases, marketing costs.

EX-POST After the fact.

FACTOR A numerical characteristic or set of characteristics common across a broad set of securities.

FOREIGN TAX CREDIT (FTC) A tax credit used to reduce or eliminate double taxation when the same income is taxed in two countries.

FOUR-FACTOR MODEL Differences in performance between diversified equity portfolios are best explained by the amount of exposure to four factors: the risk of the overall stock market, company size (market capitalization), price (book-to-market, or BtM, ratio), and momentum. Research has shown that, on erage, the four factors explain approximately 95 percent of the variation in performance of diversified U.S. stock portfolios.

FULL FAITH AND CREDIT The pledge that all taxing powers and resources, without limitation, will, if necessary, be used to repay a debt obligation.

GLAMOUR STOCKS The stocks of companies with low book-to-market values and/or high price-to-earnings ratios; another name for growth stocks.

GROWTH STOCKS The stocks of companies that have relatively high price-to-earnings (P/E) ratios or relatively low book-to-market (BtM) ratios — the opposite of value stocks because the market anticipates rapid earnings growth relative to the overall market. We are interested in a stock's earnings ratios because academic evidence indicates that investors can expect to be rewarded by investing in value companies' stocks. They are considered to be riskier investments (compared with growth companies' stocks), so investors demand a "risk premium" to invest in them.

HEDGE FUND A fund that generally has the ability to invest in a wide variety of asset classes. These funds often use leverage in an attempt to increase returns.

HIGH-YIELD BOND *See junk bond.*

HYBRID SECURITY A security with both equity and fixed-incom characteristics. Examples of hybrids are convertible bonds, preferred stocks, and junk bonds.

INDEX FUND A passively managed fund that seeks to replicate the performance of a particular index, such as the Wilshire 5000, the S&P 500, or the Russell 2000. The fund may replicate the index by buying and holding all the securities in that index in direct proportion to their weight (by market capitalization) within that index. The fund could sample the index — a common strategy for small-cap and total market index funds — and/or use index futures and other derivative instruments.

INITIAL PUBLIC OFFERING (IPO) The first offering of a company's stock to the public.

INVESTMENT GRADE A bond whose credit quality is at least adequate to maintain debt service. Moody's Investors Service investment-grade ratings are Baa and higher. Standard & Poor's are BBB and higher. Below-investment-grade ratings suggest a primarily speculative credit quality.

JUNK BOND A bond rated below investment grade; also referred to as a high-yield bond.

KURTOSIS The degree to which exceptional values, much larger or smaller than the average, occur more frequently (high urtosis) or less frequently (low kurtosis) than in a normal (bell-shaped) distribution. High kurtosis results in exceptional values called "fat tails." Low kurtosis results in "thin tails."

LARGE-CAP Large-cap stocks are those of companies considered large relative to other companies, as measured by their market capitalization. Precisely what is considered a "large" company varies by source. For example, one investment professional may define it as having a market capitalization in excess of $2 billion, while another may use $5 billion.

LEVERAGE The use of debt to increase the amount of assets that can be acquired (for example, to buy stock). Leverage increases the riskiness as well as the expected return of a portfolio.

LIQUIDITY A measure of the ease of trading a security in a market.

MANAGEMENT FEES Total amount charged to an account for the management of a portfolio.

MARKET BETA The sensitivity of the return of a stock, mutual fund, or portfolio relative to the return of the overall equity market. Because this was the original form of beta, some refer to market beta as just "beta."

MARKET CAP/MARKET CAPITALIZATION For an individual stock, this is the total number of shares of common stock outstanding multiplied by the current price per share. For example, if a company has 100 million shares outstanding and its current stock price is $30 per share, the market cap of the company is $3 billion.

MATURITY The date on which the issuer of a bond promises to repay the principal.

MICRO-CAP The smallest stocks by market capitalization represented by the ninth and 10th CRSP deciles. Other definitions used are the smallest 5 percent of stocks by market capitalization and stocks with a market capitalization of less than about $200 million.

MODERN PORTFOLIO THEORY (MPT) A body of academic work founded on four concepts. First, markets are too efficient to allow expected returns in excess of the market's overall rate of return to be achieved consistently through trading systems. Active management is therefore counterproductive. Second, over sustained periods, asset classes can be expected to achieve returns commensurate with their level of risk. Riskier asset classes, such as small companies and value companies, will produce higher returns as compensation for their higher risk. Third, diversification across asset classes can increase returns and reduce risk. For any given level of risk, a portfolio can be constructed to produce the highest expected return. Fourth, there is no one right portfolio for every investor. Each investor must choose an asset allocation that results in a portfolio with an acceptable level of risk for that investor's specific situation.

MONOTONIC Changing in such a way that is either never increasing or never decreasing.

MPT *See modern portfolio theory.*

MSCI EAFE INDEX *See EAFE Index.*

NASDAQ The National Association of Securities Dealers Automatic Quotation System, which is a computerized marketplace in which securities are traded, frequently called the "over-the-counter market."

NEGATIVE CORRELATION OF RETURNS When one asset experiences above average returns, the other tends to experience below average returns, and vice versa.

NYSE The New York Stock Exchange, which traces its origins to 1792, is the world's leading equities market. A broad spectrum of market participants — including listed companies, individual investors, institutional investors, and member firms — participate in the NYSE market.

PASSIVE ASSET CLASS FUNDS Mutual funds that buy and hold common stocks within a particular domestic or international asset class. The amount of each security purchased is typically in proportion to its capitalization relative to the total capitalization of all securities within the asset class. Each stock is held until it no longer fits the definition and guidelines established for remaining in that asset class. Passive asset class funds provide the building blocks needed to implement a passive management strategy.

P/E RATIO The ratio of stock price to earnings per share. Stocks with high P/E ratios are considered growth stocks; stocks with low P/E ratios are considered value stocks.

PRUDENT INVESTOR RULE A doctrine imbedded within the American legal code stating that a person responsible for the management of someone else's assets must manage those assets in a manner appropriate to the beneficiary's financial circumstances and tolerance for risk.

PUT An option contract giving the holder the right, but not the obligation, to sell a security at a predetermined price on a specific date (European put) or during a specific period (American put).

REBALANCING The process of restoring a portfolio toward its original asset allocation. Rebalancing can be accomplished either through adding newly investable funds or by selling portions of the best performing asset classes and using the proceeds to purchase additional amounts of the underperforming asset classes.

REAL ESTATE INVESTMENT TRUST (REIT) A company that owns or finances real estate. As represented by REITs, real estate is a separate asset class. REITs have their own risk and reward characteristics, as well as relatively low correlation with other equity and fixed income asset classes. Investors can purchase shares of a REIT in the same way they would purchase other equities, or they can invest in a REIT mutual fund that is either actively or passively managed.

RISK PREMIUM The higher expected (not guaranteed) return for accepting a specific type of non-diversifiable risk.

R-SQUARED A statistic that represents the percentage of a fund's or security's movements that can be explained by movements in a benchmark index or set of factors.

RUSSELL 2000 INDEX The smallest 2,000 of the largest 3,000 publicly traded U.S. stocks; a common benchmark for small-cap stocks.

SECURITIES AND EXCHANGE COMMISSION (SEC) A government agency created by Congress to regulate the securities markets and protect investors. The SEC has jurisdiction over the operation of broker-dealers, investment advisors, mutual funds, and companies selling stocks and bonds to the investing public.

SHARPE RATIO A measure of the return earned above the rate of return on a riskless asset, usually taken as one-month U.S. Treasury bills, relative to the amount of risk taken, with risk being measured by the standard deviation of returns. For example: The average return earned on an asset was 10 percent. The average rate of a one-month U.S. Treasury bill was 4 percent. The standard deviation was 20 percent. The Sharpe ratio would be equal to 10 percent minus 4 percent (6 percent) divided by 20 percent, or 0.3.

SHORT INTEREST The quantity of stock shares that investors have sold short but not yet covered or closed out.

SHORT SELLING Borrowing a security for the purpose of immediately selling it. This is done with the expectation that the investor will be able to buy the security back at a later date (and lower price), returning it to the lender and keeping any profit.

SKEWNESS A measure of the asymmetry of a distribution. Negative skewness occurs when the values to the left of (less than) the mean are fewer but farther from it than values to the right of (more than) the mean. For example: The return series of –30 percent, 5 percent, 10 percent, and 15 percent has a mean of 0 percent. There is only one return less than 0 percent, and three higher; but the negative one is much farther from zero than the positive ones. Positive skewness occurs when the values to the right of (more than) the mean are fewer but farther from it than values to the left of (less than) the mean.

SMALL-CAP Small-cap stocks are those of companies considered small relative to other companies, as measured by their market capitalization. Precisely what is considered a "small" company varies by source. For example, one investment professional may define it as having a market capitalization of less than $2 billion, while another may use $5 billion. We are interested in a stock's capitalization because academic evidence indicates that investors can expect to be rewarded by investing in smaller companies' stocks. They are considered to be riskier investments than larger companies' stocks, so investors demand a "risk premium" to invest in them.

SPREAD The difference between the price a dealer is willing to pay for a bond (the bid) and the price a dealer is willing to sell the bond (the offer).

S&P 500 INDEX A market-cap weighted index of 500 of the largest U.S. stocks, designed to cover a broad and representative sampling of industries.

STANDARD DEVIATION A measure of volatility or risk. The greater the standard deviation, the greater the volatility of a security or portfolio. Standard deviation can be measured for varying time periods, such as monthly, quarterly, or annually.

STYLE DRIFT Occurs when a portfolio moves away from its original asset allocation, either by the purchase of securities outside the particular asset class a fund represents or by not rebalancing to adjust for significant differences in performance of the various asset classes in the portfolio.

SYSTEMATIC RISK Risk that cannot be diversified away. The market must reward investors for assuming systematic risk or they would not take it. That reward is in the form of a risk premium, a higher expected return than could be earned by investing in a less risky instrument.

THREE-FACTOR MODEL Differences in performance between diversified equity portfolios, which are best explained by three factors: the amount of exposure to the risk of the overall stock market, company size (market capitalization), and price (book-to-market, or BtM, ratio) characteristics. Research has shown that, on average, the three factors explain more than 90 percent of the variation in performance of diversified U.S. stock portfolios.

TRACKING ERROR The amount by which the performance of a fund differs from the appropriate index or benchmark. More generally, when referring to a whole portfolio, it is the amount by which the performance of the portfolio differs from a widely accepted benchmark, such as the S&P 500 Index or the Wilshire 5000 Index.

TREASURY BILLS U.S. Treasury instruments with a maturity of up to one year. Bills are issued at a discount to par. The interest is paid in the form of the price rising toward par until maturity.

TREASURY BONDS U.S. Treasury instruments whose maturity is more than 10 years.

TREASURY NOTE U.S. Treasury instruments with a maturity of between one and 10 years.

T-STAT Short for *t*-statistic, it is a measure of statistical significance. A value greater than about 2.0 is generally considered meaningfully different from random noise, with a higher number indicating even greater confidence.

TURNOVER The trading activity of a fund as it sells securities and replaces them with new ones.

UNCOVERED INTEREST PARITY (UIP) The theory that there should be an equality of expected returns on otherwise comparable financial assets denominated in two different currencies. Rate differentials would be offset by currency appreciation or depreciation such that investor returns would be the same across markets. However, empirical evidence does not support the theory, resulting in the UIP puzzle.

VALUE STOCKS   The stocks of companies with relatively low price-to-earnings (P/E) ratios or relatively high book-to-market (BtM) ratios — the opposite of growth stocks. The market anticipates slower earnings growth relative to the overall market. They are considered to be riskier investments than growth companies' stocks, so investors demand a "risk premium" to invest in them.

VOLATILITY   The standard deviation of the change in value of a financial instrument within a specific time horizon. It is often used to quantify the risk of the instrument over that time period. Volatility is typically expressed in annualized terms.

WEIGHT   Percentage value of a security or asset class held in a portfolio, relative to the value of the total portfolio.

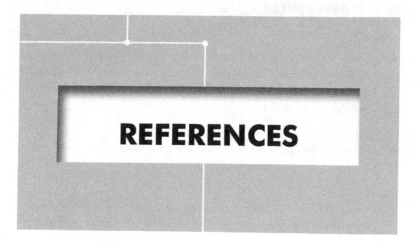

REFERENCES

1. Alberg, John and Michael Seckler, "Misunderstanding Buffett," Advisor Perspectives, August 12, 2014. Available at http://www.advisorperspectives.com/articles/2014/08/12/misunderstanding-buffett

2. Anderson, Keith and Tomasz Zastawniak, "Glamour, Value and Anchoring on the Changing P/E," European Journal of Finance, February 2016, 1–32.

3. AQR Capital Management, "Volatility Targeting," December 2012.

4. Asness, Clifford, "Momentum in Japan: The Exception That Proves the Rule," Journal of Portfolio Management, Summer 2011, 37(4): 67–75.

5. Asness, Clifford S., "The Interaction of Value and Momentum Strategies," Financial Analysts Journal, March/April 1997, 53(2).

6. Asness, Clifford S., Andrea Frazzini, Ronen Israel, and Tobias J. Moskowitz, "Fact, Fiction and Momentum Investing," Journal of Portfolio Management, Fall 2014, 40(5): 75–92.

7. Asness, Clifford S., Andrea Frazzini, Ronen Israel, Tobias J. Moskowitz, and Lasse Heje Pedersen, "Size Matters, If You Control Your Junk," Fama-Miller Working Paper, January 2015. Available at http://papers.ssrn.com/sol3/papers.cfm?abstract_id=2553889.

8. Asness, Clifford S., Robert Krail, and John Liew, "Do Hedge Funds Hedge?" Journal of Portfolio Management, Fall 2001, 28(1): 6–19.

9. Asness, Clifford S., Tobias Moskowitz, and Lasse Pedersen, "Value and Momentum Everywhere," Journal of Finance, June 2013, 68(3): 929–985.

10. Asvanunt, Attakrit and Scott Richardson, "The Credit Risk Premium," June 2016. Available at http://papers.ssrn.com/sol3/papers.cfm?abstract_id=2563482.

11. Atanasov, Victoria and Thomas Nitschka, "Foreign Currency Returns and Systematic Risks," Journal of Financial and Quantitative Analysis, April 2015, 50(1-2), 231–250.

12. Bai, Jennie, Pierre Collin-Dufresne, Robert S. Goldstein, and Jean Helwege, "On Bounding Credit-Event Risk Premia," Review of Financial Studies, March 2015, 28(9): 2608–2042.

13. Baker, Malcolm, Brendan Bradley, and Jeffrey Wurgler, "Benchmarks as Limits to Arbitrage: Understanding the Low-Volatility Anomaly," Financial Analysts Journal, January/February 2011, 67(1): 40–54.

14. Baker, Nardin L. and Robert A. Haugen, "Low Risk Stocks Outperform within All Observable Markets of the World," April 2012. Available at http://papers.ssrn.com/sol3/papers.cfm?abstract_id=2055431.

15. Ball, Ray, Joseph Gerakos, Juhani Linnainmaa, and Valeri Nikolaev, University of Chicago working paper "Accruals, Cash Flows, and Operating Profitability in the Cross-Section of Stock Returns," Journal of Financial Economics, July 2016, 121(1): 28–45.

16. Baltas, Akindynos-Nikolaos and Robert Kosowski, "Momentum Strategies in Futures Markets and Trend-Following Funds," January 2013. Available at http://papers.ssrn.com/sol3/papers.cfm?abstract_id=1968996.

17. Baltzer, Markus, Stephan Jank, and Esad Smajlbegovic, "Who Trades on Momentum?" Bundesbank Discussion Paper, January 2015. Available at http://papers.ssrn.com/sol3/papers.cfm?abstract_id=2517462.

18. Bansal, Naresh, Robert A. Connolly, and Chris Stivers, "Equity Volatility as a Determinant of Future Term-Structure Volatility," Journal of Financial Markets, September 2015, 25: 33–51.

19. Banz, Rolf W., "The Relationship Between Return and Market Value of Common Stocks," Journal of Financial Economics, March 1981, 9(1): 3–18.

20. Barberis, Nicholas and Ming Huang, "Mental Accounting, Loss Aversion, and Individual Stock Returns," Journal of Finance, August 2001, 56: 1247–1292.

21. Barberis, Nicholas and Ming Huang, "Stocks as Lotteries: The Implications of Probability Weighting for Security Prices," American Economic Review, December 2008, 98(5): 2066–2100.

22. Barroso, Pedro and Pedro Santa-Clara, "Momentum Has Its Moments," Journal of Financial Economics, April 2015, 116(1): 111–120.

23. Basu, Sanjoy, "The Relationship Between Earnings' Yield, Market Value and Return for NYSE Common Stocks: Further Evidence," Journal of Financial Economics, June 1983, 12(1): 129–156.

24. Berkshire Hathaway Annual Shareholders letter, 2012. Available at http://www.berkshirehathaway.com/letters/2012ltr.pdf.

25. Bhansali, Vineer, Joshua Mark Davis, Matt Dorsten, and Graham Rennison, "Carry and Trend in Lots of Places," Journal of Portfolio Management, Summer 2015, 41(4): 82–90.

26. Black, Angela J., Bin Mao, and David G. McMillan, "The Value Premium and Economic Activity: Long-run Evidence from the United States," Journal of Asset Management, December 2009, (10)5: 305–317.

27. Black, Stanley and Philipp Meyer-Brauns, "Dimensions of Equity Returns in Europe," Dimensional Fund Advisors, November 2015. Available at https://my.dimensional.com/csmedia/cms/papers_library/2015/11/dimensio/Dimensions_of_Equity_Returns_in_Europe.pdf.

28. Blitz, David, Eric Falkenstein, and Pim van Vliet, "Explanations for the Volatility Effect: An Overview Based on the CAPM Assumptions," Journal of Portfolio Management, Spring 2014, 40(3): 61–76.

29. Blitz, David, Juan Pang, and Pim van Vliet, "The Volatility Effect in Emerging Markets," Emerging Markets Review, September 2013, 16: 31–45.

30. Blitz, David, Bart van der Grient, and Pim van Vliet, "Interest Rate Risk in Low-Volatility Strategies," June 2014. Available at http://www.robeco.com/images/interest-rate-risk-in-low-volatility-strategies-june%202014.pdf.

31. Blitz, David C. and Pim van Vliet, "The Volatility Effect: Lower Risk without Lower Return," Journal of Portfolio Management, Fall 2007, 34(1): 102–113.

32. Bouchaud, Jean-Philippe, Stefano Ciliberti, Augustin Landier, Guillaume Simon, and David Thesmar, "The Excess Returns of "Quality" Stocks: A Behavioral Anomaly," Journal of Investment Strategies, June 2016, 5(3): 51–61.

33. Boudoukh, Jacob, Roni Michaely, Matthew Richardson, and Michael R. Roberts, "On the Importance of Measuring Payout Yield: Implications for Empirical Asset Pricing," Journal of Finance, April 2007, 62(2): 877–915.

34. The Brandes Institute, "Value vs. Glamour: A Long-Term Worldwide Perspective." Available at https://www.brandes.com/docs/default-source/brandes-institute/value-vs-glamour-worldwide-perspective.

35. Calluzzo, Paul, Fabio Moneta, and Selim Topaloglu, "Anomalies Are Publicized Broadly, Institutions Trade Accordingly, and Returns Decay Correspondingly," December 2015. Available at http://papers.ssrn.com/sol3/papers.cfm?abstract_id=2660413.

36. Carhart, Mark M., "On Persistence in Mutual Fund Performance," Journal of Finance, March 1997, 52(1): 57–82.

37. de Carvalho, Raul Leote, Patrick Dugnolle, Lu Xiao, and Pierre Moulin, "Low-Risk Anomalies in Global Fixed Income: Evidence from Major Broad Markets," Journal of Fixed Income, Spring 2014, 23(4); 51–70.

38. Chaves, Denis B., "Idiosyncratic Momentum: U.S. and International Evidence," Journal of Investing, Summer 2016, 25(2): 64–76.

39. Cheng, Nai-fu and Feng Zhang, "Risk and Return of Value Stocks," Journal of Business, October 1998, 71(4): 501–535.

40. Chordia, Tarun, Avanidhar Subrahmanyam, and Qing Tong, "Have Capital Market Anomalies Attenuated in the Recent Era of High Liquidity and Trading Activity," Journal of Accounting and Economics, June 2014, 58(1): 41–58.

41. Chow, Tzee-man, Jason C. Hsu, Li-lan Kuo, and Feifei Li, "A Study of Low Volatility Portfolio Construction Methods," Journal of Portfolio Management, Summer 2014, 40(4): 89–105.

42. Christiansen, Charlotte, Angelo Ranaldo, and Paul Söderlind, "The Time-Varying Systematic Risk of Carry Trade Strategies," Journal of Financial and Quantitative Analysis, August 2011, 46(4): 1107–1125.

43. Chu, Yongqiang, David A. Hirshleifer, and Liang Ma, "The Causal Effect of Limits to Arbitrage on Asset Pricing Anomalies," July 2016. Available at http://papers. ssrn.com/sol3/papers.cfm?abstract_id=2696672.

44. Clare, Andrew, James Seaton, Peter N. Smith, and Stephen Thomas, "Carry and Trend Following Returns in the Foreign Exchange Market," May 2015. Available at https://editorialexpress.com/cgi-bin/conference/download.cgi?db_name= MMF2015&paper_id=148.

45. Clarke, Roger G., Harindra de Silva, and Steven Thorley, "Fundamentals of Efficient Factor Investing," July 2016. Available at http://papers.ssrn.com/sol3/ papers.cfm?abstract_id=2616071.

46. Da, Zhi, Umit G. Gurun, and Mitch Warachka, "Frog in the Pan: Continuous Information and Momentum," Review of Financial Studies, July 2014, 27(7): 2171–2218.

47. Dimson, Elroy, Paul Marsh, and Mike Staunton, "Equity Premiums Around the World," October 2011. Available at https://www.cfainstitute.org/learning/products/publications/rf/Pages/rf.v2011.n4.5.aspx.

48. D'Souza, Ian, Voraphat Srichanachaichok, George Jiaguo Wang, and Chelsea Yaqiong Yao, "The Enduring Effect of Time-Series Momentum on Stock Returns over Nearly 100 Years," January 2016. Available at http://papers.ssrn.com/sol3/papers.cfm?abstract_id=2720600.

49. Elgammal, Mohammed and David G. McMillan, "Value Premium and Default Risk," Journal of Asset Management, February 2014, 15(1): 48–61.

50. Elton, Edwin J., Martin J. Gruber, Deepak Agrawal, and Christopher Mann, "Explaining the Rate Spread on Corporate Bonds," Journal of Finance, February 2001, 56(1): 247–277.

51. Fama, Eugene F. and Kenneth R. French, "The Cross-Section of Expected Stock Returns," Journal of Finance, June 1992, 4(2): 427–465.

52. Fama, Eugene F. and Kenneth R. French, "Incremental Variables and the Investment Opportunity Set," Journal of Financial Economics, April 2015, 117(3): 470–488.

53. Fama, Eugene F. and Kenneth R. French "Profitability, Investment, and Average Returns," Journal of Financial Economics, December 2006, 82(3): 491–518.

54. Fama, Eugene F. and Kenneth R. French, "Size, Value, and Momentum in International Stock Returns," Journal of Financial Economics, September 2012, 105(3): 457–72.

55. Frazzini, Andrea and Lasse Heje Pedersen, "Betting Against Beta," Journal of Financial Economics, January 2014, 111(1): 1–25.

56. Frazzini, Andrea, Ronen Israel, and Tobias J. Moskowitz, "Trading Costs of Asset Pricing Anomalies," Fama-Miller Working Paper, Chicago Booth Research Paper No. 14-05, December 2012. Available at http://ssrn.com/abstract=2294498.

57. Fridson, Martin S., "Do High-Yield Bonds Have an Equity Component?" Financial Management, Summer 1994, 23(2): 82–84.

58. Geczy, Christopher C. and Mikhail Samonov, "215 Years of Global Multi-Asset Momentum: 1800-2014 (Equities, Sectors, Currencies, Bonds, Commodities and Stocks)," May 2015. Available at http://papers.ssrn.com/sol3/papers.cfm?abstract_id=2607730.

59. Gordon, Masha, "The Profitability Premium in EM Markets," December 2013. Available at http://media.pimco.com/Documents/PIMCO_In_Depth_EM_Profitability_Dec2013.pdf.

60. Goyal, Amit and Ivo Welch, "Predicting the Equity Premium with Dividend Ratios," Management Science, May 2003, 49(5): 639–654.

61. Gray, Wesley R. and Jack Vogel, "Enhancing the Investment Performance of Yield-Based Strategies," Journal of Investing, Summer 2014, 23(2): 44–50.

62. Grobys, Klaus and Jari-Pekka Heinonen, "Is There a Credit Risk Anomaly in FX Markets?" Financial Research Letters, May 2016.

63. Grullon, Gustavo and Roni Michaely, "Dividends, Share Repurchases, and the Substitution Hypothesis," Journal of Finance, August 2002, 57(4): 1649–1684.

64. Harvey, Campbell R., Yan Liu, and Heqing Zhu, "...and the Cross-Section of Expected Returns," February 2015. Available at http://papers.ssrn.com/sol3/papers.cfm?abstract_id=2249314.

65. Hjalmarsson, Erik, "Portfolio Diversification Across Characteristics," Journal of Investing, Winter 2011, 20(4): 84–88.

66. Hou, Kewei, Chen Xue, and Lu Zhang, "Digesting Anomalies: An Investment Approach," Review of Financial Studies, March 2015, 28(3): 650–705.

67. Hurst, Brian K., Yao Hua Ooi, Lasse H. Pedersen, "A Century of Evidence on Trend-Following Investing," September 2014. Available at https://www.aqr.com/library/aqr-publications/a-century-of-evidence-on-trend-following-investing.

68. Hutchinson, Mark C. and John O'Brien, "Is This Time Different? Trend Following and Financial Crises," Journal of Alternative Investments, Fall 2014, 17(2): 82–102.

69. Ilmanen, Antti and Jared Kizer, "The Death of Diversification Has Been Greatly Exaggerated," Journal of Portfolio Management, Spring 2012, 38(3): 15–27.

70. Israel, Ronen and Tobias J. Moskowitz, "The Role of Shorting, Firm Size, and Time on Market Anomalies," Journal of Financial Economics, May 2013, 108(2): 275–301.

71. Jacobs, Heiko and Sebastian Müller, "Anomalies Across the Globe: Once Public, No Longer Existent?" July 2016. Available at http://papers.ssrn.com/sol3/papers.cfm?abstract_id=2816490.

72. Jegadeesh, Narasimhan and Sheridan Titman, "Returns to Buying Winners and Selling Losers: Implications for Stock Market Efficiency," Journal of Finance, March 1993, 48(1): 65–91.

73. Jensen, Gerald R. and Jeffrey M. Mercer, "Monetary Policy and the Cross-Section of Expected Returns," Journal of Financial Research, Spring 2002, 25(1): 125–139.

74. Jiang, Hao and Zheng Sun, "Equity Duration: A Puzzle on High Dividend Stocks," October 2015. Available at http://papers.ssrn.com/sol3/papers.cfm?abstract_id=2678958.

75. Jordan, Bradford D. and Timothy B. Riley, "The Long and Short of the Vol Anomaly," April 2016. Available at http://papers.ssrn.com/sol3/papers.cfm?abstract_id=2442902.

76. Kim, Moon K. and David A. Burnie, "The Firm Size Effect and the Economic Cycle," Journal of Financial Research, Spring 2002, 25(1): 111–124.

77. Koijen, Ralph S. J., Tobias J. Moskowitz, Lasse Heje Pedersen, and Evert B. Vrugt, "Carry," Fama-Miller Working Paper, August 2015. Available at http://papers.ssrn.com/sol3/papers.cfm?abstract_id=2298565.

78. Kozlov, Max and Antti Petajisto, "Global Return Premiums on Earnings Quality, Value, and Size," January 2013. Available at http://papers.ssrn.com/sol3/papers.cfm?abstract_id=2179247.

79. Lakonishok, Josef, Andrei Shleifer, and Robert W. Vishny, "Contrarian Investment, Extrapolation, and Risk," Journal of Finance, December 1994, 49(5): 1541–1578.

80. Lam, F.Y. Eric C., Shujing Wang, and K.C. John Wei, "The Profitability Premium: Macroeconomic Risks or Expectation Errors?" March 2016. Available at http://papers.ssrn.com/sol3/papers.cfm?abstract_id=2479232.

81. Lettau, Martin, Matteo Maggiori, and Michael Weber, "Conditional Risk Premia in Currency Markets and Other Asset Classes," Journal of Financial Economics, November 2014, 114(2): 197–225.

82. Lev, Baruch and Theodore Sougiannis, "Penetrating the Book-to-Market Black Box," Journal of Business Finance and Accounting, April/May 1999, 26(3-4): 419–449.

83. Levi, Yaron and Ivo Welch, "Long-Term Capital Budgeting," March 2014. Available at http://papers.ssrn.com/sol3/papers.cfm?abstract_id=2327807.

84. Li, Xi, Rodney N. Sullivan, and Luis Garcia-Feijóo, "The Limits to Arbitrage and the Low-Volatility Anomaly," Financial Analysts Journal, January/February 2014, 70(1): 52–63.

85. Liu, Ryan, "Profitability Premium: Risk or Mispricing?" November 2015. Available at http://faculty.haas.berkeley.edu/rliu/Job%20Market%20Paper%20Ryan%20Liu.pdf.

86. Lustig, Hanno, Nikolai Roussanov, and Adrien Verdelhan, "Common Risk Factors in Currency Markets," Review of Financial Studies, November 2011, 24(11): 3731–3777.

87. McLean, R. David and Jeffrey Pontiff, "Does Academic Research Destroy Stock Return Predictability," Journal of Finance, January 2016, 71(1): 5–32.

88. Menkhoff, Lukas, Lucio Sarno, Maik Schmeling, and Andreas Schrimpf, "Carry Trades and Global Foreign Exchange Volatility," Journal of Finance, August 2012, 67(2): 681–718.

89. Miller, Merton H. and Franco Modigliani, "Dividend Policy, Growth, and the Valuation of Shares," Journal of Business, October 1961, 34(4): 411–433.

90. Moskowitz, Tobias J., "Asset Pricing and Sports Betting," July 2015. Available at http://papers.ssrn.com/sol3/papers.cfm?abstract_id=2635517.

91. Moskowitz, Tobias J., "Explanations for the Momentum Premium," AQR Capital Management White Paper, 2010.

92. Novy-Marx, Robert, "The Other Side of Value: The Gross Profitability Premium," Journal of Financial Economics, April 2013, 108(1): 1–28.

93. Novy-Marx, Robert, "Understanding Defensive Equity," March 2016. Available at http://rnm.simon.rochester.edu/research/UDE.pdf.

94. Novy-Marx, Robert and Mihail Velikov, "A Taxonomy of Anomalies and Their Trading Costs," Review of Financial Studies, 2016, 29(1): 104–147.

95. Pedersen, Niels, Sébastien Page, and Fei He, "Asset Allocation: Risk Models for Alternative Investments," Financial Analysts Journal, May/June 2014, 70(3): 34–45.

96. Peterkort, Robert F. and James F. Nielsen, "Is the Book-to-Market Ratio a Measure of Risk?" Journal of Financial Research, Winter 2005, 28(4): 487–502.

97. Petkova, Ralitsa, "Do the Fama-French Factors Proxy for Innovations in Predictive Variables?" Journal of Finance, April 2006, 61(2): 581–612.

98. Piotroski, Joseph D. and Eric C. So, "Identifying Expectation Errors in Value/ Glamour Strategies: A Fundamental Analysis Approach," Review of Financial Studies, September 2012, 25(9): 2841–2875.

99. Rosenberg, Barr, Kenneth Reid, and Ronald Lanstein, "Persuasive Evidence of Market Inefficiency," Journal of Portfolio Management, Spring 1985, 11(3): 9–16.

100. Sarno, Lucio, Paul Schneider, and Christian Wagner, "Properties of Foreign Exchange Risk Premiums," Journal of Financial Economics, August 2012, 105(2): 279–310.

101. Shah, Ronnie R., "Understanding Low Volatility Strategies: Minimum Variance," Dimensional Fund Advisors, August 2011. Available at https://my.dimensional.com/csmedia/cms/papers_library/2011/08/understa/Minimum_Variance.pdf.

102. Shefrin, Hersh M. and Meir Statman, "Explaining Investor Preference for Cash Dividends," Journal of Financial Economics, June 1984, 13(2): 253–282.

103. van Vliet, Pim, "Enhancing a Low-Volatility Strategy is Particularly Helpful When Generic Low Volatility is Expensive," January 2012. Available at https://www.robeco.com/en/professionals/insights/quantitative-investing/low-volatility-investing/enhancing-a-low-volatility-strategy-is-particularly-helpful-when-generic-lowvolatility-is-expensive.jsp.

104. Wang, Huijun and Jianfeng Yu, "Dissecting the Profitability Premium," December 2013. Available at http://papers.ssrn.com/sol3/papers.cfm?abstract_id=1711856.

105. Yogo, Motohiro, "A Consumption-Based Explanation of Expected Returns," Journal of Finance, April 2006, 61(2): 539–580.

106. Zhang, Lu, "The Value Premium," Journal of Finance, February 2005, 60(1): 67–103.